GREAT
IS THY
Faithfulness

GREAT
IS THY

365 DEVOTIONS FROM
Our Daily Bread.®

Discovery House.®
from Our Daily Bread Ministries

ISBN: 978-1-62707-906-8

Printed in the United States of America
First printing of this edition in 2018

Strength for today
and bright hope for tomorrow.

---

from "Great Is Thy Faithfulness"
Thomas O. Chisholm

Beginning Again

Read: Colossians 1:9–14

We have redemption through His blood, the forgiveness of sins.
Colossians 1:14

It was New Year's Day 1929. The University of California at Berkeley was playing Georgia Tech in college football's Rose Bowl. Roy Riegels, a California defender, recovered a Georgia Tech fumble, then turned and scampered sixty-five yards in the wrong direction! One of Riegels's own teammates tackled him just before he reached the wrong goal line. On the next play, Georgia Tech scored and went on to win.

From that day on, Riegels was saddled with the nickname "Wrong-way Riegels." For years afterward, whenever he was introduced, people would exclaim, "I know who you are! You're the guy who ran the wrong way in the Rose Bowl!"

Our failures may not be as conspicuous, but we've all gone the wrong way, and we have memories that haunt us. Recollections of sin and failure rise up to taunt us at three o'clock in the morning. If only we could forget! If only we could begin again!

We can. When we confess our sins and repent before God, He forgives our past and puts it away. In Christ, "we have redemption through His blood, the forgiveness of sins"—all our sins (Colossians 1:14; 2:13).

It's never too late to begin again.   DHR

THINKING IT OVER

What past sins are you carrying today?

God's forgiveness is the door to a new beginning.

Strength for Today

Read: Philippians 4:8–13

I can do all things through Christ
who strengthens me. Philippians 4:13

M ost people own a calendar or an appointment book in which they record details of future commitments. A Christian friend of mine uses one in the opposite way. He doesn't record key activities until after they've taken place.

Here's his approach: Each morning he prays, "Lord, I go forth in Your strength alone. Please use me as You wish." Then, whenever he accomplishes something unusual or difficult, he records it in his diary in the evening.

For example, he may write, "Today I was enabled to share my testimony with a friend." "Today God enabled me to overcome my fear through faith." "Today I was enabled to help and encourage a troubled person."

My friend uses the word *enabled* because he knows he couldn't do these things without God's help. By recording each "enabling," he is giving God all the glory. Relying constantly on God's strength, he can testify with the apostle Paul, "I can do all things through Christ who strengthens me" (Philippians 4:13).

As you enter each new day, ask God to strengthen and use you. You can be sure that as you look back on your day, you'll praise and glorify the Lord as you realize what He has enabled you to do.   JY

Lord, give me strength for this day's task,
Not for tomorrow would I ask;
At twilight hour, oh, may I say,
"The Lord has been my guide today." — Nillingham

God always gives enough strength for the next step.

The Need for Nourishment

Read: Psalm 37:1–11

Trust in the Lord, and do good; dwell in the land,
and feed on His faithfulness. Psalm 37:3

Our grandson Cameron was born six weeks prematurely. Undersized and in danger, he became a resident of the hospital's neonatal unit for about two weeks until he gained enough weight to go home. His biggest challenge was that, in the physical exercise of eating, he burned more calories than he was taking in. This obviously hindered his development. It seemed that the little guy took two steps backward for every step of progress he made. No medicine or treatment could solve the problem; he just needed the strength-giving fortification of nourishment.

As followers of Christ, we are constantly finding our emotional and spiritual reserves drained by the challenges of life in a fallen world. In such times, we need nourishment to strengthen us. In Psalm 37, David encouraged us to strengthen our hearts by feeding our souls. He wrote, "Trust in the Lord, and do good; dwell in the land, and feed on His faithfulness" (v. 3).

When weakness afflicts us, the reassurance of God's never-ending faithfulness can enable us to carry on in His name. His faithful care is the nourishment we need, giving us, as the hymn "Great Is Thy Faithfulness" says, "strength for today, and bright hope for tomorrow."   BC

Feed on God's faithfulness to find the strength you need.

Eagle Flight

Read: Isaiah 40:29–31

He gives power to the weak. Isaiah 40:29

I was watching an eagle in flight when for no apparent reason it began spiraling upward. With its powerful wings the great bird soared ever higher, dissolved into a tiny dot, and then disappeared.

Its flight reminded me of Isaiah's uplifting words: "Even the youths shall faint and be weary, and the young men shall utterly fall, but those who wait on the Lord shall renew their strength; they shall mount up with wings like eagles" (40:30–31).

Life's heartbreaks and tragedies can put an end to our resilience, our endurance, our nerve, and bring us to our knees. But if we put our hope in the Lord and rely on Him, He renews our strength. The key to our endurance lies in the exchange of our limited resources for God's limitless strength. And it is ours for the asking.

With God's strength we can "run and not be weary," even when days become hectic and demanding. With His strength we can "walk and not faint," even though tedious, dull routine makes the way seem dreary and long. The psalmist exclaimed in the midst of his weary, tearful pilgrimage, "Blessed is the man whose strength is in You" (Psalm 84:5).

Oh, what an exchange—God's infinite strength for our finite weakness!   DHR

If you are helpless in life's fray,
God's mighty power will be your stay;
Your failing strength He will renew,
For He's a God who cares for you. —DJD

God gives strength in proportion to the strain.

Blues-Chasers

Read: Psalm 42:1–11

My God shall supply all your need according to His riches
in glory by Christ Jesus. Philippians 4:19

Do you ever get the blues? You know the times—when the press of day-to-day life gets you down. Too much to do. Too many problems. Too little of some necessity but an abundance of some difficulty. No matter the cause, the result is the same: Your strength is zapped, your joy is crushed, and your hope needs to be rejuvenated. Whenever the blues threaten your day, try some of these blues-chasers:

Problem: Things seem impossible. *Answer*: All things are possible with God (Luke 18:27).

Problem: Life is often exhausting. *Answer*: Jesus offers rest for your soul (Matthew 11:28–30).

Problem: You can't forgive yourself. *Answer*: The Lord forgives all who confess their sins to Him (1 John 1:9).

Problem: You are afraid. *Answer*: God will strengthen and help you (Isaiah 41:10).

Problem: You are worried and anxious. *Answer*: Cast all your cares on God, for He cares for you (1 Peter 5:7).

Problem: You feel alone in this world. *Answer*: The Lord promises never to leave nor forsake you (Hebrews 13:5).

Trust God's answers for the problems that come into your life. They'll help to chase the blues away. DB

No burden is too heavy for God's almighty arms.

Good Medicine

Read: Proverbs 17:17–22

A merry heart does good, like medicine. Proverbs 17:22

In a *Better Homes and Gardens* article titled "Laugh Your Way to Good Health," Nick Gallo made an observation that echoes what Solomon wrote thousands of years ago: "A merry heart does good, like medicine" (Proverbs 17:22). Gallo said, "Humor is good medicine—and can actually help keep you in good health." He quoted William F. Fry, M.D., who describes laughter as "inner jogging" and says that it's good for a person's cardiovascular system.

Comparing laughter to exercise, Gallo pointed out that when a person laughs heartily several physical benefits occur. There's a temporary lowering of blood pressure, a decreased rate of breathing, and a reduction in muscle tension. He said that many people sense a "relaxed afterglow." He concluded, "An enduring sense of humor, especially combined with other inner resources such as faith and optimism, appears to be a potent force for better health."

Christians, above all others, should benefit from laughter because we have the greatest reason to be joyful. Our faith is firmly rooted in God, and our optimism is based on the assurance that our lives are under His wise control.

Don't be afraid to enjoy a good laugh—it's good medicine.

RDH

Laughter is a remedy
For sorrow and for care;
It brings joy to troubled souls,
To damaged hearts, repair. —Sper

He who laughs, lasts.

Looking Ahead

Read: Philippians 3:7–14

Forgetting those things which are behind . . . ,
I press toward the goal. Philippians 3:13–14

The month of January is named after Janus, the Roman god of beginnings. He was symbolized as a man with two faces, one looking back and the other looking ahead.

Some people have trouble looking ahead with hope because they keep looking back and moping over the mistakes of the past. Their outlook for the future is dimmed, and their enthusiasm is dampened. But there is no use "crying over spilled milk." History is likely to repeat itself if they keep on brooding over failures of the old year, or continue complaining about the injustices they suffered during the last twelve months. Nothing is gained by continually grieving over the past.

On this day early in the new year, begin by confessing your sins to the Lord and accepting the gracious forgiveness He offers (1 John 1:9–10). Make right what needs correcting, and then, "forgetting those things which are behind," press onward with confidence and trust in your heavenly Father (Philippians 3:13–14). That was Paul's secret, and it worked.

Let's stop looking back and brooding over past failures. Rather, with a forward look, let's move ahead with hope and joy.   RDH

THINKING IT OVER

What mistakes of the past are still burdening you?

Have you confessed them to God and accepted His complete forgiveness?
(1 John 1:9). When you do, your future will hold great promise.

Instead of living in the shadows of yesterday,
walk in the light of today and the hope of tomorrow.

Dial 91:1

Read: Psalm 91:1–16

*He who dwells in the secret place of the Most High shall
abide under the shadow of the Almighty. Psalm 91:1*

Most people know that dialing the numbers 911 in the United States will get them in touch with emergency help. It's so simple that even preschoolers have saved the lives of family members by using it. Three numbers do it all.

In one case, a woman's car had been hijacked with her and her infant son inside. She dialed 911 on her cellular phone, but the hijacker was totally unaware of what she had done. With the police dispatcher listening, the young mother cleverly included clues about her location as she talked to the hijacker. Police were able to locate her and her baby and arrest the criminal.

In an emergency, help is as close as three pushes on the phone keypad. Often, though, the situations we face cannot be remedied by human rescuers. Many times our crisis requires divine assistance. When that happens, we can call a different kind of 911—Psalm 91:1. There we find the help and protection of our Almighty God. This verse reminds us that God is our "shelter" and that we can rest in His shadow.

When we face the crises of life, we often try to survive on our own. We forget that what we need most, God's protection and the comfort of His presence, are available for the asking. The next time spiritual danger strikes, dial Psalm 91:1. DB

*Under His wings, I am safely abiding,
Though the night deepens and tempests are wild;
Still I can trust Him—I know He will keep me,
He has redeemed me and I am His child. —Cushing*

We need not fear life's dark shadows when we abide
under the shadow of God's wings.

Take My Hand

Read: 2 Corinthians 1:2–6

Blessed be the God and Father of our Lord Jesus Christ,
the Father of mercies and God of all comfort.
2 Corinthians 1:3

Y ou never know when you'll need the Lord's comfort the most—
when God's care will be your only hope to face tomorrow.

One day in 1932, pianist, singer, and songwriter Thomas A. Dorsey discovered his need for God's comfort. He left his pregnant wife, Nettie, at home in Chicago while he drove his Model A to St. Louis to sing at a revival meeting. All went well, and the crowd responded enthusiastically. At the end of Dorsey's performance, he received a telegram with the tragic news that his wife had died in childbirth. Within hours, the baby boy also died.

Filled with grief, Dorsey sought answers. Should he have stayed in Chicago and not gone to St. Louis? Had God done him an injustice? A few days after Nettie's death, Dorsey sat down at the piano and began to play. Finally sensing God's peace and closeness, he began to sing some new words and play a new song:

Precious Lord, take my hand,
Lead me on, let me stand;
I am tired, I am weak, I am worn;
Through the storm, through the night,
Lead me on to the light;
Take my hand, precious Lord, lead me home.

Is there a problem too big for you to handle alone? Or a grief too great to bear? Put your hand in the Lord's. Let the "God of all comfort" lead you home.   DB

When God permits trials, He also provides comfort.

January 10

"The Best Is Yet to Be"

Read: Romans 8:25–39

*I am persuaded that neither death nor life . . . shall be able
to separate us from the love of God. Romans 8:38–39*

Oswald Chambers loved the poetry of Robert Browning and often quoted a phrase from the poem "Rabbi Ben Ezra": "The best is yet to be, the last of life for which the first was made. Our times are in His hand."

As principal of the Bible Training College in London from 1911 to 1915, Chambers often said that the school's initials, B.T.C., also stood for "Better To Come." He believed that the future was always bright with possibility because of Christ. In a letter to former students written during the dark days of World War I, Chambers said, "Whatever transpires, it is ever 'the best is yet to be.'"

For the Christian, this is certainly true when we think about going to heaven. But can we believe that our remaining days on earth will be better than the past? If our hope is centered in Christ, the answer is a resounding yes!

The apostle Paul concluded the stirring eighth chapter of Romans with the assurance that nothing in the present or the future can separate us from the love of God which is in Christ Jesus our Lord (vv. 38–39). Because we are held in God's unchanging love, we can experience deeper fellowship with Him, no matter what difficulties come our way.

In Christ, "the best is yet to be."　　　　　　　　　　DCM

When we are walking with the Lord,
The future's always bright;
It matters not what comes our way
When faith replaces sight. —Sper

You can be confident about tomorrow
if you walk with God today.

Sorrow's Aftermath

Read: Psalm 73:21–28

Whom have I in heaven but You? And there is none upon earth that I desire besides You. Psalm 73:25

A cynic asked an elderly believer who had endured great physical pain for twenty years, "What do you think of your God now?" The godly sufferer replied, "I think of Him more than ever."

Sorrow can be the means of bringing us heart-to-heart with God. When repeated strokes of adversity have robbed us of health, friends, money, and favorable circumstances, God then becomes the only thing in life for us. We come to love Him for who He is and not merely for what He has to give.

In those times we cry out with the psalmist, "Whom have I in heaven but You? And there is none upon earth that I desire besides You" (Psalm 73:25). The path of sorrow leads us to the place where we can say, "My flesh and my heart fail; but God is the strength of my heart and my portion forever" (v. 26).

We also must remember that on ahead lies heaven, where "God will wipe away every tear from [our] eyes; there shall be no more death, nor sorrow, nor crying. There shall be no more pain" (Revelation 21:4). The path of pain will have led us to the land where loss is unknown—a place where there is no grief, but only joy and the service for which we've been fully prepared. This is what puts our pain in perspective. This is the sweet aftermath of sorrow.   DHR

When we have nothing left but God,
we find that God is enough.

The Answers Can Wait

Read: Luke 4:14–22

This is a faithful saying and worthy of all acceptance,
that Christ Jesus came into the world to save sinners,
of whom I am chief. 1 Timothy 1:15

David Herwaldt, a thoughtful, reflective pastor friend of mine, was slowly dying after fifty years of faithful ministry. He often talked with me about the nature of God and the eternity he would soon enter. We realized that we had only a superficial grasp of these mysteries, but we were not distressed. We knew that God had rescued us from our sin and guilt, and we rejoiced in our salvation. We had all we needed to obey the Lord gladly, live confidently, and serve Him gratefully.

When we are distressed by our inability to answer life's most vexing questions, we must remember that Christ did not come to satisfy our curiosity. Rather, He saw us as fallen and hurt, and He came to lift and heal.

When Jesus read Isaiah 61:1–2 to the people in the synagogue (Luke 4:16–21), He presented himself as the promised Messiah, whose primary purpose for coming was spiritual. He came to deliver us from the helplessness of our spiritual poverty, to release us from the shackles of our guilt, to heal our sin-caused blindness, and to set us free from sin's enslaving power.

Let us therefore trust Him and make obeying Him our highest goal. This is the path to a grateful, joyous, and hope-filled life. The answers can wait.   HVL

When trouble seeks to rob your very breath,
When tragedy hits hard and steals your days,
Recall that Christ endured the sting of death;
He gives us hope, and merits all our praise. —Gustafson

Christ came not to satisfy our curiosity but to save our souls.

What's in a Smile?

Read: Psalm 4:1–8

You have put gladness in my heart.
Psalm 4:7

According to an article in the *New York Times*, the act of smiling can promote good feelings. Writer Daniel Goleman cites experiments in which researchers found that saying the word *cheese* caused a person to smile, which in turn created pleasant feelings. On the other hand, saying the word *few* created a different facial expression, which resulted in negative emotions.

Interesting as such a study may be, there's a better way to have peace and gladness. It works from the inside out, not from the outside in.

In Psalm 4, David set forth several courses of action he took when he was feeling deeply distressed. He asked God for relief and mercy (v. 1). He took comfort in knowing that he was favored by Him and that the Lord heard him when he called (v. 3). David was quiet before God (v. 4). He did what was right and put his trust in Him (v. 5). He rested in the assurance of God's peace and safety (v. 8). David was confident that he would receive gladness in his heart (v. 7) as a gift from God, not as the result of some forced smile that might bring a temporary good feeling.

"Father, help us in our low moments to look up to you. Grant us the peace and gladness that David experienced when he called on you."

MRD

A smile may help to lift our load
When filled with anxious care,
But trusting God brings inner peace
And joy beyond compare. —Sper

The heart touched by God's grace brings joy to the face.

January 14

Finding Rest

Read: Psalm 23

He restores my soul; He leads me in the paths of
righteousness for His name's sake. Psalm 23:3

According to a survey conducted by an insurance company, one of every six workers in the U.S. feels too busy to take all the vacation days he or she has earned. Even though studies show that a week's holiday each year can dramatically reduce stress and the risk of heart attack, many people just keep working.

A vacation can be good for body and soul. But many people don't have the luxury of time away from work and daily responsibilities. What can we do when we must remain in demanding circumstances?

Psalm 23 paints a beautiful word picture of a caring shepherd, secure sheep, and a tranquil scene of quiet meadows and still waters. But it is the Lord, our shepherd, who gives rest, not the green grass or the flowing stream. "He restores my soul; He leads me in the paths of righteousness for His name's sake" (v. 3).

Rest is a place of peace that our spirits find in God. Neither the presence of those who oppose us nor the dark valley of death can keep us from what hymn writer Cleland McAfee called "a place of quiet rest, near to the heart of God." Through prayer and meditation on His Word, we can commune with Him. In the Lord's presence we can experience the rest and renewal we so desperately need.   DCM

There is a place of comfort sweet,
Near to the heart of God,
A place where we our Savior meet,
Near to the heart of God. —McAfee

Spending quiet time with God will bring quiet rest from God.

Too Much to Do?

Read: Luke 10:38–42

*One thing I have desired of the Lord, . . . that I may dwell
in the house of the Lord all the days of my life. Psalm 27:4*

I'm usually a happy person. Most of the time I can take on as
much work as anyone can give me. But some days there just
seems to be too much to do. The schedule may be so full of meetings, appointments, and deadlines that there's no room to breathe.
Life often contains too much work, parenting, home improvement,
and other responsibilities for one person to handle.

When that happens to me—as it may happen to you—I have
some options. I can retreat into a shell of inactivity and leave everyone who is depending on me out in the cold. I can slug my way
through, moaning as I go and making everyone wish I had chosen
option one. Or I can get my perspective realigned by reminding
myself what Jesus said to Martha (Luke 10:38–42).

Jesus told Martha that she had become "distracted with much
serving" (v. 40). He reminded her that her sister Mary had chosen
the one thing that would never be taken away (v. 42). Like many of
us, Martha got so wrapped up in her service that she forgot the most
important thing—fellowship with her Lord.

Are you overwhelmed? Don't lose sight of your priorities. Spend
time with the Lord. He will lift your load and give you the right
perspective.   DB

*The many tasks we face each day
Can burden and oppress,
But spending time with God each day
Can bring relief from stress.* —Sper

To keep your life in balance, lean on the Lord.

He Lights the Way

Read: Psalm 112

*Unto the upright there arises light
in the darkness. Psalm 112:4*

A missionary in Peru went to visit a group of believers one evening. She knew that the house where they were meeting was located on a cliff and that the path would be treacherous. She took a taxi as far as it could go, and then she began the hazardous ascent to the house on foot. The night was dark and the way was very difficult. As she rounded a bend, she suddenly came upon several believers carrying bright lanterns. They had come out to light the way. Her fears were relieved, and she ascended the path easily.

In a similar way, God lights our path. When we trust Jesus as our Savior, He who is the Light of the World enters our lives and removes the darkness of our sin and despair. This light continues to comfort us through times of sorrow. In the midst of sadness, trouble, illness, or disappointment, the Lord brightens the way and encourages His children by giving hope.

This may come through a word of exhortation from a fellow believer. It may be the illumination of God's Word by the ministry of the Holy Spirit. It may be calm reassurance in response to heartfelt prayer. Or it may be the miraculous supply of a specific need. Whatever the case, God sends light when we are engulfed in darkness. Jesus gives light in the darkest night!   DCE

*No darkness have we who in Jesus abide—
The Light of the World is Jesus;
We walk in the Light when we follow our Guide—
The Light of the World is Jesus. —Bliss*

God sometimes puts us in the dark to show us that
Jesus is the light.

Free-Falling

Read: Deuteronomy 32:1–14

*The eternal God is your refuge, and underneath
are the everlasting arms. Deuteronomy 33:27*

In the tender song of Moses found in today's Bible reading, God is portrayed as a dedicated mother eagle who can be trusted by her young, even in the scary experience of their learning to fly (Deuteronomy 32:11–12).

A mother eagle builds a comfortable nest for her young, padding it with feathers from her own breast. But the God-given instinct that builds that secure nest also forces the eaglets out of it before long. Eagles are made to fly, and the mother eagle will not fail to teach them. Only then will they become what they are meant to be.

So one day the mother eagle will disturb the twigs of the nest, making it an uncomfortable place to stay. Then she will pick up a perplexed eaglet, soar into the sky, and drop it. The little bird will begin to free-fall. Where is Mama now? She is not far away. Quickly she will swoop under and catch the fledgling on one strong wing. She will repeat this exercise until each eaglet is capable of flying on its own.

Are you afraid of free-falling, unsure of where or how hard you will land? Remember, God will fly to your rescue and spread His everlasting arms beneath you. He will also teach you something new and wonderful through it. Falling into God's arms is nothing to fear. JY

*He will ever keep your soul,
What would harm, He will control;
In the home and by the way
He will keep you day by day. —Psalter*

God's love does not keep us from trials
but sees us through them.

Known Unto God

Read: Psalm 77:1–15

*Has God forgotten to be gracious? Has He in anger
shut up His tender mercies? Psalm 77:9*

While visiting a World War I military cemetery in France, I was struck by the number of grave markers bearing only these words:

A SOLDIER OF THE GREAT WAR: KNOWN UNTO GOD

The cemetery was surrounded on three sides by stone panels bearing the names of 20,000 soldiers who fell in nearby battles. Imagining the loneliness of men dying in war and the anguish of families grieving at home was overpowering.

There may be times in life when we feel forgotten and alone. Like the psalmist we cry out: "Will the Lord cast off forever? And will He be favorable no more?... Has God forgotten to be gracious? Has He in anger shut up His tender mercies?" (Psalm 77:7, 9).

The psalmist's answer to feeling abandoned came in remembering all that God had done in the past, meditating on His wonderful work, and speaking of it to others (vv. 11–12).

In our darkest moments, we can remember the words of Jesus: "Are not five sparrows sold for two copper coins? And not one of them is forgotten before God. But the very hairs of your head are all numbered. Do not fear therefore; you are of more value than many sparrows" (Luke 12:6–7).

We are never forgotten by God.   DCM

*When trials loom or death is near,
In Christ we can confide;
We never need to feel alone—
He's always at our side. —Sper*

In every desert of trial, God offers an oasis of comfort.

Naomi

Read: Ruth 4:13–22

The women said to Naomi, "Blessed be the Lord, who has not left you this day without a close relative." Ruth 4:14

A wise person once told me, "Never be quick to judge whether something is a blessing or a curse." The story of Naomi reminds me of this.

The name *Naomi* means "my delight." But when bad things happened to her, Naomi wanted to change her name to match her circumstances. After her husband and sons died, Naomi concluded, "The hand of the Lord has gone out against me!" (Ruth 1:13). When people greeted her, she said, "Do not call me Naomi; call me Mara, for the Almighty has dealt very bitterly with me" (v. 20).

Rather than judge her circumstances in light of her identity as a follower of the one true God who had proclaimed unfailing love for His people, Naomi did what most of us tend to do: She judged God in light of her circumstances. And she judged wrongly. The hand of the Lord had not gone out against her. In fact, Naomi had a God-given treasure she had not yet discovered. Although Naomi lost her husband and two sons, she was given something totally unexpected—a devoted daughter-in-law and a grandchild who would be in the lineage of the Messiah.

As Naomi's life shows us, sometimes the worst thing that happens to us can open the door for the best that God has to give us.   JAL

Loving Father, help me not to judge your love for me on the basis of whether today brings good news or bad. Help me remember that you desire to use my circumstances to make me more like Jesus. Amen.

God's purpose for today's events may
not be seen till tomorrow.

Can We Rejoice?

Read: Habakkuk 3:17–19

Yet I will rejoice in the Lord. . . . The Lord God is my strength.
Habakkuk 3:18, 19

I'll never forget the question our Bible-study leader asked: "What do you fear would test your faith in God the most?" We were studying Habakkuk 3:17–18, where the prophet said that even if God sent suffering or loss, he would still rejoice.

As a single woman in my twenties, my answer was "I don't know if I could stand the pain of losing my parents." But I told God that day that even when they died I would rejoice in Him. I found out too soon that it's easier said than done.

A month later, Dad learned he had heart disease and didn't have long to live. He didn't know Jesus as his Savior, so I begged God not to let him die without coming to know Him. Not only did he die that year, so did Mom, who was a believer. I didn't know if my prayer for Dad was answered. I couldn't rejoice; I wondered if God had even heard my prayer.

As I wrestled with Him about my questions, I experienced the Lord as my "refuge and strength, a very present help in trouble" (Psalm 46:1). I found hope in the truth that God, "the Judge of all the earth," would do what was right by everyone (Genesis 18:25).

We can rejoice—when we are rejoicing in the Lord, our strong refuge and righteous Judge.   AC

Why must I bear this pain? I cannot tell;
I only know my Lord does all things well.
And so I trust in God, my all in all,
For He will bring me through, whate'er befall. —Smith

God tries our faith so that we may try His faithfulness.

Hold Hands and Jump!

Read: Ecclesiastes 4:8–12

Two are better than one. Ecclesiastes 4:9

When Leo and Amy opened a three-hundred-seat, fine-dining restaurant, Leo admitted he was "scared of everything." Amy equates their leap of faith in starting their business to holding hands while jumping off a mountain. But if you're going to do something scary, "you want to do it with someone you know and trust," Leo continued.

Chris and Karie, another couple who took a risk to own and run a restaurant together, say they have "a good working relationship, as well as mutual admiration for each other's work."

Solomon, the wisest man who ever lived, knew how crucial it is to have companions in life. He wrote, "Two are better than one" (Ecclesiastes 4:9). When one falls during a difficult time, another provides comfort and support (vv. 10–12). We need our spouses and friends to help us through the scary times and to provide emotional support. Loners make life harder for themselves (v. 8). But those who recognize their need for others find help and encouragement.

If you need to take a leap of faith—something involving finances, a career change, a new ministry—invite someone trustworthy to hold your hand as you make that jump. Or give that same encouragement to someone close to you. Because two *really are* better than one. AC

We are dependent on the strength
We draw from one another;
Words spoken give encouragement,
Love practiced draws us closer. —Sper

Those who trust God can help others to do the same.

How Long?

Read: Psalm 13

How long, O Lord? Will You forget me forever? How long will You hide Your face from me? Psalm 13:1

My friends Bob and Delores understand what it means to wait for answers—answers that never seem to come. When their son Jason and future daughter-in-law Lindsay were murdered in August 2004, a national manhunt was undertaken to find the killer and bring him to justice. After two years of prayer and pursuit, there were still no tangible answers to the painful questions the two hurting families wrestled with. There was only silence.

In such times we are vulnerable to wrong assumptions and conclusions about life, about God, and about prayer. In Psalm 13, David wrestled with the problem of unanswered prayer. He questioned why the world was so dangerous and pleaded for answers from God.

It's a hard psalm that David sang, and it seems to be one of frustration. Yet, in the end, his doubts and fears turned to trust. Why? Because the circumstances of our struggles cannot diminish the character of God and His care for His children. In verse 5, David turned a corner. From his heart he prayed, "But I have trusted in Your mercy; my heart shall rejoice in Your salvation."

In the pain and struggle of living without answers, we can always find comfort in our heavenly Father. BC

When we pray, God wraps us in His loving arms.

Killing Time

Read: Ephesians 5:1–17

Walk circumspectly, not as fools but as wise,
redeeming the time. Ephesians 5:15–16

A friend of mine was sitting on a park bench with his hands folded, staring into the distance. When I asked what he was doing, he replied, "Oh, just killing time."

What a cruel thing to do to something as valuable as time! Why kill it? Time is given to us to be cultivated, not murdered. Time should never be wasted but used to the best advantage.

Of course, there are times when we must relax and rest. Even Jesus said to His disciples, "Come aside... and rest a while" (Mark 6:31). But that was not "killing time"; it was using time for restoration. After they had rested, they would be able to use their time more fruitfully and profitably.

If a fraction of the time we waste could be used to pray, read the Bible, witness to others, visit a friend in distress, or comfort someone who is grieving, what a difference it would make! Today, when you have leisure time, ask yourself how you can best improve those extra moments. You may think I am being narrow-minded, but the Bible is clear—we are to be "wise, redeeming the time" (Ephesians 5:15–16).

Today, see how much good you can do for God and others—not how little you can get by with. It is not true that we can "make up lost time." It is gone forever!   MRD

God's people have so much to do
In serving Christ today
That they should use their precious time
To share, to love, to pray. —JDB

Time—use it or lose it!

Mandy Just Listened

Read: Job 2:11–13

They sat down with him on the ground seven days and seven nights, and no one spoke a word to him. Job 2:13

Marty had gotten an unexpected "thank you" for service to the company—a terse note that concluded, "Your position has been terminated."

After Marty had spent months fruitlessly searching for a job, his frustration finally got to him. Angrily, he screamed at God, "Why did you do this to me? Don't you care?" He continued his tirade until he noticed his dog Mandy cowering by a chair. Composing himself, he said, "Come here, pup. You should be glad you're a dog. At least you can't get fired from being man's best friend." As he poured out his woes and talked to Mandy, his bitterness disappeared.

David Biebel, the author who told this story, wrote: "You might think the relief came from all the things he said to God, and certainly that was part of it. But Mandy played a big part too... [She] didn't argue or offer solutions or advice. She just listened, wagging her tail and licking her master's hand."

When Job's three friends saw his misery, they just sat with him, wept, and said nothing for seven days. But then they abandoned the wisdom of their silence.

Sometimes we need to just "weep with those who weep" (Romans 12:15). Our listening ear may be what they need, so they can hear what God is saying to them. DJD

When our friends encounter suffering,
We can help them if we're near;
Some may need a word of comfort,
Others just a listening ear. —Sper

Listening may be the most important thing you do today.

Eclipse

Read: Psalm 148:1–14

*Let them praise the name of the Lord, for His name
alone is exalted. Psalm 148:13*

A friend who experienced a total solar eclipse in England described the incredible sensation of being engulfed by the rushing shadow of darkness, then being awed by the rapidly approaching dawn. Some observers saw it as merely a coincidence that the moon was in the exact position to shut out the sun's light from reaching the earth at that particular time and place. My friend, though, called it an amazing show put on by God. She saw it as evidence of God's design, order, and precise control in the universe that He created.

Psalm 148 calls upon all creation to shout God's glory: "Praise Him, sun and moon; praise Him, all you stars of light!... Praise the Lord... kings of the earth and all peoples" (vv. 3, 7, 11).

God's creation sings His praise and reminds us of His sovereign purposes and control of all things in our lives. We are to "praise the name of the Lord, for His name alone is exalted; His glory is above the earth and heaven" (v. 13).

These truths can be comforting when the sunlight of our lives is eclipsed by a time of darkness and difficulty. We can trust and praise the sovereign God, knowing that His design is perfect, that His timing is exact, and that He is in complete control.   DCM

This is my Father's world,
O let me ne'er forget
That though the wrong seems oft so strong
God is the ruler yet. —Babcock

Because God is in control, we have nothing to fear.

Knowing God

Read: Psalm 96:1–13

*Let him who glories glory in this, that he understands
and knows Me, that I am the Lord. Jeremiah 9:24*

It's one thing to know about God, but it's quite another to know
Him personally. Let's see how this distinction applies when considering some of God's attributes.

The thought that God is present everywhere is staggering. But to
be aware of His presence in times of need brings comfort and hope.

The thought that God knows everything is mind-boggling. But
to have the confidence that no detail of our lives escapes His attention is to enjoy a peace that endures through every trial.

The thought that the Lord is all-powerful makes us marvel at
His greatness. But to have Him actually work in, through, and for
us encourages us to relax in His mighty arms.

The thought that God never changes is a reassuring truth. But
to commit ourselves to the care of this never-changing One is to
know the stability of His faithfulness.

The thought that God is love is wonderful to contemplate. But
to know Him as a loving Redeemer through personal faith in His
Son, Jesus Christ, brings the joy of sins forgiven.

The writer of Psalm 96 knew God, and that relationship was
reflected in his words. His heart poured out praise, and he longed
for others to know the Lord and worship Him as well.

Do you know God personally? Does it show?   RDH

Sing praise to God who reigns above,
The God of all creation,
The God of power, the God of love,
The God of our salvation. —Schutz

Knowing about God is fascinating; knowing God personally
is life-changing.

The Power of Prayer

Read: Ephesians 6:10–18

*The effective, fervent prayer of a righteous
man avails much. James 5:16*

While crossing the Atlantic on a ship many years ago, Bible teacher and author F. B. Meyer was asked to speak to the passengers. An agnostic listened to Meyer's message about answered prayer and told a friend, "I didn't believe a word of it."

Later that same day, the agnostic went to hear Meyer speak to another group of passengers. But before he went to the meeting, he put two oranges in his pocket. On his way, he passed an elderly woman who was fast asleep in her deck chair. Her arms were outstretched and her hands were wide open, so as a joke he put the two oranges in her palms. After the meeting, he saw the woman happily eating one of the pieces of fruit.

"You seem to be enjoying that orange," he remarked with a smile. "Yes, sir," she replied. "My Father is very good to me." "What do you mean?" pressed the agnostic. She explained, "I have been seasick for days. I was asking God somehow to send me an orange. I fell asleep while I was praying. When I awoke, I found He had sent me not only one but two oranges!" The agnostic was amazed by the unexpected confirmation of Meyer's talk on answered prayer. Later, he put his trust in Christ.

Yes, God answers prayer! HGB

*For answered prayer we thank You, Lord,
We know You're always there
To hear us when we call on You;
We're grateful for Your care. —JDB*

God always gives us what we ask—or something better.

God Help Me!

Read: Jeremiah 2:26–37

Where are your gods that you have made for yourselves? Let them arise, if they can save you in the time of your trouble. Jeremiah 2:28

Ever notice how people react to tragedy? Even the nonreligious try to get the attention of God, whom they have previously ignored. Accounts of plane crashes, floods, tornadoes, or hurricanes often tell of someone who calls on the Lord for help.

It would be nice to think that the heavenly Father is just waiting for such times of panic so He can send all the emergency equipment of heaven to the rescue. But the Bible indicates otherwise. Through Jeremiah, the Lord challenged His people who were in trouble to get help in the hour of death from the idols they had worshiped. He wanted them to see the futility of trusting false gods.

The Lord may ask the same question of us. In an hour of distress He may say, "Why do you cry for me now? Where are your sports heroes and movie stars? Why not seek help from the TV, appeal to your paycheck, take comfort in your possessions, or rely on your credit cards? Let these gods whom you've served so faithfully now serve you!"

God doesn't want us to think we can go on trusting false gods and still expect Him to protect us from trouble. He graciously grants forgiveness to us if we are truly repentant. And He offers hope and help to those who have learned to depend on Him all the time.   MD

The gods of this world are empty and vain,
They cannot give peace to one's heart;
The Living and True One deserves all our love—
From Him may we never depart. —DJD

Those who walk with God always find Him close at hand.

When We're Wronged

Read: 1 Peter 2:19–23

When you do good and suffer, if you take it patiently,
this is commendable before God. 1 Peter 2:20

It's natural to want to defend ourselves against injustice and to strike back. But if we're quiet and peaceful when others mistreat and persecute us, we are responding in a Christlike way. God wants to develop in us qualities that are unnatural for us. Anyone can be patient when everything's going his or her way. The greater virtue is to remain calm and controlled under provocation (1 Peter 2:20).

François Fénelon, a seventeenth-century theologian, put it this way: "Don't be so upset when evil men and women defraud you. Let them do as they please; just seek to do the will of God... Silent peace and sweet fellowship with God will repay you for every evil thing done against you. Fix your eyes on God." He allows painful situations to come into your life and, according to Fénelon, "He does this for your benefit."

For our benefit? Indeed! As we respond to injustice in a Christlike way, our anxiety, insecurity, and pessimism will be transformed into tranquility, stability, and hope.

Why do we lash out when we're mistreated? Why are we so quick to defend ourselves or to seek revenge? Is it not that we place too much value on our own comfort and rights?

If so, we must pray, echoing the words of Augustine, "Heal me of this lust of mine to always vindicate myself." DHR

Life can be lived with joy and peace
Amid its heartache and pain,
For with God's help our hate can cease
And peace and justice will reign. —DJD

The best way to respond to wrong is to do what's right.

Bridges of Grace

Read: Acts 5:33–42

*They departed..., rejoicing that they were counted worthy
to suffer shame for His name. Acts 5:41*

Imagine for a moment that you are driving through the desert in Southern California and you see the magnificent Golden Gate Bridge spanning the dried-up bed of "Three Frogs Creek" on the outskirts of "Turtle Soup Junction." What a ridiculous sight that would be!

So too, the Lord never displays His power and grace at an inappropriate time or place, but He always provides according to the difficulty of the hour. He does not impart strength until it is needed.

We shudder when we think of what some of God's children are enduring because of their faithfulness to the Savior. Many have chosen the path of intense suffering rather than follow the line of least resistance. I wonder, would we do the same?

Of course, the Lord does not ask us to make such a commitment before it is necessary. And we can be sure that when we "suffer for His sake" (Philippians 1:29), He will provide whatever we need to endure the pain.

As servants of Christ, we can take one step at a time and be confident that whether we come to a dried-up gulch or a surging river, the Lord's bridges of grace will be just right to allow us safe passage to the other side.   MD

God gives enough grace for each trial we face.

Happy Adversity?

Read: James 1:1–12

Count it all joy when you fall into various trials. James 1:2

On the back of a wedding anniversary card were some wiggly lines drawn by our three-year-old grandson. Alongside was a note from our daughter explaining that Trevor told her what he had written: "I'm writing a letter for your love and happy adversity."

Trevor's "mistake" has become our watchword, because "happy adversity" embodies the biblical principle of facing difficulties with joy: "Count it all joy when you fall into various trials, knowing that the testing of your faith produces patience" (James 1:2–3).

From our perspective, adversity is anything but happy. We have the idea that the Christian life is supposed to be trouble-free, and we see little value in hardship. But God sees it differently.

J. B. Phillips's translation of James 1:2–3 reads: "When all kinds of trials and temptations crowd into your lives, my brothers, don't resent them as intruders, but welcome them as friends! Realize that they come to test your faith and to produce in you the quality of endurance."

Affliction does not come as a thief to steal our happiness, but as a friend bringing the gift of staying power. Through it all, God promises us His wisdom and strength.

So don't be offended if I wish you "Happy Adversity" today.

DCM

Life's burdens are designed not to break us but to bend us toward God.

February 1

A Difficult Hill

Read: Isaiah 40:25–31

*He gives power to the weak, and to those who have
no might He increases strength. Isaiah 40:29*

Researchers at the University of Virginia have found that most people perceive a hill to be steeper than it really is, especially if they're tired or carrying a heavy load. When asked to estimate the slope of a hill, test participants consistently misjudged it, thinking a ten-degree slant was about thirty degrees, and rating a five-degree slope as nearly twenty degrees. Hardly any of them believed they could be that far off.

When we're burdened and exhausted, even a minor problem can seem too big for us to handle. As we encounter a trial in life, we're tempted to sit down at the base of that difficult hill and stay there, convinced that the grade is too steep for us.

That is why we need the encouragement of God's Word. It draws our attention to our untiring God, who knows our need. Isaiah wrote, "The Creator of the ends of the earth neither faints nor is weary. His understanding is unsearchable. He gives power to the weak, and to those who have no might He increases strength" (Isaiah 40:28–29).

Because we so easily misjudge life's difficulties, we need courage to keep going when we are tempted to quit. Take a step of faith today and join those who depend on the Lord, who run and are not weary, who walk and do not faint (v. 31). In His strength, you can conquer any difficult hill.   DCM

*As we live for Christ and follow Him,
The way may seem quite steep;
But if we trust His grace and strength,
Our steps He'll guide and keep. —Fitzhugh*

God always gives enough strength for the next step.

Running Well

Read: Isaiah 40:27–31

*Do you not know that those who run in a race all run,
but one receives the prize? Run in such a way that
you may obtain it. 1 Corinthians 9:24*

A computer study of 5,000 racehorses has revealed a way to predict whether or not a young horse will develop into a good runner. A professor at the Massachusetts Institute of Technology used computers and high-speed cameras to find out how a good horse runs. He discovered that the legs of a fast horse operate much like the spokes of a wheel. Each leg touches down only as the leg before it pushes off. The effect is peak efficiency of effort and speed.

In the Old Testament, Isaiah talked about running well in the course of life. He said that the person who runs the best is the one who learns to "wait on the Lord" (Isaiah 40:31). He doesn't waste energy trying to do things on his own. He looks to the Lord for his strength and hope.

In the New Testament, the Christian life is likened to a race. The apostle Paul indicated that those who run well are characterized by self-control and self-discipline (1 Corinthians 9:24–27). The author of Hebrews said, "Let us lay aside every weight, and the sin which so easily ensnares us, and let us run with endurance the race that is set before us" (Hebrews 12:1).

Do you want to earn an imperishable crown? Then wait on the Lord. Practice self-control. Lay aside sinful burdens. These are the secrets of running well. — MD

*To run the race of life in Christ,
This must become your daily goal:
Confess your sins, trust God for strength,
Use discipline and self-control. —Sper*

Those who wait on the Lord run without the weight of sin.

The Power of Weakness

Read: 2 Corinthians 1:3–11

I can do all things through Christ who
strengthens me. Philippians 4:13

I received a letter from a woman who read about the way I had learned to live a life dependent on God. She was challenged as she read that Christ's strength was manifested through my weakness, particularly when I started a Bible study while recovering from a nervous condition.

She read about my trembling hands, and how my neighbors were encouraged to admit their own weaknesses and to depend on Christ as they saw me learning to do. She wrote, "I laughed and cried as I read your story. I feel deeply encouraged that God can use me, even though I feel weak."

We may think that we attract others to Christ more effectively through our strengths than through our weaknesses. But the Lord used trouble and weakness in the apostle Paul's life to teach him to rely on God's power (2 Corinthians 1:9). He testified, "When I am weak, then I am strong" (12:10).

When Christians act as if they hardly know what weakness is, needy people often think, "I could never be like that." But when Christians admit they experience Christ's strength in their weakness, they proclaim this hope: "The strength Christ gives to me, He can give to you!" Whose strength will you proclaim today—your own, or God's?   JY

God uses weakness to reveal
His great sufficiency;
So if we let Him work through us,
His power we will see. —Sper

To experience God's strength, we must first
admit our weakness.

No Greater Love!

Read: James 4:1–6

He gives more grace. James 4:6

Pastor and author F. B. Meyer once confided to a friend that he felt welcome in any home in England except his own. His loveless marriage was a source of deep heartache. Yet Meyer believed that he, by his aching soul, was being prepared to give love and strength to others, and especially to his wife at the end of her days. He wrote these words to her:

If then your future life should need
A strength my love can only gain
Through suffering—or my heart be freed
Only by sorrow from some stain,
Then you shall give, and I will take
This crown of fire for Love's dear sake.

You too may feel unloved. If so, don't try to find love by befriending this world (James 4:4–5). Rather, give yourself to knowing and loving God. Let Him meet your deep need for affection and caring. "He gives more grace" (v. 6)—more than anything you could ever gain on your own.

And here is multiplied grace: When you know and experience God's unconditional love, you can then give yourself to others— even to those who have caused you great pain.

Allow God by His grace to work through your heartache, to control your intentions and desires. Allow Him to draw you in His direction and hold you with His affection, molding you to His perfect design. There is no greater love! DHR

No one is beyond the reach of God's love.

Dangerous Crossings

Read: Psalm 77:16–20

*Your way was in the sea, Your path in the great waters,
and Your footsteps were not known. Psalm 77:19*

I don't wade in swift streams anymore. The bottom's too slippery, the current's too strong, and my old legs aren't what they used to be.

So many challenges that I once took on readily are now too difficult for me. Like the psalmist, I lose sleep sometimes, wondering how I can negotiate them (Psalm 77:1–4).

Then I remember the "works of the Lord," His "wonders of old" (v. 11). His "way was in the sea, [His] path in the great waters," though He left no footprints behind (v. 19).

That's the way it is with God. Although you can't see Him, He is surely there. Unseen, He leads His people "like a flock" (v. 20). He does not fear the currents and storms of life, for His strength and courage are infinite.

And there's more: The Shepherd leads us through the help of other people. He led Israel "by the hand of Moses and Aaron" (v. 20). He leads us through the wise counsel of a father or mother, the strong grip of a godly friend, the loving encouragement of a caring husband or wife, the gentle touch of a young child.

Good hands are reaching out to us. Our Lord is a tough and tender Shepherd who leads through perilous crossings to the other side. Have you put your hand in His?   DHR

THINKING IT OVER

*What causes you to lose sleep?
Why not leave it in God's hands?*

God tells us to burden Him with what burdens us.

Nothing Left But God

Read: 2 Chronicles 20:1–17

*Do not be afraid nor dismayed because
of this great multitude, for the battle is not yours,
but God's. 2 Chronicles 20:15*

A wise Bible teacher once said, "Sooner or later God will bring self-sufficient people to the place where they have no resource but Him—no strength, no answers, nothing but Him. Without God's help, they're sunk."

He then told of a despairing man who confessed to his pastor, "My life is really in bad shape." "How bad?" the pastor inquired. Burying his head in his hands, the man moaned, "I'll tell you how bad—all I've got left is God." The pastor's face lit up. "I'm happy to assure you that a person with nothing left but God has more than enough for great victory!"

In today's Bible reading, the people of Judah were also in trouble. They admitted their lack of power and wisdom to conquer their foes. All they had left was God! But King Jehoshaphat and the people saw this as reason for hope, not despair. "Our eyes are upon You," they declared to God (2 Chronicles 20:12). And their hope was not disappointed as He fulfilled His promise: "The battle is not yours, but God's" (v. 15).

Are you in a position where all self-sufficiency is gone? As you turn your eyes on the Lord and put your hope in Him, you have God's reassuring promise that you need nothing more.   JY

*In You, O Lord, we take delight,
Our every need You will supply;
We long to do what's good and right,
So, Lord, on You we will rely. —DJD*

When all you have is God, you have all you need.

Musical Interludes

Read: Mark 6:30–34

He said to them, "Come aside by yourselves to
a deserted place and rest a while." Mark 6:31

God writes the music for our lives. Our role is to follow His lead—humming, harmonizing, blending, and singing in tune.

Serving the Lord, like singing, can be stirring and rewarding. But when we are set aside by illness, or replacement, or retirement, the interludes can be frustrating and unfulfilling. When God says to us, "Come... rest a while" (Mark 6:31), we may not want to stop. It seems that our performance is over, that we've come to the end of our song.

If we allow ourselves to be overwhelmed with our inactivity, it will cause us to focus on our defects and our circumstances. But we need to remind ourselves that the Lord may be using our time of rest to make our music better.

The Great Conductor is counting time with precision. There is more to the arrangement than we know. If we keep our eyes on Him, in time He'll enable us to chime in again.

In the meantime we can enjoy the rest. The quiet times are opportunities to quiet our souls and compose ourselves for the measures that lie ahead. The rest is not a mistake, nor an omission, but a necessary part of the symphony God wrote in the beginning and is conducting for us every day.

The Conductor knows best. Wait on Him.   DHR

God uses life's stops to prepare us for the next start.

Are Good Times Bad?

Read: Jeremiah 32:1–2, 16–30

*You show lovingkindness to thousands.... You are great in
counsel and mighty in work. Jeremiah 32:18, 19*

In books and sermons, Christians are often asked whether their
faith is strong enough to withstand *bad* times. I'm wondering,
though, if a better question is this: "Is my faith strong enough to
survive *good* times?"

I keep hearing about people who drift away from the Lord not
when life is bad but when it's good. That's when God seems unnecessary.

Too often we interpret His blessing as an indication of our goodness, not His. We assume we deserve everything pleasant that happens, and we fail to appreciate what He is telling us about himself
through the good gifts He lets us enjoy.

In *The Problem of Pain*, C. S. Lewis wrote, "God whispers to us
in our pleasures... but shouts in our pains." If we refuse to listen
when He whispers to us, He may use shouts to get our attention.
That happened to the Israelites. Although God had given them "a
land flowing with milk and honey," they turned from Him, so He
caused "calamity to come upon them" (Jeremiah 32:22–23).

The goodness of God is a reason to obey Him, not an opportunity to disobey. When we realize that, our relationship with the
Lord will be strengthened, not weakened, by His wonderful bounty
and blessing.   JAL

THINKING IT OVER

*Do you draw closer to God when life is good,
or when troubles come your way? Why?
What is God saying to you through His goodness today?*

The goodness of God speaks volumes about His character.

God Still Rules

Read: Habakkuk 2:1–14

Look among the nations and watch—
be utterly astounded! Habakkuk 1:5

As the year 1999 came to a close, great leaders of the century were remembered, including Prime Minister Winston Churchill and President Franklin Roosevelt. During World War II, they led Great Britain and the United States to defeat Nazism and Fascism.

Did you know that both men nearly lost their lives before the war began? In December 1931, Churchill was struck by a car as he crossed Fifth Avenue in New York City. In Miami in December 1933, an assassin's bullet barely missed Roosevelt and killed the man standing beside him.

Both leaders could have died, but they survived. Why? I believe God wanted these two men alive to lead their respective nations to victory over the enemy.

The Bible teaches that God causes nations and their leaders to rise and fall (Daniel 2:21; 4:32–35; 5:21). When Habakkuk complained that it didn't seem right for God to use wicked Babylon to discipline Israel, the Lord assured the prophet that this did not mean evil would triumph. God was still in control and would one day bring about perfect justice (Habakkuk 2:13–14).

We too can be sure that our times are in God's hands. No matter what may happen in this world, God still rules!   DCE

This is my Father's world—
Oh, let me ne'er forget
That though the wrong seems oft so strong,
God is the Ruler yet. —Babcock

God's sovereignty overrules any calamity.

God's Song

Read: Ephesians 2:1–10

We are His workmanship, created in Christ Jesus
for good works. Ephesians 2:10

A church organist was practicing a piece by Felix Mendelssohn and not doing too well. Frustrated, he gathered up his music and started to leave. He had not noticed a stranger come in and sit in a rear pew.

As the organist turned to go, the stranger came forward and asked if he could play the piece. "I never let anyone touch this organ!" came the blunt reply. Finally, after two more polite requests, the grumpy musician reluctantly gave him permission.

The stranger sat down and filled the sanctuary with beautiful, flawless music. When he finished, the organist asked, "Who are you?" The man replied, "I am Felix Mendelssohn." The organist had almost prevented the song's creator from playing his own music!

There are times when we too try to play the chords of our lives and prevent our Creator from making beautiful music. Like that stubborn organist, we only reluctantly take our hands off the keys. As His people, we are "created in Christ Jesus for good works, which God prepared beforehand" (Ephesians 2:10). But our lives won't produce beautiful music unless we let Him work through us.

God has a symphony written for our lives. Let's allow Him to have His way in us. DCE

Once we stop our own devising,
Quit the schemes of our own choosing,
Cease from all our fruitless striving,
God steps in with grace and power! —DJD

God's ability is not limited by our inability.

Refusing the Easy Way

Read: Daniel 1:1–8

*Daniel purposed in his heart that he would
not defile himself. Daniel 1:8*

Looking out the window of an airplane, you can see the winding paths of rivers below. Except for some man-made waterways, all rivers have one thing in common—they all are crooked. The reason is simple—they follow the path of least resistance. Rivers find their way around anything that blocks their flow because they take the easy way.

The same can be said for some people. Because they fail to resist the devil, they yield to temptation and deviate from the path God would have them follow. Unlike Daniel, who "purposed in his heart that he would not defile himself" (Daniel 1:8), they bend to worldly pressures and compromise what they know is right.

Writing to followers of Christ, John said that we can be victorious in our struggle against evil because "He who is in you is greater than he who is in the world" (1 John 4:4). Rather than being overcome, we can be overcomers. Nothing should deter us from the course God wants us to travel. We don't have to yield to any temptation or foe. The Holy Spirit who lives in us will strengthen us so that we can remain steadfast.

We won't become "crooked" if we refuse to follow the path of least resistance. RDH

You won't go astray on the straight and narrow way.

God Sees You

Read: Genesis 16:1–13

She called the name of the Lord who spoke to her,
You-Are-the-God-Who-Sees. Genesis 16:13

Hagar, Sarah's handmaid, was being treated unkindly by Sarah, so she fled into the wilderness. As Hagar stood beside a spring in that desolate and lonely place, the Angel of the Lord visited her. He assured her that God himself was aware of her situation. Hagar responded, "You-Are-the-God-Who-Sees" (Genesis 16:13). She found great comfort in knowing that the Lord God saw her and knew about her distress.

You and I can have that same confidence in God's watchful care. We can be sure that the Lord God is with us wherever we go, and that He knows everything that happens to us. As the All-Powerful One, He is able to solve every problem, no matter how overwhelming or perplexing it may be. We are never alone, never forgotten, and never beyond hope.

Whatever your troubling circumstances are, whether you're afflicted by illness or injury, brokenhearted over the loss of a loved one, or disillusioned because your dearest friend has betrayed or rejected you, God knows and cares. You may be deeply depressed, or perhaps you're plagued by loneliness and discouragement. But you can be confident that you are under God's watchful eye. Yes, like Hagar, you can know that God sees you. RDH

Beneath His watchful eye
His saints securely dwell;
That hand which bears all nature up
Shall guard His children well. —Doddridge

We need not fear the perils around us because
the eye of the Lord is always upon us.

The Advantage of Weakness

Read: 2 Corinthians 12:1–10

*He said to me, "My grace is sufficient for you, for My strength
is made perfect in weakness." 2 Corinthians 12:9*

I always enjoy talking with my old college friend Tom and getting caught up on what the Lord has been teaching us since we
last met.

One day Tom began with a sheepish grin, "You know, I can't
believe how many years it has taken me to learn my latest lesson—
and I'm a Bible teacher!" He went on to list some of the trials and
testings he and his family had been facing and how unworthy he felt
teaching an adult Sunday school class. "Week after week I felt I was
a total failure," he confided, "and kept wondering if this might be
my last Sunday before announcing my resignation."

Then one Sunday a young woman stayed after class to speak to
Tom. She was a friend of his family, so she knew what they had
been going through. "Tom," she said, "I hope you won't take this
the wrong way, but you're a much better teacher when you're going
through tough times."

Tom smiled as he told me, "Only then did I feel that I grasped
the Lord's response to Paul's thorn in the flesh: 'My grace is sufficient for you, for My strength is made perfect in weakness'" (2 Corinthians 12:9).

When we recognize how much we need God, He will strengthen
us. That's the advantage of weakness.   JY

Inadequate but mighty—
How strange, yet wholly true;
Weak servants filled with power
The Lord's great work can do. —Bosch

In tough times, God teaches us to trust.

Hope in God

Read: Psalm 42

*Why are you cast down, O my soul? . . . Hope in God, for I shall
yet praise Him for the help of His countenance. Psalm 42:5*

Looking at the western shores of Sri Lanka, I found it hard to
imagine that a tsunami had struck just a few months earlier.
The sea was calm and beautiful, couples were walking in the bright
sunshine, and people were going about their business—all giving
the scene an ordinary feeling I wasn't prepared for. The impact of
the disaster was still there, but it had gone underground into the
hearts and minds of the survivors. The trauma itself would not be
easily forgotten.

It was catastrophic grief that prompted the psalmist to cry out
in anguish: "My tears have been my food day and night, while they
continually say to me, 'Where is your God?'" (Psalm 42:3). The
struggle of his heart had likewise been turned inward. While the
rest of the world went on with business as usual, he carried in his
heart the need for deep and complete healing.

Only as we submit our brokenness to the good and great Shepherd of our hearts can we find the peace that allows us to respond
to life: "Why are you cast down, O my soul? And why are you dis-
quieted within me? Hope in God, for I shall yet praise Him for the
help of His countenance" (v. 5).

Hope in God—it's the only solution for the deep traumas of the
heart.   BC

The Christian's hope is in the Lord,
We rest secure in His sure Word;
And though we're tempted to despair,
We do not doubt that God is there. —DJD

No one is hopeless whose hope is in God.

Midnight Encouragement

Read: Judges 7:1–23

Your hands shall be strengthened to go down
against the camp. Judges 7:11

The Midianites and their allies had invaded Israel. It was the time of the judges, and Gideon could muster only 32,000 men against an army "as numerous as locusts" (Judges 7:12). Then God cut the army of Israel down to 300 (vv. 2–7). Gideon was afraid, so God sent him into the enemy camp at night. Crouching behind cover, the Israelite captain heard one soldier tell another about a dream (vv. 13–14). A loaf of barley bread had tumbled into the Midianite camp, destroying one of its tents. His friend saw it as a sure sign that Gideon would win the battle.

Gideon was greatly encouraged. After worshiping God, he returned to the camp, organized his 300 men with their trumpets and lamps, and routed the superior Midianite forces (vv. 15–22).

As Christ's followers we're not battling armies, but we are at war. Spiritual foes attack us (Ephesians 6:10–12). They undermine our confidence and sap our strength. We're also battling ourselves—our weaknesses, fears, and doubts (Romans 7:15–25). After a while, we can get discouraged.

But our God is the great Encourager. When our resolve weakens or our vision fades, by His power He will give us the strength we need (Ephesians 3:16)—even when the enemy seems more numerous than a swarm of locusts. DCE

As we meet fierce foes on the pathway of life,
Whether Satan or self or sin,
Let us look to the Lord for encouragement;
If we do, the battle we'll win! —Fitzhugh

To trust is to triumph, for the battle is the Lord's.

February 16

He's Been Faithful

Read: Psalm 119:89–96

Your faithfulness endures to all generations. Psalm 119:90

J im and Carol Cymbala prayed and praised and preached their way through a personal two-year nightmare. Their teenage daughter Chrissy had turned her back on the God they loved and served so faithfully. Although their hearts were breaking, Jim and Carol continued ministering to the people of the Brooklyn Tabernacle in New York City.

Some people think that Carol wrote the song "He's Been Faithful" after her daughter's dramatic return to God, but she didn't. She wrote it before. Carol refers to it as "a song of hope born in the midst of my pain." While hurting deeply, Carol said that her song "became like a balm to my heart, strengthening me once again." The words she wrote during that time helped her to move forward. Although her daughter had not yet come back to the Lord, Carol could praise Him for His loving faithfulness in her own life.

Later, when Chrissy showed up at home and fell to her knees begging forgiveness, the truth of Psalm 119:90 became real to Carol: God is faithful not just to our generation, but to all generations! Carol also experienced in a new way a line of her own song that has blessed so many: "What I thought was impossible, I've seen my God do!"   JAL

When we have nothing left but God,
we find that God is enough.

Being Realistic

Read: Psalm 27

Whenever I am afraid, I will trust in You.
Psalm 56:3

Few of us are traveling to heaven in a state of freedom from all fear. Who can honestly testify that they always practice this verse: "In God I have put my trust; I will not be afraid" (Psalm 56:11)? We do trust, and yet we may be troubled at times by gnawing worries. Our common experience is that our trust in God is mingled with episodes of worry.

Even the apostle Paul, who wrote many of the New Testament letters, had some anxieties. He confessed to the Corinthians, "I was with you in weakness, in fear, and in much trembling" (1 Corinthians 2:3).

So don't worry that you have worries! Don't pretend you never have them. If you are troubled by anxieties, admit them to yourself. Share them with a trusted friend. Above all, talk to the all-compassionate friend, Jesus Christ, who knows your every thought and emotion (Psalm 139:4). With compassion, He says to you, "Do not fear" (Luke 12:32). Ask Him for the grace to help you overcome your fears and worries. Then, "wait on the Lord; be of good courage, and He shall strengthen your heart" (Psalm 27:14).

On your journey through life, whenever you're afraid, trust in the Lord (Psalm 56:3).   VCG

THINKING IT OVER

What worry do you need to talk to the Lord about?

Trusting God's faithfulness dispels our fearfulness.

Living Life to the Maximum

Read: John 10:7–11

I have come that they may have life, and that they
may have it more abundantly. John 10:10

Aveteran mountain climber was sharing his experiences with a group of novices preparing for their first major climb. He had conquered many of the world's most difficult peaks, so he was qualified to give them some advice. "Remember this," he said, "your goal is to experience the exhilaration of the climb and the joy of reaching . . . the peak. Each step draws you closer to the top. If your purpose for climbing is just to avoid death, your experience will be minimal."

I see an application to the Christian's experience. Jesus did not call us to live the Christian life just to escape hell. It's not to be a life of minimum joy and fulfillment, but a life that is full and over-flowing. Our purpose in following Christ should not be merely to avoid eternal punishment. If that's our primary motivation, we are missing the wonders and joys and victories of climbing higher and higher with Jesus.

The Lord promised us "life... more abundantly" (John 10:10). We cannot experience a full and abundant life if we are living in fear. When we walk by faith, we will see each day of the Christian life as a challenge to be met, and as one more upward step to glory!

Do not live minimally. Live life to the maximum! Climb that mountain with confidence!   DCE

God has given life abundant—
Live it fully every day;
Though our time on earth is fleeting,
He goes with us all the way. —Hess

We get the most out of life when we live for Christ.

"Joy Stealers"

Read: Philippians 1:1–11

He who has begun a good work in you
will complete it. Philippians 1:6

Why do many Christians fail to experience real joy, which is listed as a fruit of the Holy Spirit in Galatians 5:22?

In his book *Laugh Again*, Charles Swindoll suggests three common "joy stealers"—worry, stress, and fear. He defines worry as "an inordinate anxiety about something that may or may not occur." (And it usually doesn't.) Stress, says the author, is "intense strain over a situation we can't change or control." (But God can.) And fear, according to Swindoll, is a "dreadful uneasiness over danger, evil, or pain." (And it magnifies our problems.)

Swindoll says that to resist these "joy stealers" we must embrace the same confidence that Paul expressed in his letter to the Philippians. After giving thanks for the Philippian believers (1:3–5), the apostle assured them "that He who has begun a good work in you will complete it until the day of Jesus Christ" (v. 6).

Whatever causes us worry, stress, and fear cannot ultimately keep God from continuing His work in us. With this confidence we can begin each day knowing that He is in control. We can leave everything in His hands.

Resist those "joy stealers" by renewing your confidence in God each morning. Then relax and rejoice.   JY

Although our joy will wane at times
From worry, stress, and fear,
God keeps on working in our heart
And tells us He is near. —DJD

Happiness depends on happenings; joy depends on Jesus.

He's Never Grumpy

Read: Luke 11:5–10

Ask, and it will be given to you. Luke 11:9

While driving my car the other day, I saw a sign that said, "Sometimes I wake up grumpy—but usually I let him sleep." It reminded me of the night my pregnant wife awakened me saying we had to get to the hospital because the baby was on the way. Half-awake, I replied, "Let's go back to sleep and take care of things in the morning." Then suddenly I realized what she had said, and I was up in a flash.

In Luke 11, a man who needed food for a guest went to a friend's house at midnight and asked for three loaves of bread. The awakened friend may have replied somewhat as I did. After all, it was the middle of the night. Yet he got up and provided the requested food (v. 8). I don't think the man gave his friend what he wanted just because he wouldn't go away. Rather, he got up because he realized that this friend would not have had the boldness to wake him if he hadn't been desperate.

The point is this: If an earthly friend will overcome his reluctance to meet your need, will not your heavenly Father, who is never reluctant, do far more than that? He never sleeps, He is never grumpy, and He wants the very best for you. Therefore, do not hesitate to ask, seek, and knock (v. 9). He will always be there for you.

HVL

Pray on, then, child of God, pray on;
This is your duty and your task.
To God the answering belongs;
Yours is the simpler part—to ask. —Chisholm

God is never inconvenienced by our prayers.

Living Water

Read: Jeremiah 2:4–13

Jesus stood and cried out, saying, "If anyone thirsts,
let him come to Me and drink." John 7:37

Lee Atwater was a well-known figure in U.S. politics. He engineered the successful 1988 presidential campaign of George H. W. Bush and was the head of the Republican National Committee (1988–1991). But in the midst of all his activities he developed an inoperable brain tumor and died at the age of forty.

During his illness, Atwater came to realize that wealth, honor, and power are not life's supreme values. Admitting to a deep emptiness within himself, he urged people to work at filling up the "spiritual vacuum in American society." In an insightful comment, he confessed, "My illness helped me to see that what was missing in society is what is missing in me—a little heart, a lot of brotherhood."

In his day, Jeremiah perceived that same kind of vacuum in many of his fellow Israelites. He warned them against the danger of personal and national emptiness. They were digging cisterns, he said, "broken cisterns that can hold no water" (Jeremiah 2:13).

What about your own life? Is it spiritually dried up? Ask Jesus, the fountain of living water (John 7:37), to fill you with His presence. Then joy and peace will begin to bubble up and even overflow. VCG

I heard the voice of Jesus say,
"Behold, I freely give the living water,
Thirsty one, stoop down
And drink and live." —Bonar

The only real thirst quencher is Jesus—the living water.

February 22

Worrier or Warrior?

Read: Ephesians 3:14–21

*[God] is able to do exceedingly abundantly above
all that we ask or think. Ephesians 3:20*

A missionary wrote a newsletter to thank his supporters for being "prayer warriors." Because of a typing error, though, he called them "prayer *worriers.*" For some of us, that might be a good description.

In his book *Growing Your Soul,* Neil Wiseman writes, "Prayer must be more than a kind of restatement of fretting worries or a mulling over of problems. Our petitions must move beyond gloomy desperation, which deals mostly with calamity and despair."

During an anxious time in my life, I became a "prayer worrier." I would beg, "Lord, please keep my neighbor from causing me problems tomorrow." Or, "Father, don't let that ornery person spread gossip about me."

But then the Lord taught me to pray *for* people, rather than *against* them. I began to say, "Lord, bless and encourage my neighbor, and help him to sense Your love." Then I watched to see what God would do. The Lord's amazing answers not only helped others but also helped to cure my own anxiety!

Paul was no "prayer worrier." He prayed for God's people that they might know the strength, love, and fullness of God, who is able to do far more than we can ask or even think (Ephesians 3:14–21). Such confidence made Paul a true "prayer warrior." Are your prayers like that?   JY

*As we resolve to live for Christ
In actions, words, and deeds,
We'll yield our anxious hearts to Him
And pray for others' needs. —Branon*

Fervent prayer dispels anxious care.

Above Your Problems

Read: Isaiah 40:15–31

*Those who wait on the Lord . . . shall mount up
with wings like eagles. Isaiah 40:31*

One of the pitfalls of living in our troublesome world is that we can become problem-centered rather than God-centered. When this happens, we lose the proper perspective. Gradually, all our problems begin to look huge and the strength of almighty God seems small. Instead of moving mountains by faith, we become constant worriers, creating mountains of needless pressure for ourselves and others.

Isaiah 40 is an effective prescription for those of us whose God seems small. God reminds us that He is much bigger than the world He created. He points out that compared to Him, "the nations are as a drop in a bucket" (v. 15) and the inhabitants of earth "are like grasshoppers" (v. 22). His words aren't meant to belittle us, but rather to encourage us to look to Him and gain His perspective of life.

Yet, God offers us more than a new perspective. He offers us something that will enable us to live by that view. If we will depend on Him instead of brooding over our problems, He will renew our strength, and wings of faith will lift our hearts above our difficulties. Some of them may be huge, but we can see them as smaller than our great God. And that makes all the difference.   JY

*Lord, give us wings to soar above
Our problems great and small,
With strengthened faith and confidence
To trust You with them all. —Sper*

Worry ends where faith begins.

Our God Is Marching On

Read: Habakkuk 2:6–20

The Lord is in His holy temple. Let all the earth
keep silence before Him. Habakkuk 2:20

In 1861, during the U.S. Civil War, author and lecturer Julia Ward Howe visited Washington, D.C. One day she went outside the city and saw a large number of soldiers marching. Early the next morning she awoke with words for a song in her mind.

She was aware of all the ugliness of the war, but her faith led her to write: "Mine eyes have seen the glory of the coming of the Lord." She saw, I believe, that in spite of and through all the ugliness, God was "marching on" toward the day when He will right the wrongs of the ages.

The prophet Habakkuk came to a similar conclusion. Chapter 1 of his book tells us how troubled he was when he learned that God was going to punish the people of Judah by letting them be conquered by the wicked Babylonians. In chapter 2, God assured His servant that—in spite of and through all the ugliness and wrongs of history—He is "marching on" toward the day when "the earth will be filled with the knowledge of the glory of the Lord" (v. 14).

If we believe that God is "marching on," in spite of all the brutal conflicts that mark our day, we will not despair. We can quietly await the final verdict from our Lord, who rules the universe from "His holy temple" (v. 20). HVL

God rules as Sovereign on His throne,
He judges great and small;
And those who would His earth destroy
Beneath His rod shall fall. —DJD

Someday the scales of justice will be perfectly balanced.

February 25

Celebrate Winter

Read: Psalm 42

Why are you cast down, O my soul? . . . Hope in God, for I shall
yet praise Him for the help of His countenance. Psalm 42:5

I love living where there are four seasons. But even though I love settling down with a good book by a crackling fire when it's snowing, I must admit that my love for the seasons grows a little dim when the long gray days of winter drone on into February.

Yet regardless of the weather, there is always something special about winter: Christmas! Thankfully, long after the decorations are down, the reality of Christmas still lifts my spirits no matter what's happening.

If it weren't for the reality of Christ's birth, not only would winter be dark and dreary, but our hearts would be bleak and have nothing to hope for. No hope for the freedom from guilt and judgment. No hope of His reassuring and strengthening presence through dark and difficult times. No hope for a future secured in heaven.

In the winter of a troubled life, the psalmist asked, "Why are you cast down, O my soul?" The remedy was clear: "Hope in God, for I shall yet praise Him for the help of His countenance" (Psalm 42:5).

In C. S. Lewis's tales of Narnia, Mr. Tumnus complains that in Narnia it is "always winter and never Christmas." But for those of us who know the God who made the seasons, it is always Christmas in our hearts!   JS

When our lives are heavy-laden,
Cold and bleak as winter long,
Stir the embers in our hearts, Lord;
Make Your flame burn bright and strong. —Kieda

Let the reality of Christmas chase away the blahs of winter.

Help for the Helpless

Read: Hebrews 4:14–16

Let us therefore come boldly to the throne of grace, that we may obtain mercy and find grace to help in time of need. Hebrews 4:16

I sometimes ask people, "Where does it say in the Bible, 'God helps those who help themselves'?" Most say they're not sure, but the concept is so familiar that they think it must be somewhere in God's Word.

Actually, the Bible doesn't say that at all. It tells us just the opposite: God helps the helpless.

When you read the Gospels, you find that Jesus did not refuse to help the helpless. He did not withhold forgiveness and compassion from those who acknowledged their sin. He did not turn away from those who had no power to change. In fact, the people who distressed Him most were those who thought they didn't need any help at all.

God's thoughts are higher than ours (Isaiah 55:9), and He sees things differently than we do. We see our own ability to deal with problems; He shows us our weaknesses to teach us to rely on His strength. We take pride in our successes and begin to think we don't need God's help; He allows us to fail so He can teach us that true success comes through His grace.

Are you feeling helpless today? God's grace is available for those who recognize that they cannot help themselves. "Come boldly to the throne of grace" to find help in your time of need (Hebrews 4:16). DHR

God helps those who know they are helpless.

Our Unseen Helpers

Read: Hebrews 1:5–14

Are [angels] not all ministering spirits
sent forth to minister? Hebrews 1:14

At one point in Martin Luther's stormy career, he received some discouraging news. But he responded by saying, "Recently I have been looking up at the night sky, spangled and studded with stars, and I found no pillars to hold them up. Yet they did not fall." Luther was encouraged as he reminded himself that the same unseen God who was upholding the universe was caring for him.

There is another unseen source of help from which God's children can take courage when facing a physical or spiritual crisis—angels! Those heavenly hosts are called "ministering spirits" (Hebrews 1:14), and they are instantly responsive to God's command. Little do we know what powerful protection and help they provide. When Jesus was enduring agony in Gethsemane, "an angel appeared to Him from heaven, strengthening Him" (Luke 22:43).

But you say, "I've never seen an angel." No need of that! It's enough to know that they do their quiet, protecting work beyond the realm of physical sight. They call no attention to themselves, lest we focus on them instead of Jesus. But their presence is real. Just knowing that these unseen helpers are on our side strengthens our trust in God, whom they faithfully serve.   DJD

The angels of God assist the people of God
as they do the work of God.

Finding Security

Read: Psalm 59

You have been my defense and refuge in
the day of my trouble. Psalm 59:16

After a man shot and killed two people at Los Angeles International Airport in 2002, some began insisting that armed guards be placed at every check-in area. Others said that individuals should be screened before entering an airport terminal. But a consultant on airport security said, "If you move the checkpoint, all you're going to do is push the problem to another part of the airport. There will always be a public area that is vulnerable to these kinds of attacks."

In a world where violence and terrorism may strike anytime, anyplace, where can we find security? Where can we be safe?

The Bible says that our security is not in human protection but in God himself. The book of Psalms contains more than forty references to taking refuge in the Lord, many of them from David's experience of being pursued by his enemies. In his prayers for help, he centered his hope in the Lord: "You have been my defense and refuge in the day of my trouble. To You, O my Strength, I will sing praises; for God is my defense, my God of mercy" (Psalm 59:16–17).

God doesn't guarantee to protect us from difficulty and physical harm, but He does promise to be our refuge in every situation. In Him we find real security.   DCM

Though danger lurks on every side,
In Christ our Lord we will abide;
Our God is strong, our hope is sure—
In Him alone we are secure! —Fitzhugh

No one is more secure than the one who rests in God's hands.

February 29

Trouble with People

Read: Psalm 56

In God I have put my trust; I will not be afraid.
What can man do to me? Psalm 56:11

Was David paranoid? Did he think the whole world was out to get him? You might get that impression as you read through some of his psalms. Look at a few of the statements he made:

"Strangers have risen up against me, and oppressors have sought after my life" (Psalm 54:3).

"There are many who fight against me" (56:2).

"They lie in wait for my life; the mighty gather against me" (59:3).

Of course, during this time David was being hotly pursued by Saul and his men, so it's easy to see why he felt as he did. Nonetheless, his observations about people may echo the way we feel on occasions when others criticize and oppose us. Perhaps it's those with whom we work. They seem to disagree with us no matter what we do or say. Maybe it's family members who apparently enjoy irritating us. Or people at church who seem to be critical and faultfinding. We just feel as if everyone is against us.

If this describes your situation, it's time to do what David did. He declared, "In God I have put my trust; I will not be afraid. What can man do to me?" (56:11).

When you have trouble with people, turn to God. He understands.

DB

God is stronger than our strongest foe.

Our Lifeline

Read: Psalm 91

He is my refuge and my fortress; my God,
in Him I will trust. Psalm 91:2

In his book *The Fisherman and His Friends*, Louis Albert Banks tells of two men who were assigned to stand watch on a ship out at sea. During the night the waves from a raging storm washed one of them overboard. The sailor who drowned had been in the most sheltered place, while the one who survived was more exposed to the elements. What made the difference? The man who was lost had nothing to hold on to.

What a picture of the way some people are affected by the trials of life! When life is peaceful, they are very self-sufficient; but when the going gets rough, they are swept off their feet. Because they have refused God's help and have nothing to hold on to, they are easily overwhelmed.

People who cling to the Lord, though, can weather the fiercest storms of adversity. They are often heard to say, "I don't know what I would do without the Lord." They know that the heavenly Father is always with them to strengthen, guard, and protect them.

Those who have put their hope in God have Someone they can rely on in every circumstance of life. They can say of the Lord, "He is my refuge and my fortress; my God, in Him I will trust" (Psalm 91:2). Can you?　　　　　RDH

He cannot fail, your faithful God,
He'll guard you with His mighty power;
Then fear no ill, though troubles rise,
His help is sure from hour to hour. —Bosch

God has not promised to keep us from life's storms,
but to keep us through them.

The Power of Our Limits

Read: Exodus 4:10–12

*Go, and I will be with your mouth and teach you
what you shall say. Exodus 4:12*

When God called Moses to serve, he replied, "O my Lord, I am not eloquent, neither before nor since You have spoken to Your servant; but I am slow of speech and slow of tongue" (Exodus 4:10). The language used here suggests that Moses may have had a speech impediment. Perhaps he stuttered.

The Lord said to him, "Who has made man's mouth? Or who makes the mute, the deaf, the seeing, or the blind? Have not I, the Lord?" (v. 11).

Our impairments, our disabilities, our handicaps are used by God for His own glory. His way of dealing with them may not be to remove them but to endow us with strength and use our limitations for good.

If our weaknesses cause us to seek God and rely on Him, they actually help us instead of hinder us. In fact, they become the best thing that could happen to us, because our growth in courage, power, and happiness depends on our relationship with the Lord and how much we are relying on Him.

Three times the apostle Paul pleaded with the Lord to remove his impediment, but the Lord answered, "My grace is sufficient" (2 Corinthians 12:9). Paul then gloried in his limitations, for he realized that they did not limit him. As he put it, "When I am weak, then I am strong" (v. 10). DHR

*God uses weakness to reveal
His great sufficiency;
So if we let Him work through us,
His power we will see. —Sper*

God's strength is best seen in our weakness.

March 3

Joy—Even in Poverty

Read: Habakkuk 3:14–19

Though the labor of the olive may fail, and the fields yield no food;...
yet I will rejoice in the Lord. Habakkuk 3:17–18

In the book *450 Stories for Life,* Gust Anderson tells about visiting a church in a farming community of eastern Alberta, Canada, where there had been eight years of drought. The farmers' economic situation looked hopeless. But in spite of their poverty, many of them continued to meet together to worship and praise God.

Anderson was especially impressed by the testimony of a farmer who stood up and quoted Habakkuk 3:17–18. With deep feeling, he said, "Though the fig tree may not blossom, nor fruit be on the vines; though the labor of the olive may fail, and the fields yield no food; though the flock may be cut off from the fold, and there be no herd in the stalls—yet I will rejoice in the Lord, I will joy in the God of my salvation." Anderson thought, *That dear saint has found the secret of real joy!*

It's not wrong to find pleasure in the good things money can buy, but we should never rely on them for happiness. If our fulfillment depends on material possessions, we are crushed when we lose them. But if our joy is found in the Lord, nothing can disrupt it, not even economic distress.

Yes, those who know and trust the Lord can rejoice—even in poverty! RDH

Happiness depends on happenings; joy depends on Jesus!

Dying for Encouragement

Read: Deuteronomy 3:23–29

Command Joshua, and encourage him and
strengthen him. Deuteronomy 3:28

In Deuteronomy 3 we read that Moses encouraged Joshua as he was about to assume leadership of the Israelites. No doubt Joshua was filled with fear and a feeling of inadequacy to fill Moses's shoes. The Lord therefore told Moses to encourage Joshua.

All of us need a word of encouragement from time to time to spur us on when we are facing a major new challenge. But we also need words of appreciation and commendation as we carry out our daily responsibilities, whether at home or at work.

When a corporate accountant committed suicide, an effort was made to find out why. The company's books were examined, but no shortage was found. Nothing could be uncovered that gave any clue as to why he took his life—that is, until a note was discovered. It simply said: "In thirty years I have never had one word of encouragement. I'm fed up!"

Many people crave some small sign of approval. They need a word of recognition, a caring smile, a warm handshake, and an honest expression of appreciation for the good we see in them or in their work.

Every day let's determine to encourage (not flatter) at least one person. Let's do our part to help those around us who are dying for encouragement. RDH

It may seem insignificant
To say a word or two;
But when we give encouragement,
What wonders it can do! —K. DeHaan

A word of encouragement can make the difference between giving up or going on.

Load Limit

Read: 1 Corinthians 10:1–13

God is faithful, who will not allow you to be tempted beyond
what you are able. 1 Corinthians 10:13

We've all seen load-limit signs on highways, bridges, and elevators. Knowing that too much strain can cause severe damage or complete collapse, engineers determine the exact amount of stress that various materials can safely endure. Posted warnings tell us not to exceed the maximum load.

Human beings also have their load limits, which vary from person to person. Some people, for example, can bear the pressure of trial and temptation better than others; yet everyone has a breaking point and can take only so much.

At times, circumstances and people seem to be pushing us beyond what we can bear. But the Lord knows our limitations and never allows any difficulties to enter our lives that exceed our strength and ability to endure. This is especially true when we're enticed by sin. According to 1 Corinthians 10:13, "God is faithful, who will not allow you to be tempted beyond what you are able."

So when trials and temptations press down on you, take courage. Remember, your heavenly Father knows the limits of your ability to stand up under life's pressures. Draw on His strength; no temptation will ever be greater than that! RDH

If you yield to God, you won't give in to sin.

What Will Last?

Read: 2 Corinthians 4:16–18

The things which are seen are temporary, but the things which are not seen are eternal. 2 Corinthians 4:18

I have a friend who was denied a doctorate from a prestigious West Coast university because of his Christian worldview. As he was approaching the conclusion of his studies, his advisor invited him to come into his office and informed him that his dissertation had been rejected.

My friend's first thought was of thousands of dollars and five years of his life taking flight, and his heart sank. But then he thought of the words of the hymn by Rhea Miller: "I'd rather have Jesus than silver or gold, I'd rather be His than have riches untold... I'd rather have Jesus than anything this world affords today." And then my friend laughed—for he realized that nothing of eternal value had been lost.

How we respond to loss is all a matter of perspective. One person is absorbed with the permanent; the other with the passing. One stores up treasure in heaven; the other accumulates it here on earth. While one believes that happiness is found in being rich and famous, Christ's followers are willing to suffer poverty, hunger, indignity, and shame because of "the glory that will be revealed" (1 Peter 5:1).

Wouldn't you "rather have Jesus"?   RDH

Living only for temporary gain leads to eternal loss.

A Weeping World

Read: Lamentations 3:1–9, 24

"The Lord is my portion," says my soul, "therefore I hope in Him!"
Lamentations 3:24

A mother was told that her son had been killed in an accident on the job. In that moment, her life was flooded with tears. In another family, a sudden heart attack snatched away a husband, leaving a wife to face life alone. More tears! We live in a weeping world.

The book of Lamentations was written by Jeremiah, who is called the weeping prophet. The citizens of Judah had been taken into captivity (1:3); Jerusalem lay in ruins (2:8–9); the people were destitute (2:11–12); their suffering was horrible beyond belief (2:20); and the prophet wept continually (3:48–49). Yet Jeremiah still affirmed the mercies, the compassions, and the faithfulness of God. From deep within him, his soul was saying, "The Lord is my portion, therefore I hope in Him!" (3:24).

What realism in those tear-saturated words! It's the reality that weeping and lamentations do not necessarily reflect a weak faith or a lack of trust in God. Some of us may think that a Christian must feel joyful even when the heart is breaking—or at least try to appear that way. But Jeremiah's experience refutes that. Tears are a natural part of a Christian's life. But thank God, one day in Glory our blessed Savior will wipe them all away (Revelation 21:4).　　　　DJD

The soul would have no rainbow if the eyes had no tears.

Self-Pity or Rejoicing?

Read: Philippians 4:1–8

Rejoice in the Lord always. Again I will say, rejoice!
Philippians 4:4

Temperament seems to be something that each of us is born with. Some of us have upbeat dispositions, while others play the music of life in a minor key. Yet how we respond to life's trials also affects our overall disposition.

For example, Fanny Crosby lost her sight when she was only six weeks old. She lived into her nineties, composing thousands of beloved hymns. On her 92nd birthday she cheerfully said, "If in all the world you can find a happier person than I am, do bring him to me. I should like to shake his hand."

What enabled Fanny Crosby to experience such joy in the face of what many would term a "tragedy"? At an early age she chose to "rejoice in the Lord always" (Philippians 4:4). In fact, Fanny carried out a resolution she made when she was only eight years old: "How many blessings I enjoy that other people don't. To weep and sigh because I'm blind, I cannot and I won't."

Let's remember that "the joy of the Lord is [our] strength" (Nehemiah 8:10). Let's also take comfort in the teachings of Jesus, who said, "These things I have spoken to you, that My joy may remain in you, and that your joy may be full" (John 15:11). When faced with the choice of self-pity or rejoicing, let's respond with rejoicing. VCG

Rather than complain about the thorns on roses,
be thankful for roses among the thorns.

A Reason for Hope

Read: Lamentations 3:19–33

His compassions fail not. They are new every morning;
great is Your faithfulness. Lamentations 3:22–23

It's one of the saddest stories of the Bible, yet it inspired one of the most hopeful hymns of the twentieth century.

The prophet Jeremiah witnessed unimaginable horrors when the Babylonians invaded Jerusalem in 586 BC. Solomon's temple was reduced to ruins, and with it went not only the center of worship but also the heart of the community. The people were left with no food, no rest, no peace, no leader. But in the midst of suffering and grief, one of their prophets found a reason for hope. "Through the Lord's mercies we are not consumed," wrote Jeremiah, "because His compassions fail not. They are new every morning; great is Your faithfulness" (Lamentations 3:22–23).

Jeremiah's hope came from his personal experience of the Lord's faithfulness and from his knowledge of God's promises in the past. Without these, he would have been unable to comfort his people.

This hope of Lamentations 3 is echoed in a hymn by Thomas Chisholm (1866–1960). Although suffering sickness and setbacks throughout his life, he wrote "Great Is Thy Faithfulness." It assures us that even in times of great fear, tragic loss, and intense suffering we can find comfort and confidence as we trust in God's great faithfulness.   JAL

The best reason for hope is God's faithfulness.

March 10

Living with Grace

Read: 1 Peter 5:5–11

Be clothed with humility, for "God resists the proud,
but gives grace to the humble." 1 Peter 5:5

Kevin Rogers, pastor of a church in Canada, has likened the grace of God to an imaginary secretary who compels him to treat other people as God does. Rogers writes: "Grace is my secretary, but she won't let me obey my Day-Timer. She lets the strangest people into my workspace to interrupt me. Somehow she lets calls get through that I would prefer to leave for a more convenient time. Doesn't Grace know that I have an agenda? Some days I wish that Grace weren't here. But Grace has an amazing way of covering my mistakes and turning the office into a holy place. Grace finds good in everything, even failures."

By God's grace—His unmerited love and favor—we have been forgiven in Christ. God tells us that instead of relating to others from a position of superiority, we must put others ahead of ourselves. We should wear the clothes of humility because He "resists the proud, but gives grace to the humble" (1 Peter 5:5).

When "the God of all grace" (v. 10) controls our lives, He can transform interruptions into opportunities, mistakes into successes, pride into humility, and suffering into strength. That's the amazing power of God. That's the evidence of His grace!   DCM

THINKING IT THROUGH

How have you seen grace at work in your life lately?
In what areas of life do you see a need for grace?
To whom can you demonstrate God's grace today?

When you know God's grace, you'll want
to show God's grace.

When It's Hard to Pray

Read: Romans 8:26–27

There is not a word on my tongue, but behold,
O Lord, You know it altogether. Psalm 139:4

The Bible tells us that God knows our every thought and every word on our tongue (Psalm 139:1–4). And when we don't know what to pray for, the Holy Spirit "makes intercession for us with groanings which cannot be uttered" (Romans 8:26).

These biblical truths assure us that we can have communication with God even without a word being spoken, because He knows the intentions and desires of our heart. What a comfort when we are perplexed or in deep distress! We don't have to worry if we can't find the words to express our thoughts and feelings. We don't have to feel embarrassed if sometimes our sentences break off half-finished. God knows what we were going to say. We don't have to feel guilty if our thoughts wander and we have to struggle to keep our minds focused on the Lord.

And for that matter, we don't have to worry about a proper posture in prayer. If we are elderly or arthritic and can't kneel, that's okay. What God cares about is the posture of our heart.

What a wonderful God! No matter how much you falter and stumble in your praying, He hears you. His heart of infinite love responds to the needs and emotions of your own inarticulate heart. So keep on praying! VCG

Prayer is the soul's sincere desire,
Unuttered or expressed,
The motion of a hidden fire
That trembles in the breast. —Montgomery

Prayer does not require eloquence but earnestness.

Suffering's Reward

Read: Romans 5:1–5

*We also glory in tribulations, knowing that tribulation
produces perseverance. Romans 5:3*

A young Christian went to an older believer and asked, "Will
you pray that I may be more patient?" So they knelt together
and the man began to pray, "Lord, send this young man tribulation
in the morning; send him tribulation in the afternoon; send him—"
Just then the young believer blurted out, "No, not *tribulation!* I asked
for *patience*." "I know," said the wise Christian, "but it's through
tribulation that we learn patience."

The word *perseverance* in today's Scripture can mean the ability
to remain steadfast under difficulties without giving in. John A.
Witmer wrote, "Only a believer who has faced distress can develop
steadfastness. That in turn develops character."

When the apostle Paul told the Christians in Rome that "tribulation produces perseverance" (Romans 5:3), he was speaking from
personal experience. He had suffered beatings, whippings, stoning,
shipwreck, and persecution. Yet he remained steadfast in his faith
and did not shrink from his responsibility to preach the gospel.

If you are facing a difficult test, praise God! Under His wise
control, everything that happens to us—whether pleasurable or
painful—is designed to develop Christlike character. That's why
we can glory in tribulation.   RDH

He who waits on the Lord will not be crushed
by the weight of adversity.

A Bad Habit

Read: Exodus 17:1–7

They tempted the Lord, saying, "Is the Lord among us or not?"
Exodus 17:7

Most people have a bad habit or two. Some habits are just irritating, such as talking too much or too fast. Others are much more serious.

Consider, for example, the bad habit developed by the people of ancient Israel. They had just been delivered from slavery (Exodus 14:30), and they ought to have been thankful. Instead, they started to complain to Moses and Aaron, "Oh, that we had died by the hand of the LORD in the land of Egypt!" (16:3).

We read in Exodus 17 that their complaining escalated into a quarrel. In reality, their complaint was with God, but they picked a fight with Moses because he was the leader. They said, "Why is it you have brought us up out of Egypt, to kill us and our children and our livestock with thirst?" (v. 3). The people even began questioning if God was really with them (v. 7). Yet He always met their needs.

If we're honest, we would have to admit that we sometimes complain when God isn't coming through for us the way we want. We accuse Him of being absent or disinterested. But when our heart is concerned with God's purposes rather than our own, we will be patient and trust Him to provide all that we need. Then we won't develop the bad habit of complaining.　　　　AL

Those Christians who with thankful hearts
Praise God throughout the day
Won't tend to grumble and complain
When things don't go their way. —Branon

To conquer the habit of complaining, count your blessings.

Pigeon Walk

Read: Daniel 6:1–10

He knelt down on his knees three times that day, and prayed and gave thanks before his God, as was his custom. Daniel 6:10

Have you ever wondered why a pigeon walks so funny? It's so it can see where it's going. A pigeon's eyes can't focus as it moves, so the bird actually has to bring its head to a complete stop between steps in order to refocus. It proceeds clumsily—head forward, stop, head back, stop.

In our spiritual walk with the Lord, we have the same problem as the pigeon: We have a hard time seeing while we're on the go. We need to stop between steps—to pause and refocus on the Word and the will of God. That's not to say we have to pray and meditate about every little decision in life. But certainly our walk with the Lord needs to have built into it a pattern of stops that enable us to see more clearly before moving on.

Daniel's practice of praying three times a day was an essential part of his walk with God (Daniel 6:10). He knew there's a certain kind of spiritual refocusing that we can't do without stopping. His stops gave him a very different kind of walk—one that was obvious to those around him.

What about us? At the risk of being thought of as different, as Daniel was, let's learn this valuable lesson from the pigeon: "Looking good" isn't nearly as important as "seeing well."   MD

There is a blessed calm at eventide
That calls me from a world of toil and care;
How restful, then, to seek some quiet nook
Where I can spend a little time in prayer. —Bullock

Time in Christ's service requires time out for renewal.

March 15

A Circle of Compassion

Read: 2 Corinthians 1:1–4; Philippians 2:1–4

Rejoice with those who rejoice, and weep with
those who weep. Romans 12:15

Following the death of our seventeen-year-old daughter in a car accident in June 2002, each member of our family handled the loss differently. For my wife, among the most helpful sources of comfort were visits from moms who had also lost a child in an accident.

Sue found strength in their stories, and she wanted them to tell her how God had been faithful in their lives, despite the deep sorrow that comes with losing a precious child.

Soon Sue became part of a circle of compassion, a small group of moms who could weep, pray, and seek God's help together. That cadre of grieving moms formed a bond of empathy and hope that provided encouragement in the face of her daily sorrow.

Each person grieves uniquely, yet we all need to share our hearts, our burdens, our questions, and our sadness with someone else. That's why it's vital that we find others with whom to discuss our pain and sorrow.

In our relationship with Christ, we find encouragement, consolation, love, fellowship, affection, and mercy (Philippians 2:1). God comforts us so that we can comfort others (2 Corinthians 1:4). So let's "rejoice with those who rejoice, and weep with those who weep" (Romans 12:15). Then others will find a circle of compassion too. DB

A heartfelt tear can show our love
As words can never do;
It says, "I want to share your pain—
My heart goes out to you." —DJD

We must learn to weep before we can dry another's tears.

March 16

In Partnership with God

Read: Matthew 6:5–15

Your Father knows the things you have need of
before you ask Him. Matthew 6:8

A man had transformed an overgrown plot of ground into a beautiful garden and was showing a friend what he had accomplished. Pointing to a bed of flowers, he said, "Look at what I did here." His companion corrected him, "You mean, 'Look at what God and I did here.'" The gardener replied, "I guess you're right. But you should have seen the shape this plot was in when He was taking care of it by himself."

We chuckle at the man's reply, but it expresses a wonderful spiritual truth—we are coworkers with God. This applies to every area of life, including prayer. It answers a question that naturally comes to mind when we reflect on Jesus's statements in Matthew 6. He said we don't need to pray on and on with vain repetitions like the pagans, because our Father knows what we need before we ask (Matthew 6:7–8).

The question is, then, why pray? The answer is simple and comforting. God has graciously chosen to give us the privilege of being His partners in both the physical and spiritual areas of life. Through prayer we work with Him in defeating the powers of evil and in bringing about the fulfillment of His loving purposes in the world. Partners with God—what a privilege! What an incentive to pray! HVL

Although God knows our every need,
His work He wants to share;
He takes us into partnership
By calling us to prayer. —DJD

God's work is done by those who pray.

Ripples on the Pond

Read: Colossians 3:1–8

*Set your mind on things above, not on things
on the earth. Colossians 3:2*

A young boy made a toy boat and then went to sail it on a pond. While he was playing with it along the water's edge, the boat floated out beyond his reach. In his distress he asked an older boy to help him. Without saying a word, the older child picked up some stones and started to throw them toward the boat.

The little boy became upset, for he thought that the child he had turned to for help was being mean. Soon, though, he noticed that instead of hitting the boat, each stone was directed beyond it, making a small ripple that moved the vessel a little nearer to the shore. Every throw of the stone was planned, and at last the treasured toy was brought back to his waiting hands.

Sometimes it seems as if God allows circumstances into our lives that are harming us and are without sense or plan. We may be sure, though, that these waves of trial are intended to bring us nearer to God, to encourage us to set our minds "on things above, not on things on the earth" (Colossians 3:2). Because we are prone to drift away from Him, the Lord must discipline us to get us back on the right course (Hebrews 12:9–11).

How are you responding to life's difficulties? They are God's loving way of drawing you closer to Him.   HGB

Lightly hold earth's joys so transient,
Lightly hold to things of clay,
Grasp perfections everlasting,
Where Christ dwells in heaven's day! —Bosch

God uses the waves of trial to draw us closer to himself.

He Can Be Trusted

Read: Psalm 84

*O Lord of hosts, blessed is the man who
trusts in You! Psalm 84:12*

I was sitting in my chair by the window, staring out through fir and spruce trees to the mountains beyond, lost in thought. I looked down and saw a young fox, staring up at my face. She was as still as a stone.

Days before, I had seen her at the edge of the woods, looking nervously over her shoulder at me. I went to the kitchen for an egg and rolled it toward the place I had last seen her. Each day I put another egg on the lawn, and each day she ventured out of the trees just long enough to pick it up. Then she would dart back into the woods.

Now she had come on her own to my door to get an egg, convinced, I suppose, that I meant her no harm.

This incident reminded my wife of David's invitation: "Oh, taste and see that the Lord is good" (Psalm 34:8). How do we start doing that? By taking in His Word. As we read and reflect on His compassion and lovingkindness, we learn that He can be trusted (84:12). We lose our dread of getting closer to Him. Our fear becomes a healthy respect and honor of Him.

You may at times distrust God, as the fox was wary of me at first. But give Him a chance to prove His love. Read about Jesus in the Gospels. Read the praises to God in the Psalms. Taste and see that He is good! DHR

*O taste and see that God is good
To all that seek His face;
Yea, blest the man that trusts in Him,
Confiding in His grace. —Psalter*

No one is beyond the reach of God's love.

Cut Off?

Read: Psalm 31:14–24

*You heard the voice of my supplications when
I cried out to You. Psalm 31:22*

During Antarctica's nine-month winter, the continent is engulfed in darkness and the temperature sinks to -115° F (-82° C). Flights are halted from late February to November, leaving workers at scattered research stations isolated and virtually cut off from outside help. Yet, in 2001, two daring rescue missions penetrated the polar winter and airlifted people with serious medical conditions to safety.

We all feel helpless and cut off at times. It may seem that not even God can hear or answer our cries for help. The psalmist David said in a time of trouble, "I am cut off from before Your eyes" (Psalm 31:22). But David discovered that the Lord had not forgotten him, and he rejoiced, "You heard the voice of my supplications when I cried out to You" (v. 22).

What circumstances make you feel helpless or hopeless today? Poor health, broken relationships, a family member in great need? In Jesus Christ, God has pierced the dark winter of our world in a daring rescue through His redeeming love. He is therefore able to reach us and calm our fears in the most desperate circumstances.

We are never cut off from the mighty power and sustaining peace of God. DCM

*The Lord is near to all who call;
He promised in His holy Word
That if we will draw near to Him,
Our faintest heart cry will be heard. —Hess*

God's help is only a prayer away.

God, My Glory

Read: Psalm 3

*You, O Lord, are a shield for me, my glory and the
One who lifts up my head. Psalm 3:3*

Is God your glory? (Psalm 3:3). The word *glory* is the translation of a Hebrew word meaning "weight" or "significance."

Some people measure their worth by beauty, intelligence, money, power, or prestige. But David, who wrote Psalm 3, found his security and worth in God. He said that many stood against him. He heard their cruel voices and was tempted to believe them, to give way to discouragement and depression. Nevertheless, he comforted and strengthened his heart with these words: "You, O Lord, are a shield for me, my glory and the One who lifts up my head" (v. 3).

What a change that realization made! He had God, and his enemies did not. So he could hold up his head with confidence.

Verses like Psalm 3:3 can bring peace to your heart even in the midst of a storm of trouble. God is your shield and deliverer. He will deal with your adversaries in due time.

Meanwhile, tell God all about your troubles. Let Him be your glory. You don't have to defend yourself. Ask Him to be your shield—to protect your heart with His overshadowing love and care. Then, like David, you can lie down in peace and sleep, though tens of thousands are against you (vv. 5–6).   DHR

*Though many be against me
And would attack my name,
I'll glory in my Savior
And trust Him just the same. —Fitzhugh*

No one is more secure than the one
who is held in God's hands.

The Joy of Waiting

Read: 1 Samuel 1:19–28

*For this child I prayed, and the Lord has granted
me my petition. 1 Samuel 1:27*

Nine months can seem like forever for a mother-to-be. In the first trimester, hormonal changes sometimes cause lingering morning sickness. Emotions rise to the surface, prolonging afternoon blues. Then a changing appetite stretches out evening hours with late-night cravings for pizza, chocolate, and dill pickles.

During the next three months, the expectant mother outgrows her clothes and spends long hours looking for a new wardrobe. The last trimester turns normal activity into a chore as the final watch begins.

Then, suddenly the endless waiting is over. Nine months become like yesterday's newspaper. They are gone. They become insignificant, a faint memory—overcome by joy. Ask the new mom if she regrets enduring her pregnancy. Never!

Hannah's wait began even more slowly. For years she was unable to have a child. She felt so unfulfilled, so dishonored (1 Samuel 1). But the Lord remembered her, and she conceived. Her joy was complete.

Hannah waited patiently and saw the Lord turn her sorrow into overflowing joy. Her song (2:1–10) is a reminder that disappointment and the most bitter distress can lead to fulfillment and delight. For those who wait on the Lord, long hours of enduring will one day give way to rejoicing.   MD

Let patience have her perfect work;
Let God refine your gold;
For in His time He'll show you why,
And blessings great unfold. —Bosch

God's gift of joy is worth the wait.

You Are Never Alone

Read: John 14:15–21

I will not leave you orphans; I will come to you. John 14:18

Jesus is just as real today as He was when He walked on this earth. Even though He doesn't move among us physically, by the Holy Spirit He is here, there, everywhere—a continuous, living presence—outside of us and inside of us.

That may be a terrifying thought for some. Perhaps you don't like yourself, or you're contemplating all the bad things you've done. Insecurity and sin can create a sense of fear, awkwardness, and clumsiness in Jesus's presence. But think of what you know about Him.

Despite what you are or what you may have done, He loves you (Romans 5:8; 1 John 4:7–11). He will never leave you nor forsake you (John 14:18; Hebrews 13:5). Others may not think much of you or invite you to spend time with them, but Jesus does (Matthew 11:28). Others may not like the way you look, but He looks at your heart (1 Samuel 16:7; Luke 24:38). Others may think you're a bother because you're old and in the way, but He will love you to the end (Romans 8:35–39).

Jesus loves you in spite of all the conditions that cause others to turn away. He wants to change you to be like Him, but He loves you as you are and will never abandon you. You are family; you will never, ever be alone.   DHR

Jesus shares your worries and cares,
You'll never be left all alone,
For He stands beside you to comfort and guide you,
He always looks out for His own. —Brandt

If you know Jesus, you'll never walk alone.

Effective Praying

Read: Matthew 7:7–11

Everyone who asks receives, and he who seeks finds. Matthew 7:8

A twelve-year-old Cambodian boy named Lem Cheong began to question his family's religious beliefs. He had been taught that a person seeking guidance should go to a temple and shake a container of numbered bamboo slivers until one fell out. The priest then interpreted the meaning of the number. But this practice didn't satisfy Cheong's longing for clear answers, nor did it fill the void in his heart that only God could fill.

According to Harold Sala in his book *Touching God*, Cheong asked his uncle, a priest, if he had ever had a prayer answered. The man was shocked by the brashness of his nephew's question, but he admitted that he couldn't remember a single time one of his prayers had been answered.

Later Cheong asked a Christian if God had ever answered his prayers. The man recounted several instances. Cheong was so impressed that he accepted Jesus as his Savior that day. Since then, prayer has become a vital part of his life.

Jesus said, "Ask, and it will be given to you; seek, and you will find; knock, and it will be opened to you" (Matthew 7:7). Christian prayer is effective because God is the living and true God who hears and answers according to His will. And His will is always good. VCG

For answered prayer we thank You, Lord;
We know You're always there
To hear us when we call on You—
We're grateful for Your care. —Branon

Through prayer, finite man draws upon
the power of the infinite God.

Come to Me

Read: John 10:1–18

When he brings out his own sheep, he goes before them; and
the sheep follow him, for they know his voice. John 10:4

After a hijacked plane slammed into the Pentagon on September 11, 2001, many people inside the building were trapped by a cloud of thick, blinding smoke. Police officer Isaac Hoopi ran into the blackness, searching for survivors, and heard people calling for help. He began shouting back, over and over: "Head toward my voice! Head toward my voice!"

Six people, who had lost all sense of direction in a smoke-filled hallway, heard the officer's shouts and followed. Hoopi's voice led them out of the building to safety.

"Head toward My voice!" That's also the invitation of Jesus to each of us when we are in danger or when we have lost our way. Jesus described the true spiritual shepherd of the sheep as one who "calls his own sheep by name and leads them out. And when he brings out his own sheep, he goes before them; and the sheep follow him, for they know his voice" (John 10:3–4).

Are we listening for Jesus's voice during our times of prayer and Bible reading? When we're in difficult circumstances, are we walking toward Him instead of groping in the dark?

Jesus is "the good shepherd" (v. 11). Whatever our need for guidance or protection, He calls us to heed His voice and follow Him. DCM

When you hear the Shepherd's voice
As He calls you, "Come to Me,"
In your life make Him your choice
And a faithful follower be. —Hess

You don't need to know where you're going
if you're following the Shepherd.

Ordinary Days

Read: 2 Corinthians 6:1–10

In all things we commend ourselves as ministers of God: in much patience, in tribulations, in needs, in distresses. 2 Corinthians 6:4

Have you ever received an annual holiday letter from an acquaintance that recounts the *ordinary* events of the past year? Has anyone told you about cleaning the carpet or taking out the trash? Not likely.

An online publication called the *Journal of Mundane Behavior* says these routine events fill most of our time. The managing editor, a sociologist, says everyday life is valuable, since we spend nearly 60 percent of our lives doing things like commuting to work and shopping for groceries.

We don't often consider the apostle Paul's ordinary days, but he wrote, "In all things we commend ourselves as ministers of God" (2 Corinthians 6:4). "All things" included not only harsh persecution but also "needs, sleeplessness, purity, kindness, love," and other everyday experiences (vv. 4–10).

Oswald Chambers said that we tend to lose our enthusiasm "when there is no vision, no uplift, but just the common round, the trivial task. The thing that tells in the long run for God and for men is the steady persevering work in the unseen, and the only way to keep the life uncrushed is to live looking to God" (*My Utmost for His Highest*, March 6).

So let's live today to the fullest for the Lord, because it's such an important, ordinary day. DCM

If we commit ourselves to Christ
And follow in His way,
He'll give us life that satisfies
With purpose for each day. —Sper

To get the most out of life,
make every moment count for Christ.

March 26

Never Alone

Read: Hebrews 13:5–6

I will never leave you nor forsake you. Hebrews 13:5

Robinson Crusoe, the chief character in a novel by Daniel Defoe, was shipwrecked and stranded on an uninhabited island. Life was hard, but he found hope and comfort when he turned to the Word of God.

Crusoe said, "One morning, being very sad, I opened the Bible upon these words, 'I will never, never leave thee, nor forsake thee.' Immediately it occurred that these words were to *me; why* else should they be directed in such a manner, just at the moment when I was mourning over my condition, as one forsaken of God and man?

"'Well then,' said I, 'if God does not forsake me... what matters it, though the world should all forsake me . . . ?' From this moment I began to conclude in my mind that it was possible for me to be more happy in this forsaken, solitary condition than it was probable that I should ever have been in any other state in the world; and with this thought I was going to give thanks to God for bringing me to this place."

Have you been forsaken by a friend, a child, a spouse? God has said, "I will *never* leave you nor forsake you" (Hebrews 13:5). So you too can say with confidence, "The Lord is my helper; I will not fear. What can man do to me?" (v. 6).   DHR

Fear will leave us when we remember
that God is always with us.

March 27

Always for Us

Read: Ruth 1

If God is for us, who can be against us? Romans 8:31

Naomi, her husband, and their two sons left Israel and moved to Moab because of a famine (Ruth 1:1–2). One son married Ruth, the other married Orpah. Eventually Naomi's husband and sons died (vv. 3, 5), so she decided to return to Israel. But she felt that her daughters-in-law would be better off staying in Moab (vv. 6–13). She tried to dissuade them from going with her by saying, "No, my daughters; for it grieves me very much for your sakes that the hand of the Lord has gone out against me!" (v. 13).

Was Naomi right in her thinking about God? Perhaps the family had displayed a lack of faith by moving to pagan Moab, but God certainly was not against her. He proved this by wonderfully providing for her and Ruth after they returned to Israel. (Read the rest of the book—it's short.)

You may be unemployed, terminally ill, have a disabled child, or care for a loved one with Alzheimer's. God hasn't promised to keep us from such problems. But He has proven that He is always "for us" as Christians by what He did through Jesus (Romans 5:8–9). Nothing, not even death, can separate us from His love (8:35–39).

The Lord is never "against us," not even when He chastens us (Hebrews 12:5–6). He is always for us!   HVL

Our God is always there for us—
Receiving every prayer,
Delighting in our words of praise,
Responding with His care. —Sper

The One who died to save you will never be against you.

The Great Potter

Read: Jeremiah 18:1–6

*As the clay is in the potter's hand, so are you
in My hand. Jeremiah 18:6*

One definition of the word *attitude* is "the angle of approach" that an aircraft takes when landing. Author Chris Spicer writes: "Attitudes are to life as the angle of approach is to flying." He adds, "Attitude is the way we choose to think about things; attitudes will cause us to react and behave in a certain way." He also says that attitudes are not inborn or accidental. They are learned and absorbed reactions; therefore they can be changed.

During my thirties, the Lord began convicting me of my wrong thinking toward myself, others, and life—negative, self-pitying, and bitter thinking. With the help of God's Word, I recognized my need for change in three main areas: my attitudes, actions, and reactions. But I feared I couldn't change. One day I read in Jeremiah 18 how the potter refashioned some marred clay (which is what I felt like) into a different vessel, as it pleased the potter. What I couldn't do, my great Potter could! I only needed to be cooperative clay.

Today this vessel is far from finished. But as I put myself in the Potter's hands, He keeps working on me and shaping my attitudes and actions. I call them Christ-attitudes, Christ-actions, and Christ-reactions.

The great Potter can do the same for you.   JY

A change in the heart brings a change in behavior.

Joy List

Read: John 15:9–17

These things I have spoken to you, that My joy may remain in you, and that your joy may be full. John 15:11

Writer C. W. Metcalf was working as a hospice volunteer when he met thirteen-year-old Chuck, who was terminally ill. One day Chuck gave Metcalf half a dozen sheets of paper with writing on both sides and said, "I want you to give this to my mom and dad after I die. It's a list of all the fun we had, all the times we laughed." Metcalf was amazed that this young boy on the verge of death was thinking about the well-being of others.

Metcalf delivered the list. Years later he decided to make a list of his own. Surprisingly, he found it difficult at first to compile his "joy list." But as he began looking each day for the moments of laughter, satisfaction, and joy, his list began to grow.

Any joy list that we compile will no doubt include many references to the presence and power of Jesus Christ. No matter what our circumstances, joy is His gracious gift to all who trust Him. Even as Jesus faced the cross, He looked beyond its agony to the glad result of His sacrifice. He told His disciples, "These things I have spoken to you, that My joy may remain in you, and that your joy may be full" (John 15:11).

Why not begin your own joy list today? It can be a good reminder of the Lord's faithful love and the gladness of heart He brings.

DCM

Because life's circumstances change,
Our happiness may not remain;
But if we're walking with the Lord,
Our inner joy He will sustain. —Sper

To multiply your joy, count your blessings.

What Do You Seek?

Read: John 1:35-42

Jesus turned, and seeing them following, said to them,
"What do you seek?" John 1:38

How would you answer if Jesus were to ask you, "What do you seek?" (John 1:38).

Would you ask Him for health and fitness? A better job? A happier marriage? Financial security? Vindication from a false accusation? Salvation for a wayward loved one? An explanation of some difficult theological concept?

For two disciples of John the Baptist, this situation was more than an exercise in imagination. One day while they were with John, Jesus walked by and John announced, "Behold the Lamb of God!" (v. 36). Instead of continuing to follow John, his two disciples started following Jesus.

When Jesus saw them, He asked, "What do you seek?" (v. 38).

Apparently John had taught them well, because their answer indicated that they were not seeking something for themselves but Jesus himself. They wanted to know where Jesus was staying. Not only did Jesus show them the place, He spent the remainder of the day with them.

I wonder how often we miss an opportunity to spend time with Jesus because we're seeking something other than His presence. I know from experience that the more time I spend with Jesus, the less desire I have for a lot of things that once seemed very important.   JAL

To walk in fellowship with Christ
And sense His love so deep and true
Brings to the soul its highest joy
As nothing in this world can do. —DJD

Jesus longs for our fellowship even more than we long for His.

Learning to Rest

Read: Matthew 11:25–30

Take My yoke upon you and learn from Me, . . . and you
will find rest for your souls. Matthew 11:29

Many Christians are anxious and troubled. Although they are experiencing the "rest" of salvation that accompanies the forgiveness of sins and are looking forward to the eternal "rest" of heaven, their souls are still in turmoil. Fearful and doubting, they seem to be continually burdened by life's problems.

A closer look at their anxiety can reveal the reason for their distress. Having never learned to rest in the Lord, they fail to experience the "quietness and confidence" (Isaiah 30:15) that comes to those who daily fellowship with Him through Bible study and prayer.

An unknown author has penned a verse describing the problem:

We mutter and sputter, we fume and we spurt;
We mumble and grumble, our feelings get hurt;
We can't understand things, our vision grows dim,
When all that we need is communion with Him!

Don't let yourself become a victim of fruitless fretting. If you do, you'll lose the peace and joy that is your rightful heritage. Instead, set aside part of each day to talk with God, thanking Him for who He is and what He has done for you. Then, by reading His Word and believing His comforting promises, your faith will grow stronger and a supernatural peace will flood your soul.

Jesus said, "Come to Me . . . and I will give you rest" (Matthew 11:28). Have you learned to rest in Him? HGB

When we put our problems in God's hands,
He puts His peace in our hearts.

April 1

In God's Hands

Read: 2 Samuel 16:5–14

It may be that the Lord will look on my affliction, and that
the Lord will repay me with good. 2 Samuel 16:12

In 2 Samuel 16:5–14 we read of King David being cursed by Shimei. This happened while David was fleeing from his son Absalom, who wanted to kill him.

Unlike David, we often want to silence our critics, insist on fairness, and defend ourselves. But as we grow in our awareness of God's protective love, we become less concerned with what others say about us and more willing to entrust ourselves to our Father. Like David, we can say of each critic, "Let him alone, and let him curse" (2 Samuel 16:11). This is humble submission to God's will.

We may ask our opponents to justify their charges, or we may counter them with steadfast denial. Or, like David (v. 12), we can wait patiently until God vindicates us.

It is good to look beyond those who oppose us and look to the One who loves us with infinite love. It is good to be able to believe that whatever God permits is for our ultimate good—good, though we're exposed to the curses of a Shimei; good, though our hearts break and we shed bitter tears.

You are in God's hands, no matter what others are saying about you. He has seen your distress, and in time He'll repay you for the cursing you have received. So trust Him and abide in His love.

DHR

THINKING IT OVER

Read 1 Peter 2:20–23. How did Jesus respond
to words spoken against Him? What did He do and not do?
In what situations can you follow His example?

We can endure life's wrongs because we know
that God will make all things right.

April 2

God Will Move the Stone

Read: Mark 16:1–14

*When they looked up, they saw that the stone
had been rolled away. Mark 16:4*

The women who sought to anoint the dead body of Jesus are to be commended for their tender love and regard for the Savior. Yet, as they came near the place of burial, the practical difficulty of moving the heavy stone that sealed His tomb brought them unnecessary anxiety. Their fears were groundless; the stone had already been moved.

So too, we are often needlessly concerned over prospective difficulties that God graciously removes or helps us overcome. Let us exercise greater faith in facing possible obstructions on the pathway of duty. We may be sure of the Lord's assistance in such matters when we press on in His name and for His glory.

The following poem gives us some practical admonitions that apply to today's reading:

In today's bright sunlight basking,
Leave tomorrow's cares alone—
Spoil not present joys by asking:
"Who shall roll away the stone?"
Oft, before we've faced the trial
We have come with joy to own,
Angels have from heaven descended
And have rolled away the stone. —Anonymous

Go forward today on the pathway of service, undaunted by possible future obstacles. Let your heart be cheered by the certainty that whatever difficulty you may face, God will move the stone.

HGB

If God doesn't remove an obstacle,
He'll help you find a way around it.

Too Much Ambition

Read: Mark 10:35–45

*The Son of Man did not come to be served, but to serve,
and to give His life a ransom for many. Mark 10:45*

If you are familiar with the works of William Shakespeare, you know that Macbeth was one of his characters. Macbeth wanted so much to be king that he resorted to murder—and he paid for it with his life.

We are like that tragic character when we let our ambitions cloud our thinking and forget who is really in control of our lives. We may not use evil methods to achieve our goal, but we do allow ambition to cloud our thinking about the sovereignty of God. Instead of leaving matters in His hands, we take them into our own.

Another example of too much ambition is found in the conversation James and John had with Jesus in Mark 10. Their goal was to sit in the positions of greatest prestige and power in the kingdom. And because they weren't content to wait and see if Jesus would bestow that honor on them, they boldly requested it. They were too impatient to leave the matter in His hands.

Ambition is not always wrong. But when it consumes us so that we can't wait for God, we display a lack of faith as the disciples did.

When we submit our goals and desires to the Lord, we can be sure that He will give us what is best. DB

Be ambitious for the Lord, but be cautious
about your motives.

Money and Time

Read: Mark 12:13–17, 28–31

*Render to Caesar the things that are Caesar's, and to God
the things that are God's. Mark 12:17*

During a trip to London, I visited the Bank of England Museum, then made my way to the Clockmakers' Museum. At some point, it struck me that both money and time have been very important commodities as far back as anyone can remember. Yet they present one of the great dilemmas of life. We trade our valuable time working for money, and then we spend our money to make the most of our time off. We seldom possess the two with any degree of balance.

In contrast, our Lord never seemed perplexed by money or time. When asked if it was lawful to pay taxes to Caesar, Jesus answered: "Render to Caesar the things that are Caesar's, and to God the things that are God's" (Mark 12:17). With great demands on His time, Jesus spent early mornings and late nights in prayer, seeking to know and do His Father's will.

Hymn writer Frances Havergal wrote:

*Take my life, and let it be
Consecrated, Lord, to Thee;
Take my moments and my days,
Let them flow in ceaseless praise.
Take my silver and my gold,
Not a mite would I withhold;
Take my intellect and use
Every power as Thou shalt choose.*

We can properly balance time and money when we offer ourselves without reservation to God. DCM

Spend time and money wisely—they both belong to God.

The Beacon

Read: Mark 6:45–52

He came to them, walking on the sea. Mark 6:48

When a helicopter crashed in a cold, mountainous wilderness, the pilots survived but were seriously injured. The frozen afternoon stretched toward an even more freezing night. The situation seemed hopeless—until a rescue helicopter appeared, its searchlights illuminating the darkness. It spotted the wreckage, landed nearby, and carried the injured men off to safety.

"How did you know where we were?" one pilot asked.

"The homing device on your aircraft," the rescuers told him. "It went off automatically when you went down. All we had to do was follow it."

The disciples of Jesus also experienced the joy of being rescued. They had been struggling as they rowed their boat against wind and waves in the darkness of night on the Sea of Galilee (Mark 6:45–47). Then Jesus came to them, walking on the water, and calmed the sea (vv. 48–51).

We may experience similar times when all is dark and foreboding. We can't help ourselves, and it seems that no one else can either. No one knows how terrified and exhausted we are. No one, that is, except Jesus.

When we're trapped, hurt, lonely, or discouraged, Jesus knows it. Our cries of grief are beacons that bring Him to our side—right when we need Him most. DCE

There is only One who knows
All the answers to my woes;
He will all my needs supply
When in faith to Him I cry. —Morgan

Jesus hears even the faintest cry for help.

April 6

Thorns or Roses?

Read: Numbers 14:1–11

When the people complained,
it displeased the Lord. Numbers 11:1

Two boys were eating some grapes. One of them remarked, "Aren't they sweet!" "I guess so," the other replied, "but they're full of seeds." Wandering into a garden, the first boy exclaimed, "Look at those big, beautiful red roses!" The other commented, "They're full of thorns!" It was a warm day, so they stopped at the store for a soft drink. After several swallows, the second youngster complained, "My bottle's half-empty already." The first quickly responded, "Mine's still half-full!"

Many people are like the negative-thinking boy in this story. They always look at life through dark glasses. Like the children of Israel in today's Scripture, they complain and grumble when they should be praising the Lord for His gracious provision. But thank God, not everyone is like that. There are people who concentrate on the bright side and are radiant, happy, and grateful. They are realistic about the somber side of life, but they don't pout and fret.

You can overcome negative thinking. No matter who you are or what your circumstances, there's always much to be grateful for. Think about God's love for you. Praise Him for His providential care. Then, instead of complaining about thorns, you'll be thankful for the roses.   RDH

Some folks see so many thorns,
They scarce can see one rose,
While others count two blossoms
For every thorn that grows. —Garrison

Instead of grumbling because you don't get what you want,
be thankful you don't get what you deserve.

Arranging Your Mind

Read: Philippians 4:4-9

Rejoice in the Lord always. Again I will say, rejoice!
Philippians 4:4

Several years ago I read a story about a ninety-two-year-old Christian woman who was legally blind. In spite of her limitation, she was always neatly dressed, with her hair carefully brushed and her makeup tastefully applied. Each morning she would meet the new day with eagerness.

After her husband of seventy years died, it became necessary for her to go to a nursing home where she could receive proper care. On the day of the move, a helpful neighbor drove her there and guided her into the lobby. Her room wasn't ready, so she waited patiently in the lobby for several hours.

When an attendant finally came for her, she smiled sweetly as she maneuvered her walker to the elevator. The staff member described her room to her, including the new curtains that had been hung on the windows. "I love it," she declared. "But Mrs. Jones, you haven't seen your room yet," the attendant replied. "That doesn't have anything to do with it," she said. "Happiness is something you choose. Whether I like my room or not doesn't depend on how it's arranged. It's how I arrange my mind."

The Bible says, "Rejoice in the Lord" (Philippians 4:4). Remind yourself often of all that Jesus has given to you and be thankful. That's how to arrange your mind. — DHR

God takes delight when we rejoice
In all that He has done
And when we thank Him for the love
He shows us through His Son. —DJD

The happiness of your life depends on the quality
of your thoughts.

April 8

Loss and Gain

Read: Luke 24:13–35

Their eyes were opened and they knew Him; and He
vanished from their sight. Luke 24:31

A Texas high school football team began the 2002 season with a 57-game winning streak and hopes for an unprecedented fifth consecutive state championship. In spite of losing their long-time coach and competing against larger schools, the Celina Bob-cats remained undefeated through the regular season. But then they lost a quarterfinal playoff game by one point. It felt like the end of the world—even though they had won 68 straight games and five state championships in seven years.

When our dreams are shattered and our hearts are broken, we may feel that all has been lost and nothing has been gained. It takes the touch of God to open our eyes to the greater glory of His plan.

When the crucified and risen Christ joined two disciples on the road to Emmaus, they were grieving over His death. "We were hoping that it was He who was going to redeem Israel" (Luke 24:21), they told Jesus, whom they didn't recognize. But Jesus said, "Ought not the Christ to have suffered these things and to enter into His glory?" (v. 26). Later they realized they had been talking with Jesus. He was alive!

In our time of loss, the risen Lord comes to us with comfort and peace, revealing His glory and the eternal gain that is ours because of His cross. DCM

When circumstances overwhelm
And seem too much to bear,
Depend upon the Lord for strength
And trust His tender care. —Sper

Present pains can lead to permanent gains.

Give Him Your Burden

Read: Psalm 55:16–23

Cast your burden on the Lord, and
He shall sustain you. Psalm 55:22

A poor man in Ireland was plodding along toward home, carrying a huge bag of potatoes. A horse and wagon finally drew up alongside him on the road, and the driver invited the man to climb aboard. After getting on the wagon, he sat down but continued to hold the heavy bag.

When the driver suggested that the man set the bag down in the wagon, he replied, "I don't want to trouble you too much, sir. You are giving me a ride already, so I'll just carry the potatoes."

"How foolish of him!" we say. Yet sometimes we do the same thing when we attempt to bear the burdens of our lives in our own strength. No wonder we become weary and overwhelmed with anxiety and fear.

In Psalm 55, David spoke of the anxiety he felt because his enemies were attacking him (vv. 1–15). But then he gave his concerns to the Lord and was filled with renewed hope and confidence (vv. 16–23). That's why he could write, "Cast your burden on the Lord, and He shall sustain you" (v. 22).

When you recall the story of the man and his bag of potatoes, remember the simple lesson it illustrates: Rather than trying to bear your burdens by yourself, set them down in God's hands.   HGB

Give Him each perplexing problem,
All your needs to Him make known;
Bring to Him your daily burdens—
Never carry them alone! —Adams

God invites us to burden Him with what burdens us.

Keep on Asking

Read: Luke 11:1–13

*I say to you, ask, and it will be given
to you. Luke 11:9*

I heard a woman say that she never prayed more than once for anything. She didn't want to weary God with her repeated requests.

The Lord's teaching on prayer in Luke 11 contradicts this notion. He told a parable about a man who went to his friend's house at midnight and asked for some bread to feed his unexpected visitors. At first the friend refused, for he and his family were in bed. Finally he got up and gave him the bread—not out of friendship but because the caller was so persistent (vv. 5–10).

Jesus used this parable to contrast this reluctant friend with our generous heavenly Father. If an irritated neighbor will give in to his friend's persistence and grant his request, how much more readily will our heavenly Father give us all we need!

It's true that God, in His great wisdom, may sometimes delay His answers to prayer. It's also true that we must pray in harmony with the Scriptures and God's will. But Jesus moved beyond those facts to urge us to persist in prayer. He told us to ask, seek, and knock until the answer comes (v. 9).

So don't worry about wearying God. He will never tire of your persistent prayer!   JY

God never tires of our asking.

Unexpected Alligators

Read: Matthew 13:18–23

When tribulation or persecution arises because of the word, immediately he stumbles. Matthew 13:21

A friend of actress and comedienne Gracie Allen once sent a small, live alligator to her as a gag. Not knowing what to do with it, Gracie put it in the bathtub and then left for an appointment. When she returned home, she found a note from her maid. "Dear Miss Allen: Sorry, but I have quit. I don't work in houses where there is an alligator. I would have told you this when I started, but I never thought it would come up."

Some people who say they'll serve Christ are quick to leave when trouble comes. In Jesus's parable of the soils, He pictured the various responses that people have to the gospel. For example, a person may seem to accept God's truth, but he stumbles in his faith when difficulties arise (Matthew 13:20–21). Such troubles test the sincerity of one's faith and expose the weakness of one's commitment to Christ.

But someone may say, "Shouldn't our Lord tell us up front what is involved in following Him?" He does. He appeals to us with one invitation: "Trust Me." If we let trouble or disillusionment shake our faith, we are breaking the spirit of the trust that brought us to Christ in the first place.

"Father, when life brings us the unexpected and we feel like quitting, help us to be faithful to You." MD

Day by day and with each passing moment,
Strength I find to meet my trials here;
Trusting in my Father's wise bestowment,
I've no cause for worry or for fear. —Berg

Tough times can teach us to trust.

When You're Down

Read: Psalm 6

Depart from me, all you workers of iniquity; for the Lord
has heard the voice of my weeping. Psalm 6:8

S ometimes it doesn't take much to get us down, does it? An
unkind remark from a friend, bad news from the auto mechanic,
a financial setback, or a misbehaving child can put a cloud of gloom
over everything, even on the sunniest day. You know you should
be joyful, but everything seems to be against you, making simple
tasks a struggle.

David must have been feeling that way when he wrote Psalm 6.
He felt weak and sickly (v. 2), troubled (v. 3), forsaken (v. 4), weary
(v. 6), and grief-stricken (v. 7). But he knew what to do when he
was down. He looked up and trusted God to take care of him and
to see him through.

When we look up and focus on God, something good happens.
We get our eyes off ourselves and gain a new appreciation of Him.

Next time you're down, try looking up to God. He is sovereign
(Psalm 47:8); He loves you (1 John 4:9–10); He considers you special
(Matthew 6:26); He has a purpose for your trials (James 1:2–4).

Yes, life can seem unbearable at times. But don't let it keep you
down. Meditate on God's goodness, talk to Him, and know that He
hears you (Psalm 6:9). That will give you strength to get up when
you're down.   DB

Come, ye disconsolate, where'er ye languish—
Come to the mercy seat, fervently kneel;
Here bring your wounded hearts, here tell your anguish:
Earth has no sorrow that heav'n cannot heal. —Moore

When life knocks you to your knees,
you're in a good position to pray.

New Hope

Read: Romans 15:5–13

*May the God of hope fill you with all joy and
peace in believing, that you may abound in hope
by the power of the Holy Spirit. Romans 15:13*

G rant Murphy of Seattle was the active type, a man who ran at full throttle. Idling and coasting were not in his nature. "One might even call him hyperactive," recalled a dear friend.

Then multiple sclerosis began to slow Grant down. First he needed crutches to get around. Then he was limited to sitting in a chair. Finally he was confined to a bed.

Near the end, he was hardly strong enough to talk. His friend recalls, however, that "he expressed only joy and thankfulness with a constant anticipation of being in the Lord's presence." Not long before he died, Grant whispered Romans 15:13 to a friend. He repeated the words "in believing," then added, "I can't do anything now."

It's when we can't do anything that *God does everything.* And herein lies a profound paradox of the Christian's experience. Faith is simultaneously an exercise of our will and the impartation of divine strength. And from that marvelous mixture spring joy and peace and an abundance of hope.

Are you in a totally helpless situation? Strength gone? All options exhausted? If you have trusted Jesus as your Savior, God will strengthen you to keep on believing. As you trust Him, He'll give you not only joy and peace, but also hope when all hope is gone.   DJD

*When we are weak and in despair,
Our mighty God is near;
He'll give us strength and joy and hope,
And calm our inner fear. —Sper*

No one is hopeless whose hope is in God.

April 14

Calamity

Read: Luke 13:1–5

Do you think that they were worse sinners . . . ? I tell you, no;
but unless you repent you will all likewise perish. Luke 13:4–5

S ome Christians are quick to declare that a public disaster (such as a terrorist attack, an earthquake, or a flood) is the result of divine judgment. In reality, a complex array of factors lie behind most disasters.

In Luke 13, Jesus was asked about some people who were cruelly murdered, and about eighteen people who died when a tower collapsed on them. The people asking the questions were wondering if those who died were worse sinners than others. "I tell you, no," said Jesus, "but unless you repent you will all likewise perish" (vv. 3, 5).

Instead of reading divine judgment into tragedies, we should see them as a call to personal repentance. This is especially true for unbelievers, but it is also true for Christians. Acts of terrorism, for example, challenge us to pray earnestly for the conversion and the good of the deluded people who commit such acts.

Calamities in themselves are never good, but they can fulfill God's purposes when they serve as a wake-up call to believers, and when they bring unbelievers to repentance and faith in Jesus. Let's not ask, "Who's to blame?" but "Lord, what are You saying to me?"

HVL

When great calamity befalls,
We wonder why it's sent;
But God says, "Ask not who has sinned—
Just hear My call, 'Repent!'" —DJD

In alarming situations, listen for God's wake-up call.

April 15

God in the Thunderstorm

Read: Psalm 97:1–6

*Clouds and darkness surround Him. . . . His lightnings light
the world; the earth sees and trembles. Psalm 97:2, 4*

It had been a long Michigan winter and my three-year-old
granddaughter had forgotten all about thunderstorms. So she
was frightened one spring afternoon when the sky grew dark, lightning flashed, thunder began to roll, and rain came pouring down.
She climbed onto her dad's lap. He reassured her that God knows
all about thunderstorms, and he used the occasion to tell her about
God's awesome power.

Psalm 97:1–6 also uses the imagery of a thunderstorm to illustrate the mighty works of the Lord. The writer paints a scene of
rolling clouds, jagged forks of lightning, and rumbling thunder to
describe God's power. The thick, dark clouds that hide the sun
remind me that man cannot stand the full view of God's glory
(v. 2). In the lightning I see a picture of God's fiery wrath on His
foes (vv. 3–4). In all of these forces of nature I see the glory of God
(v. 6).

We've all witnessed the power of a thunderstorm. And sometimes we are afraid. But each storm that rolls across the sky can
bring to mind great truths: God is awesome in power, He judges
His foes, and His glory fills the earth.

So, when the next storm comes, join the psalmist in praising
God for His wondrous power and majesty. See God in the thunderstorm.   DCE

Sovereign Ruler of the skies,
Ever gracious, ever wise,
All my times are in Your hand,
All events at Your command. —Ryland

When we trust God, His power is not a danger but a comfort.

Praying and Waiting

Read: Nehemiah 1:5–11

Rest in the Lord, and wait patiently for Him.
Psalm 37:7

A Christian couple was deeply distressed because their married son and his family had quit going to church and were giving God no place in their lives. As their friend, I advised them to continue showing love, to pray, and to avoid starting arguments. But at the family's annual Christmas gathering, the father gave his son a lecture in the presence of the other siblings. The son and his family left in anger and broke off all contact with his parents.

It's hard to rely on prayer alone when you want something to happen right now. But that is what Nehemiah did. He was distraught by the news that the Israelites in Jerusalem were in grave danger (Nehemiah 1:3–4). He was a man with great leadership ability and in a favorable position to receive help from the king he served, so he was eager to help his people. But he knew that he could be executed for coming into the presence of a Persian king without being invited. Therefore, though he had asked God to give him the opportunity immediately, he trusted God enough to wait. Four months later, the king opened the door for him to make his request (2:1–8).

It's not always easy to be patient, but God can be trusted. Wait patiently for Him.　　　　　　　　　　　　　　　　　　　HVL

Praying, resting, waiting, trusting—
These are words that tell a story;
As we wait for God to lead us,
He responds, "Just seek My glory." —Hess

Delay is not denial—pray on!

One Day at a Time

Read: Matthew 6:25–34

Do not worry about tomorrow.
Matthew 6:34

Perhaps you've seen the phrase "One Day at a Time" on a bumper sticker, plaque, or refrigerator magnet. The slogan is often used by recovering alcoholics as a reminder that a person doesn't have to stay sober forever—just for today. A month, or even a week, without alcohol may seem impossible for them. But the key to success is to trust God for the strength to say no to a drink *today*.

The thread of living "one day at a time" is woven throughout the fabric of Scripture. God supplied the Israelites with manna daily (Exodus 16:4). Our heavenly Father's mercies are new every morning (Lamentations 3:22–23). Jesus taught His followers to ask for their "daily bread" (Matthew 6:11) and to refuse to worry about tomorrow (v. 34). It's a lesson we seem to learn with difficulty, but one that holds the key to life and peace.

When we face a situation that seems overwhelming, we may drift toward hopelessness or despair, wondering how we'll be able to see it through to the end. But God's words of comfort and encouragement remind us that He "daily loads us with benefits" (Psalm 68:19).

Daily bread. Daily light. Daily strength. When tomorrow seems too long to endure, God reminds us to trust Him—one day at a time. DCM

Day by day and with each passing moment,
Strength I find to meet my trials here;
Trusting in my Father's wise bestowment,
I've no cause for worry or for fear. —Berg

God doesn't ask us to bear tomorrow's burdens
with today's strength.

Inner Strength

Read: Ephesians 3:14–21

[I pray] that He would grant you, according to the riches of His glory, to be strengthened with might through His Spirit in the inner man. Ephesians 3:16

A large company uses suction to extract contaminating substances from steel drums. Powerful pumps draw the materials out of the barrels, but the workers must carefully regulate the force of these pumps. If they take out too much air, the drums will collapse like paper cups, because the outer pressure will exceed the inner pressure.

Likewise, when adversity and hardship come into our lives, God must empower us from within or we will be unable to withstand the pressures from without. True, we get solid support from loved ones and Christian friends; but it is our spiritual inner man, "strengthened with might through His Spirit" (Ephesians 3:16), that sustains us and keeps us from crumpling.

The Holy Spirit works to strengthen us and renew our minds as we read the Bible and pray. If we neglect the Scriptures, seldom talk with the Lord, and stop our fellowship with other believers, we'll grow weak and vulnerable. Then we will be unable to withstand the pressures of temptation or trouble.

Let's ask the Lord to develop our inner strength so that when life's blows and burdens press upon us we will not cave in.   DCE

Help us, O Lord, when troubles come
To trust Your Word and not succumb,
And help us not to turn aside
But in Your strength and love abide. —DJD

The power of Christ within you is greater than
the pressure of troubles around you.

April 19

"Piggies"

Read: 1 Peter 5:5–7

[Cast] all your care upon Him,
for He cares for you. 1 Peter 5:7

I recall walking along a Texas creek many years ago with my brother-in-law Ed and his three-year-old son David. David had been collecting smooth, round stones from the stream while we walked. He called them "piggies," because their rounded shape reminded him of little pigs.

David had stuffed a number of "piggies" in his pockets, and after running out of pockets he began carrying them in his arms. After a while he began to stagger under the load and lag behind. It was obvious he would never make it back to the house without help, so Ed said, "Here, David, let me carry your piggies."

Reluctance clouded David's face for a moment, and then it lit up. "I know," he said. "You carry me and I'll carry my piggies!"

I've often thought of that incident and my own childish insistence that I must carry my own load. Jesus offers to take all of my burdens but I resist out of stubbornness and pride. "You carry me," I say, "but I'll carry my 'piggies.'"

How foolish it is to try to carry all your burdens on your own when Jesus asks you to cast "all your care upon Him, for He cares for you" (1 Peter 5:7).

Have you put all of your "piggies" in Jesus's strong arms today?

DHR

I would tell the Lord my longings,
Roll on Him my every care,
Cast upon Him all my burdens,
Burdens that I cannot bear. —Weigle

God cares.

God Reigns

Read: Psalm 93

Alleluia! For the Lord God Omnipotent reigns! Let us be glad and rejoice and give Him glory. Revelation 19:6–7

I remember well the shock and grief I felt in 1968 when Senator Robert Kennedy was assassinated in Los Angeles. People everywhere, regardless of their political affiliation, were numb with grief and horror. Coming so soon after the assassination of his brother, President John F. Kennedy, made it even more tragic.

Yet after Senator Kennedy's funeral in St. Patrick's Cathedral, the walls echoed with the triumphant words of Handel's *Messiah*: "The Lord God Omnipotent reigneth … and He shall reign for ever and ever."

These words do not suggest that God willed the assassination. They are a triumphant affirmation that in spite of such events, God achieves all His good purposes. People do things that anger and grieve Him. But He is at work bringing good out of evil, light out of darkness, joy out of pain, order out of chaos, and life out of death.

In Psalm 93, the pounding waves of the seas that "have lifted up their voice" represent humanity in turmoil and opposition to God (v. 3). They sometimes seem to be winning the battle. But the Lord is "mightier than the noise of many waters" (v. 4). One day He will completely vanquish all opposition and usher in the perfect eternal world He has promised us. Our God reigns! Hallelujah!   HVL

The more clearly we see God's sovereignty, the less perplexed we are by man's calamities.

Does God Love Me?

Read: Romans 5:6–11

We love Him because He first loved us.
1 John 4:19

It's not easy to understand the depth of God's love for us. Because of our pride and fear, we fail to grasp how undeserving we are and how free His love is.

At times I struggle with pride, so I tend to believe that I have earned any love I receive. Pride tells me that I am loved only when I am lovable, respectable, and worthy.

At other times I feel the tug of fear. Deep down inside, I know that I don't deserve the love I get. My motives are never pure, and I fear I will be rejected if they are exposed. So even while I am basking in acceptance, I live with the fear of being unmasked, revealing that I am much less than what others think me to be.

When I consider my relationship with God, therefore, I tend to feel that His affection for me is based on my performance. When I do well, He loves me; but if I foul up, then I expect only His scorn.

Yet God does not love us because we deserve it. He loves us in spite of what we are. In 1 John 4:10 we read, "In this is love, not that we loved God, but that He loved us and sent His Son." Because of what Jesus Christ has done for us, we know we are always loved by God. That simple truth shatters our pride and dispels our fear.

HWR

Oh, such love, my soul, still ponder—
Love so great, so rich, so free!
Say, while lost in holy wonder,
"Why, O Lord, such love to me?" —Kent

No one is beyond the reach of God's love.

Power Outage

Read: 2 Timothy 1:6–12

*God has not given us a spirit of fear, but of power and of love
and of a sound mind. 2 Timothy 1:7*

The silence awakened me at 5:30 one morning. There was no gentle whir of fan blades, no reassuring hum from the refrigerator downstairs. A glance out the window confirmed that a power outage had left everyone in our neighborhood without electricity just as they would be preparing for work.

I realized that alarm clocks would not sound, and there would be no TV news. Coffee makers, toasters, hair dryers, and many telephones would be useless. Beginning a day without power was simply an inconvenience and a disruption of routine—but it felt like a disaster.

Then I thought of how often I rush into the day without spiritual power. I spend more time reading the newspaper than the Bible. Talk radio replaces listening to the Spirit. I react to difficult people and circumstances in a spirit of fear rather than the spirit of "power and of love and of a sound mind" that God has given us (2 Timothy 1:7). I must appear as spiritually unkempt as a person who dressed and groomed in the dark.

Our power outage was short-lived, but the lesson remains of my need to begin each day by seeking the Lord. His strength is not for my success or well-being, but so that I will glorify Christ by living in His power. DCM

*There's never a lack of God's power
In prayer and reading His Word,
For Jesus in heaven is listening—
Your prayer will always be heard. —Hess*

The human spirit fails us unless the Holy Spirit fills us.

April 23

A Bitter Attitude

Read: Deuteronomy 32:44–52

Set your hearts on all the words which I testify among you today. . . .
it is your life. Deuteronomy 32:46–47

Great emphasis is being placed on living longer and better. Advances in medical science are making it possible for more and more people. Yet in spite of this, none of us can avoid growing old. One day aging will overtake all of us, and our bodies will shut down.

What is preventable, however, is an attitude of bitterness and regret as we grow older. Look at the life of Moses. When he was 120 years old, he stood with the Israelites before they crossed the Jordan River and entered the Promised Land. He could not go with them because he had disobeyed the Lord when in anger he struck the rock in the wilderness (Numbers 20:11–12, 24).

How easily Moses could have slipped into a self-pitying and resentful frame of mind. Had he not borne the burden of a stubborn and stiff-necked people for forty years? Had he not interceded for them time after time? Yet at the end of his life he praised the Lord and urged a new generation of Israelites to obey Him (Deuteronomy 32:1–4, 45–47).

As we grow older, we can dwell on the failures and hardships of our past, or we can remember God's faithfulness, accept His discipline, and keep looking to the future in faith. It's the only way to avoid a bitter attitude.   DJD

Though wrinkles and weakness come with age
And life with its stress takes its toll,
Yet beauty and vigor can still be seen
When Jesus gives peace to our soul. —DJD

We cannot avoid growing old, but we can avoid growing cold.

Ground Squirrels

Read: Romans 8:27–39

I was at ease, but He has shattered me.
Job 16:12

Ground squirrels hibernate near our home during the winter, and they reappear when the snow melts in the spring. My wife Carolyn and I enjoy watching them scurry back and forth from one hole to another, while others stand like tiny sentries watching for predators.

In mid-May, a man from a nearby golf course arrives on a little green tractor with a tank loaded with lethal gas. The groundskeeper tells us that these little critters have to be eliminated because they dig holes in the fairways. Some survive, but most do not. It always makes us a little sad to see the tractor arrive.

If I could, I'd chase the little animals away. I'd destroy their holes and force them to settle someplace else. I'm sure they would resent my interference, but my actions would be solely for their good.

So it is with God. He may break up our comfortable nests now and then, but behind every difficult change lies His love and eternal purpose. He is not cruel or capricious; He is working for our ultimate good (Romans 8:28). He wants us to be "conformed to the image of His Son" (v. 29) and to give us glorious enjoyment in heaven forever. How then can we fear change when it comes from Someone whose love for us never changes? (vv. 38–39).   DHR

What tenderness the Father shows
To sinners in their pain!
He grants to them His strength to bear
The hurt that brings them gain. —DJD

God's love can seem harsh until we view it with hindsight.

Nothing Hidden

Read: 1 Timothy 5:24–25

Some men's sins are clearly evident.... Likewise,
the good works of some... and those that are otherwise
cannot be hidden. 1 Timothy 5:24–25

A woman had been maligned and misrepresented by an envious coworker. She was frustrated because her attempts to confront the coworker in private had only made matters worse. So she decided to swallow her pride and let the matter go. She said, "I'm glad the Lord knows the true situation." She expressed a profound truth that both warns and comforts.

Paul pointed out that nothing can be concealed forever (1 Timothy 5:24–25). This serves as a solemn warning. For example, a news report told about a highly respected person who was arrested for crimes he had been secretly committing for years.

Yet the fact that nothing can be hidden can also be a great consolation. I have known people who never held a position of honor, nor were they recognized for their service. After they died, however, I learned that in their own quiet way they had touched many lives with their kind words and helpful deeds. Their good works could not remain hidden.

We can hide nothing from God—that's a solemn warning! But it's also a great comfort, for our heavenly Father knows about every encouraging smile, every kind word, and every loving deed done in Jesus's name. And someday He will reward us.   HVL

Neither vice nor virtue can remain a secret forever.

Unfamiliar Roads

Read: Psalm 119:105–112

*Teach me Your way, O Lord, and lead me
in a smooth path. Psalm 27:11*

Trouble often lies ahead when we go down unfamiliar roads.
I know a teenager who decided to take a different way to
work one morning. As he tried to navigate unfamiliar city streets,
he went through an intersection without seeing the red octagonal
sign that said "Stop."

Within a few seconds, he did stop, but not for a stop sign. He was
pulled over by a helpful gentleman in a police car who reminded
him that he should have stopped. It cost him eighty dollars to learn
about unfamiliar roads.

What would have happened if a guide had accompanied this
young driver? What if someone had been next to him to tell him
which way to go and to alert him to danger ahead? He wouldn't be
out the eighty dollars, that's for sure.

In life, we often have to walk down unfamiliar paths—paths
that may feel threatening. So how do we do that without making
costly mistakes?

We take Someone along who knows the way. The psalmist recognized that Guide when he wrote, "Lead me, O Lord, in Your righteousness... make Your way straight before my face" (Psalm 5:8).

Does your path today seem unfamiliar? Ask your Father to travel
the road with you. DB

*Take Jesus with you as your faithful guide,
You cannot fail when He is at your side;
You may encounter trouble on life's road,
But He will help to lift your heavy load. —Hess*

The Spirit within us will faithfully guide us.

April 27

Ain't It Awful!

Read: Lamentations 3:25–42

*Let us search out and examine our ways,
and turn back to the Lord. Lamentations 3:40*

A friend told me about a man who shouted the same three words each day from his street-corner newsstand. "Ain't it awful!" he would say to passersby while extending a newspaper. People bought a paper because they just had to know what terrible thing had occurred.

Tragedy and dire predictions always make the front page, but if we become preoccupied with bad news, we will succumb to what my friend calls "awfulizing"—a pervasive pessimism that clouds every situation with gloom.

If anyone had a good reason for being despondent, it was the prophet Jeremiah. For forty years he declared God's judgment on the rebellious and unrepentant nation of Judah. Jeremiah suffered because of their disobedience, but he clung to his faith in God's goodness. Even after witnessing the destruction of Jerusalem and the captivity of his people, Jeremiah wrote: "The Lord will not cast off forever. Though He causes grief, yet He will show compassion according to the multitude of His mercies. . . . Let us search out and examine our ways, and turn back to the Lord" (Lamentations 3:31–32, 40).

Disobedience to God can cause great pain, but the doorway out of discouragement leads to the Lord, who "is good to those who wait for Him" (v. 25).   DCM

*Turn not aside, discouraged one,
Stir up your gift, pursue your goal;
In God's own time you'll see Him work,
He'll give you hope and lift your soul. —DJD*

Awful circumstances cannot alter the goodness of God.

April 28

The Pine Looper

Read: Jeremiah 17:1–10

He shall be like a tree planted by the waters, which
spreads out its roots by the river. Jeremiah 17:8

In the summer of 1992, a fire blackened 4,500 acres of forest about thirty-five miles north of Atlantic City. One homeowner saw a fireball with sixty-foot flames come roaring up across the street from his house, before veering away. The Associated Press quoted him as saying, "I've worked twenty-five years of my life here. The thought of having it gone in ten minutes makes you want to stay for the last possible minute."

The fire was difficult to contain because of dry conditions. The forest was dry despite rainfall, partly because of an insect called the pine looper, which defoliates trees.

The dry-tree condition behind this New Jersey fire has a parallel in the history of Israel. Jeremiah said that his countrymen had become like dry shrubs in a desert rather than green trees by a river (17:6–8). Even more alarming, he said they had aroused the fire of God's anger (v. 4) by trusting in man and departing from the Lord (v. 5). For Christians today, it's life's fiery trials that threaten to scorch our souls if we're trusting in our own strength.

"Father, forgive us for making ourselves dry and leafless. Without Your mercy, we would be consumed when the heat comes. Teach us to root ourselves in the river of Your sufficiency."   MD

The person who relies upon
The Lord's sufficiency
Is like a tree that's planted by
Deep waters flowing free. —Sper

The fires of life will not destroy you if
you're watered by the River of Life.

April 29

The Frog's "Blackboard"

Read: Psalm 119:33–40

Turn away my eyes from looking at worthless things,
and revive me in Your way. Psalm 119:37

As a young boy, one of my favorite pastimes was hunting frogs along the banks of a pond near our home. I was unaware of their unique visual powers that enabled them to elude me so easily. Later I learned that the frog's optical field is like a blackboard wiped clean, and that the only images it receives are objects that directly concern him. These little amphibians are never distracted by unimportant things, but are aware only of essentials and whatever may be dangerous to them.

In the Christian life we frequently become preoccupied with the vain things of the world. We allow our lives to become so cluttered with materialistic and insignificant concerns that we lose perspective of the things that endure. In our text the psalmist asked God for help in fixing his attention on what is good and lasting (Psalm 119:37).

The words of the Lord should not depart from our eyes, but must be kept in our heart always (Proverbs 4:21). Then our field of vision will be wiped clean of unnecessary things, and we will see clearly what God wants us to do.

Have you become distracted by sin so that you can no longer discern what is really important? Then take a lesson from the frog's "blackboard" and center your gaze on Christ and His will for your life.   MD

The more attracted we are to Christ,
the less we'll be distracted by the world.

Pain Is Not Pointless

Read: Isaiah 28:23–29

*This also comes from the Lord of hosts, who is wonderful in counsel
and excellent in guidance. Isaiah 28:29*

During times of hardship, I often feel like whining, "Who needs this pain? I certainly don't!" But Isaiah 28 and my own experience tell me this is a shortsighted reaction. Not that we need hardship just for its own sake, but we do need to be changed and to mature. In God's hand, hardship can be an effective tool to bring about our much-needed growth.

In verses 23–28 we read the prophet's "poetic parable," written to help the people of Israel understand how God works and what He intended to accomplish in their lives through tough times. A farmer is portrayed skillfully plowing the ground, planting his crops, and threshing the harvest. If the soil could talk, it might have whined, "Who needs this painful plowing?" But the pain is not pointless. Isaiah said that the farmer is taught by God to work in measured and well-timed ways, handling delicate crops with care and others more vigorously, but always with a sure harvest in view.

Our reassurance during tough times is that the farmer's God is our God, "who is wonderful in counsel and excellent in guidance" (v. 29). His dealings with us are always thoughtful and purposeful, producing in us "the peaceable fruit of righteousness" (Hebrews 12:11).   JY

God has a purpose in our heartaches—
The Savior always knows what's best;
We learn so many precious lessons
In every sorrow, trial, and test. —Jarvis

When you trust in God, pain is an opportunity for progress.

Choosing Joy

Read: Romans 5:1–11

We also rejoice in God through our
Lord Jesus Christ. Romans 5:11

Most of us don't choose a difficult life—it chooses us. But we can choose our response to it. As someone once said, "Pain is inevitable but misery is optional." Yet, when difficulties arise, misery often seems to be the only option.

Author Lloyd Ogilvie tells of a Christian friend who was physically and emotionally depleted because of extreme pressures. A depressed mood engulfed him. When Ogilvie asked him how he was doing, he said grimly, "Well, joy's certainly no option!" Ogilvie replied, "You're right! Joy is no option. It's your responsibility."

Shocked, the friend retorted, "You talk about joy as if it were a duty." Ogilvie responded, "Right again!" He explained that we have a duty to God, ourselves, and others to overcome our moods and to battle through to joy.

In Romans 5, Paul gave these reasons for joy: We have peace with God through Christ, access into grace, and hope of future glory (vv. 1–2). We have assurance that tribulation produces perseverance, which in turn builds character and leads to hope (vv. 3–4). We have hope that doesn't disappoint, because God's love has been poured into our hearts (v. 5).

Fill your mind with these truths. Then, no matter what your circumstances, you can choose joy. 　　　　　　　JY

When trials come and my moods descend,
When pain and sorrows seem never to end,
As I yield to You, Lord, may I see
The peace and joy You've promised me. —Fitzhugh

For the Christian, joy is a choice.

Who Are You?

Read: Galatians 3:26–4:7

*You are all sons of God through faith
in Christ Jesus. Galatians 3:26*

Have you ever experienced an identity crisis—a time when you asked yourself who you really were, and why you were here? There are three specific times when this crisis is most common.

Teens often go through a period of wondering who they are—trying to fit into their circle of friends while trying to learn the meaning of life. During middle age some people struggle with identity, perhaps out of disappointment for not having achieved all they had hoped. In later years people realize that life is approaching its final stages, and they wonder what kind of person they have become.

Because Christians are not immune to such questions, it's good to review who God says we are. This can be encouraging as we remember what Christ did when He redeemed us. The Bible tells us that because of our relationship to Christ, we are forgiven (Acts 10:43), reconciled to God (2 Corinthians 5:18–19), new creations in Christ (2 Corinthians 5:17), joint heirs with Christ (Romans 8:16–17), God's adopted children (Galatians 4:4–7), and God's witnesses and ambassadors (Matthew 28:19–20; 2 Corinthians 5:20). Best of all, we are destined to be like His Son (Romans 8:29).

Such wonderful truths should leave no doubt about who we really are and why we are here! —DB

*New life in Christ—miraculous
That we're not bound by sin!
The power of God—how glorious
That we've been changed within! —Sper*

When we know we are identified with Christ,
we will have no identity crisis.

Waiting

Read: Titus 2:11–15

*Our citizenship is in heaven, from which we also eagerly wait
for the Savior, the Lord Jesus Christ. Philippians 3:20*

In the 1940s, Samuel Beckett wrote a play called *Waiting for Godot*, which is now regarded as a classic. Two men stand on an empty stage, hands in their pockets, staring at each other. There is no action, no plot, they just stand there waiting for Godot to come.

But who is Godot? Is he a person? Does he represent God? Christian ethicist Lewis Smedes suggests, Godot "stands for the pipe dreams that a lot of people hang on to as an escape." As the play ends, those men are still standing on the stage, just waiting.

When the fiftieth anniversary of that play was celebrated, someone asked Beckett, "Now will you tell us who Godot is?" He answered, "How should I know?"

Waiting for Godot is a parable of many people's lives—empty and meaningless, a pointless matter of waiting. And if there's no God of love, grace, and wisdom, then life really is a hopeless waiting for empty time to pass.

How totally different, though, is Christian hope! We're waiting and "looking for the blessed hope and glorious appearing of our great God and Savior Jesus Christ" (Titus 2:13). That hope sustains us—a hope that beyond this world lies a life of indescribable blessing.

VCG

*We're waiting for You, Lord, to come
And take us home to be with You;
Your promise to return for us
Gives hope because we know it's true.* —Sper

The greatest joy on earth is to have the sure hope of heaven.

Profit and Loss

Read: 1 Timothy 6:17–19

Command those who are rich in this present age not to . . .
trust in uncertain riches but in the living God. 1 Timothy 6:17

Publisher Frank Doubleday had a one-of-a-kind book that was bound in red Russian leather. He called it the *Book of the Law and the Profits.* Unlike the portions of the Bible that we call the Law and the Prophets, Doubleday's book was an account of his business dealings and his financial profits. According to author George Doran, the red book contained Doubleday's morning prayers and evening vespers. In other words, it seemed that he worshiped money.

Jesus knew how easily all of us are tempted to become devotees of money and all the things it can buy. He warned, "No one can serve two master . . . You cannot serve God and mammon [money]" (Matthew 6:24).

We are idolaters if we put our trust in money as the ultimate source of our security and happiness. Our Lord also warned against being absorbed in the things that gratify our fleshly desires and self-centered ambitions. He asked, "What profit is it to a man if he gains the whole world, and loses his own soul?" (16:26).

Money can't bring us true and lasting profit. That can be found only by trusting the living God (1 Timothy 6:17). As we put our hope in Him and live in obedience to His Word, we will have eternal profit (v. 19).   VCG

If I gained the world but not the Savior,
Would my gain be worth the lifelong strife?
Are all earthly pleasures worth comparing
For a moment with a Christ-filled life? —Olander

None are so poor as those whose only wealth is money.

Our Place of Refuge

Read: Psalm 57

In the shadow of Your wings I will make my refuge,
until these calamities have passed by. Psalm 57:1

It is believed that David wrote Psalm 57 while fleeing from King Saul, who had hatred in his heart for the former shepherd boy. David ducked into a cave and barely escaped his pursuer. He was safe temporarily, but the threat was still there.

We've all been there. Maybe not in a cave, but pursued by something that strikes fear into our hearts. Perhaps it is the deep sorrow that follows the death of someone we love. Maybe it's the fear of an unknown future. Or it could be an oppressive physical illness that won't go away.

In such circumstances, God does not always remove the difficulty, but He is present to help us. We wish that He would swoop in and whisk us to safety—just as David may have wished for a quick end to Saul's pursuit. We plead with God to stop the pain and make the road to tomorrow smooth and straight. We beg Him to eliminate our struggle. But the difficulty remains. It is then that we have to take refuge in God as David did. While hiding in that cave, he said, "In the shadow of Your wings I will make my refuge, until these calamities have passed by" (Psalm 57:1).

Are you in the middle of trouble? Take refuge in the Most High God.   DB

We learn the lesson of trust in the school of trial.

Surprising Light

Read: Lamentations 3:16–33

His compassions fail not. They are new every morning;
great is Your faithfulness. Lamentations 3:22–23

If you've ever been so overwhelmed by sorrow that you couldn't speak, you can begin to understand the emotions of Jeremiah as he wrote the book of Lamentations. It is a sobbing requiem for the death of Jerusalem and the captivity of her people because of their sins. The tears of "the weeping prophet" seem to splash onto every page.

Recently, as I read Lamentations, I was so caught up in the destruction and desolation described by Jeremiah that a familiar passage took me by surprise: "Through the Lord's mercies we are not consumed, because His compassions fail not. They are new every morning; great is Your faithfulness" (3:22–23).

Those verses are so often quoted alone that I had forgotten the bleak context in which they were penned. In the midst of Jeremiah's dark night of the soul, they shine as an unexpected ray of hope and light.

There may be times in our lives when it appears that all is lost and we sink into despair. But in our deepest sorrow, we are often surprised by the light of God's never-failing love. Then, by His grace and mercy, we can echo the words of Jeremiah: "'The Lord is my portion,' says my soul, 'therefore I hope in Him!'" (v. 24).   DCM

Life's darkest trials cannot dim the light of God's love.

What Does God Require?

Read: Isaiah 1:13–17

Go and learn what this means: "I desire mercy and not sacrifice."
Matthew 9:13

The mother of four growing children went to a counselor because she felt that she was a failure. She had trained for ministry and had hoped to serve the Lord as a missionary overseas. But instead, she fell in love and married a widower with four children. Barely able to keep her household functioning, she was not able to engage in any formal ministry. She wrongly concluded that God was subjecting her to well-deserved chastisement.

A Christian counselor pointed her to Micah 6:8, which asks, "What does the Lord require of you?" Immediately that question is answered, "To do justly, to love mercy, and to walk humbly with your God." Those requirements she could meet without going to a foreign mission field. And meet them she did!

Her experience calls to mind Martin Luther's advice to people who believed they could please God by journeying to a sacred shrine: "Let anyone go on a pilgrimage who feels compelled to do so; but let him remember that God can be served a thousand times better at home by giving the money the journey would cost to his own wife and children and bearing his cross with patience."

Remember, God requires justice, mercy, and humility—no matter where we live. VCG

O Master, let me walk with Thee
In lowly paths of service free;
Tell me Thy secret, help me bear
The strain of toil, the fret of care. —*Gladden*

What God requires, God provides.

May 8

Plenty of Pencils

Read: 2 Corinthians 12:7–10

When I am weak, then I am strong. 2 Corinthians 12:10

My mother lives alone now. It's been eight years since my dad died. She can't get out by herself except to take brief walks. She's having a terrible time with her short-term memory. Conversations are limited to a few repeated comments.

Yet she told me something profound. She said, "I was thinking the other day about my troubles, and I decided that I don't have anything to complain about. God's taking care of me and I've got people who are helping. My only trouble is that I can't remember anything, and I've got plenty of pencils and paper to write everything down."

The apostle Paul struggled with what he called "a thorn in the flesh" (2 Corinthians 12:7). But he found that in his weakness he experienced "the power of Christ" (v. 9). He said, "I take pleasure in infirmities, in reproaches, in needs, in persecutions, in distresses, for Christ's sake" (v. 10).

All of us have struggles. They may be related to age, finances, relationships, or a myriad of other difficulties. But if we truly set our heart to trusting God, and if we stay thankful even in the midst of our troubles, we'll be more likely to acknowledge that we "don't have anything to complain about."   DB

Even in my darkest hour
The Lord will bless me with His power;
His loving grace will sure abound,
In His sweet care I shall be found. —*Brandt*

As you go through life, concentrate on the roses
instead of the thorns.

May 9

What Cancer Can't Do

Read: 1 Corinthians 15:35–49

Thanks be to God, who gives us the victory through
our Lord Jesus Christ. 1 Corinthians 15:57

One of the most dreaded sentences a patient can hear is, "You have cancer." These words bring a chill to the heart. Although great progress is being made in treating this disease, recovery can be long and painful, and many people do not survive.

An enthusiastic believer in Christ, Dan Richardson, lost his battle with cancer. But his life demonstrated that even though the physical body may be destroyed by disease, the spirit can remain triumphant. This poem was distributed at his memorial service:

Cancer is so limited . . .
It cannot cripple love,
It cannot shatter hope,
It cannot corrode faith,
It cannot eat away peace,
It cannot destroy confidence,
It cannot kill friendship,
It cannot shut out memories,
It cannot silence courage,
It cannot invade the soul,
It cannot reduce eternal life,
It cannot quench the Spirit,
It cannot lessen the power of the resurrection.

If an incurable disease has invaded your life, refuse to let it touch your spirit. Your body can be severely afflicted, and you may have a great struggle. But if you keep trusting God's love, your spirit will remain strong.   DCE

Our greatest enemy is not disease, but despair.

Courage to Continue

Read: Haggai 2:1–9

"Be strong, all you people of the land," says the Lord,
"and work; for I am with you." Haggai 2:4

I enjoy my job, so usually I am eager to get out of bed and go to work. But one day I became discouraged when I thought about my family's financial security. Was I providing enough? Other people seemed to be doing so much better. I grew fearful as I thought about the future, and those fears sapped my zest for life.

It would have been helpful for me to recall what God had said through Haggai to the Jews who had returned to Jerusalem from exile. Even though they had started enthusiastically to rebuild the temple, they became discouraged. Memories of Solomon's glorious temple made their work seem insignificant by comparison.

They needed courage. So God told them, "Be strong, all you people of the land... and work; for I am with you" (Haggai 2:4).

How can we find courage? Some find it in a group. Some depend on their achievements. Some try to boost their self-confidence by raising their voice. But these do nothing more than camouflage their insecurity.

As God's people, our confidence comes from our relationship with Him. He is with us. We are His people. As we keep these truths in mind, we will find courage to continue working in a way that pleases Him and brings us joy. AL

We find courage to stand when we kneel before the Lord.

Peace in the Storm

Read: Psalm 37:1–11

Commit your way to the Lord, trust also in Him,
and He shall bring it to pass. Psalm 37:5

During a terrible storm on the ocean, a small passenger ship rolled precariously in the roaring tempest. The furniture and anything else that could move was tied down, and the passengers were confined to their bunks for their own safety. Many on board thought the vessel was doomed.

Finally, a passenger who was determined to find out if there was any hope for survival set out to see the one who was in command. Clinging to the walls and handrails, he made his way to the wave-lashed deck, up a ladder, and into the wheelhouse. He noticed that the ship was nearing land and was between some jagged rocks. It became apparent that the captain was trying to reach the safety of a calm bay up ahead. Knowing he could not make himself heard above the roar of the wind and waves, the captain just turned wordlessly to the worried passenger and smiled. Reassured, the man returned to the others and said, "Don't be afraid. All is well. I've seen the captain's face, and he smiled!"

When we are battered by the storms of life, we may be tempted to give in to feelings of hopelessness. But if we look to our sovereign Captain and commit our way to Him (Psalm 37:5), we will find peace even in the midst of turmoil. We can trust Him to bring us through the storm.   HGB

God's unseen presence comforts me,
I know He's always near;
And when life's storms besiege my soul,
He says, "My child, don't fear." —DJD

God may calm the storm around you, but more often
He'll calm the storm within you.

The Hope of the Heart

Read: Romans 4:13–25

*[Abraham] did not waver at the promise of God
through unbelief. Romans 4:20*

Promises are the hope of our heart. A child's security depends on a parent's promise to keep him or her safe. A spouse can live with confidence because of a mate's promise of fidelity, loyalty, and love. Businesses depend on promises from employees, vendors, and clients. Countries remain safe when neighbors keep their promise to honor their borders.

Unfortunately, hearts and relationships are broken in all of those situations by unkept promises. There is one Promise-Maker, though, who can be trusted completely and without fear. That one is God. He has given us hundreds of promises in His Word, and He keeps every one of them.

If anyone had reason to wonder if God could or would keep His promises, it was Abraham. But "contrary to hope, in hope [Abraham] believed" (Romans 4:18). We know that what God had promised him—that he and his wife would have a child when they were both past ninety years old—could not have happened without divine intervention.

Are you looking for hope? Then search the Scriptures diligently and claim the promises of God that apply to you. Promises truly are the hope of the heart, and God always keeps His word.   DB

Standing on the promises that cannot fail,
When the howling storms of doubt and fear assail,
By the living Word of God I shall prevail,
Standing on the promises of God. —Carter

The future always looks bright when viewed
through the window of God's promises.

Just You and God

Read: Psalm 35:1–10

*Plead my cause, O Lord, with those
who strive with me. Psalm 35:1*

My friend Ron wasn't having a good week when I saw him at church. His new job had thrust him in the midst of some people who were foul-mouthed, rude, and obnoxious. Ron is one tough guy, but after two months of working in that environment, he was no longer sure he could tolerate any more ungodly, uncouth behavior.

Ron is by no means alone. Perhaps you too are in an environment that is not friendly to godliness—either at work, at home, or elsewhere. If so, what can you do? Here are some suggestions that may help you survive and even thrive:

Concentrate on God's goodness and depend on it. Our circumstances do not change the truth that the Lord is good all the time (Nahum 1:7).

Stay true to your convictions. Daniel refused to give in when he was surrounded by the ungodly (Daniel 1).

Immerse yourself in the Bible. Listen to God in His Word. It will encourage you (Psalm 119:49–50).

Do good for those who oppose you. Return good for evil (Matthew 5:44).

Trust God to be your companion. He will never leave you. And He won't forsake you (Hebrews 13:5).

When it's just you and God, that's enough.   DB

*When we are weak and in despair,
Our mighty God is near;
He'll give us strength and joy and hope,
And calm our inner fear. —Sper*

With God behind you and His arms beneath you,
you can face whatever is before you.

Taste and Say!

Read: Psalm 34:1–10

Oh, taste and see that the Lord is good; blessed is the man
who trusts in Him! Psalm 34:8

Do you believe God is good, even when life isn't? Mary did, and I gasped in amazement the day I heard her pastor share her story at her funeral.

Mary had been a widow—very poor, and housebound because of her ailments in old age. But like the psalmist, she had learned to praise God amid her hardships. Over the years she had come to savor with deep gratitude every good thing He sent her way.

Her pastor had occasionally visited her at home. Because of her crippling pain, it took her a long time to inch her way to the door to let him in. So he would call on the telephone and tell her that he was on his way and what time he would get there. Mary would then begin the slow, arduous journey to the door, reaching it about the time he arrived. Without fail, she would greet him with these triumphant words: "God is good!"

I've observed that those who speak most often about God's goodness are usually those with the most trials. They focus on the Lord's mercy and grace rather than on their troubles, and in so doing they taste His goodness. Mary's example not only challenges us to "taste and see," but also to taste and say that the Lord is good—even when life isn't. JY

Though trials come, though fears assail
Through tests scarce understood,
One truth shines clear; it cannot fail—
My God is right and good. —Hager

When you taste God's goodness,
His praise will be on your lips.

The Book of Hope

Read: Romans 5:1–11

Hope does not disappoint. Romans 5:5

Writing in *Texas Co-Op Power* magazine, Donna Chapman described the excitement generated on her family's farm in the 1940s by the arrival of the Montgomery Ward catalog. Often called "the wish book," its pages were filled with images of items ranging from clothing and cookstoves to furniture and tools. The catalog's warm, friendly tone seemed to invite people to picture themselves as they lived, worked, and dressed at the time, and as they hoped to become.

The Bible is not a spiritual mail-order catalog, but in its pages we vividly see ourselves both as we are today and as we hope to be. The Bible certainly is God's book of hope.

In Romans 5, Paul said that "we rejoice in hope of the glory of God" (v. 2), "glory in tribulations" (v. 3), and "rejoice in God through our Lord Jesus Christ" (v. 11). Even our present difficulties are an essential part of the process of becoming the people we know God wants us to be.

The Bible is far more than a book of wishful thinking; it is a book of well-founded confidence in God's purpose and plan for us as believers. Whatever we are like today, we know that in Christ we have a living hope, and it will not end in disappointment.   DCM

A strong defense to guard the soul
Is ours from heaven above;
God fills our hearts with steadfast hope
And gives us faith and love. —DJD

No one is hopeless whose hope is in God's Word.

When Things Go Wrong

Read: 2 Corinthians 4:7–18

We are hard pressed on every side, yet not crushed; we are perplexed, but not in despair. 2 Corinthians 4:8

One measure of our spiritual maturity is the way we respond when things go wrong. If we give in to despair, doubt God's existence, or strike out at some innocent person, we have some growing up to do.

Explorer Samuel Hearne (1745–1792) was on an expedition in northern Canada when a crucial piece of charting equipment broke. So he had to turn back. Then, thieves stole most of his supplies. Hearne responded in an unexpected way. In his journal he wrote, "As the ravagers had materially lightened my load,... this part of the journey was the easiest and most pleasant of any I had experienced since my leaving the fort."

Back in the first century, as the apostle Paul traveled from town to town proclaiming the gospel, he faced opposition and desperate situations (2 Corinthians 4:8–10; 11:23–33). Time and time again he found help and hope by turning to the Lord.

How about you? How did you respond the last time something went wrong? Did you fall apart? If so, ask God for patience and a positive perspective to handle life's setbacks in a mature Christian way (James 1:2–5). When things go wrong, ask God for strength and wisdom. Then thank Him for working to increase your faith.

DCE

Oh, give me a grateful heart,
A heart that's tried and true,
So that when troubles and trials come
I'll still be praising You. —Hawkes

Tough times teach trust.

Joy and Peace

Read: Romans 1:18–23; 5:1–11

*Having been justified by faith, we have peace with God
through our Lord Jesus Christ. Romans 5:1*

Lucky Lawrence thought he had it all. Like so many who seek
fulfillment in fame, money, and success, he struggled to find
real joy despite having all those things. His real name was Larry
Wright, and he was the number one rock-and-roll radio personality
in Phoenix in the 1960s. But his family life was a mess, and he was
fast becoming an alcoholic.

As Mike Yorkey tells it in his book *Touched by the Savior*, the
solution came to Lucky Lawrence when his wife, Sue, trusted Jesus
as her Savior. Larry noticed the peace and joy in her life and the
obvious change in her attitude toward him. Soon he too asked Jesus
to forgive him and be his Savior.

Gone was the frustrating search for peace. In its place was the
joy and peace of God. Larry and Sue have now served the Lord for
more than thirty years.

In Romans we see the contrast between the two kinds of existence possible in this life. In Romans 1:18–32, we read about the
sad, frightening life of those who refuse to live for God. It's a life
full of trouble and turmoil. But in Romans 5:1–11, we see what
happens when a person trusts Christ. "We have peace," it says. "We
rejoice," we're told. And we have hope, love, and salvation. What
a contrast!

Which of these two worlds are you living in?   DB

HOW TO HAVE JOY AND PEACE
Believe God and His Word (Romans 5:1; 15:13).
Live by the power of God's Spirit (Galatians 5:16, 22–23).
With God's help, always do what is right (Romans 14:17).

No God, no peace; know God, know peace.

What's the Good News?

Read: Matthew 28:1–10, 16–20

*As cold water to a weary soul, so is good news
from a far country. Proverbs 25:25*

What's the good news today? I ask that question sometimes of people I know. If the person is a Christian, he might smilingly reply, "The same as it was yesterday. God loves us." And both he and I rejoice that it will be the same tomorrow.

Those who don't know Christ, though, don't have such good news to share. We can understand why pessimistic novelist T. C. Boyle says, "If God doesn't exist... and you have no purpose on Earth, then it's a mighty mean place, ruled by accident.... I'd like to have a lot better news for everybody, but I don't."

Despite personal disappointments and the evils we see in this world, life is not just a series of accidents. Our God is in ultimate control, making even man's wrath contribute to the fulfillment of His wise and loving purposes.

Faith in the One who died on Calvary's cross and rose from the tomb is the antidote to dark despair. Faith in our Lord Jesus Christ gives a realistic reason for hope.

When Jesus rose from the grave, He told two women to tell His disciples He was alive. Later He commanded His followers to take that news to all nations (Matthew 28:9–10, 19).

That's the good news we can proclaim to others. It's the answer to the riddle of our existence.   VCG

*Oh, may our lives ring loud and clear
With God's good news for all,
So people who are lost in sin
Will clearly hear His call. —Sper*

The good news is not that Jesus lived and died,
but that He died and lives.

May 19

Such a Hope

Read: Romans 8:18–27

This hope we have as an anchor of the soul,
both sure and steadfast. Hebrews 6:19

Two women. One a former coworker I had known for twenty years. The other, the wife of a former student from my days as a school teacher. Both dedicated moms of two young children. Both missionaries. Both incredibly in love with Jesus Christ.

Then suddenly, within the space of a month—both were dead. The first, Sharon Fasick, died in a car accident, attracting little attention though deeply affecting family and friends. The second, Roni Bowers, died with her daughter Charity when their plane was shot down over the jungles of Peru—a situation that thrust her story into the international spotlight.

Their deaths filled many people with inexpressible sorrow. But there was something else—hope. Both women's husbands had the confident expectation that they would see their wives again in heaven. What happened after they died demonstrates that the Christian faith works. Both men, Jeff Fasick and Jim Bowers, have spoken about the peace God has given them. They have testified that this kind of hope has allowed them to continue on in the midst of the unspeakable pain.

Paul said that our present sufferings "are not worthy to be compared with the glory which shall be revealed" (Romans 8:18). Such a hope comes only from Christ.   DB

When peace like a river attendeth my way,
When sorrows like sea billows roll;
Whatever my lot, Thou hast taught me to say,
"It is well, it is well with my soul." —Spafford

The hope of heaven is God's solution for sorrow.

Prayer's Effects

Read: James 5:13–20

The effective, fervent prayer of a righteous
man avails much. James 5:16

For many years, researchers have tried to determine if prayer has any effect on physical healing. An assistant professor at George Washington University School of Medicine says that "trying to scientifically determine prayer's effect on health is nearly impossible."

Even Christians who agree that God heals may differ widely on how, when, and why He does. We struggle to understand why the Lord restores some to health while others suffer and die.

James addressed the matter in a way that is worthy of careful study and attention. He discussed healing in the context of a fellowship of believers and said: "Confess your trespasses to one another, and pray for one another, that you may be healed. The effective, fervent prayer of a righteous man avails much" (James 5:16).

James's purpose was not to stir up controversy or to prove a scientific point. Instead, he focused on the privilege and power of prayer. While speaking of physical healing, he also included a call for restoration to spiritual health through repentance and confession (v. 15).

Science tries to prove cause and effect. Faith directs us to call on the power of our loving God, whose ways we can rarely understand but can always trust.   DCM

My prayer is a simple one, Lord:
Whatever is best for me, do;
In sickness, in health I desire
What brings the most glory to You. —Fasick

Prayer is the soil in which hope and healing grow best.

"God Makes No Mistakes"

Read: Romans 12:14–21

*Do not be overcome by evil, but overcome
evil with good. Romans 12:21*

A few days after arriving on the campus of Texas A&M University in 1984, Bruce Goodrich was awakened at 2:00 a.m. Upperclassmen roused him out of bed to initiate him into the Corps of Cadets, a military-style training program.

Bruce was forced to exercise and run several miles in hot and humid conditions. When he eventually collapsed, he was told to get up and keep going. He collapsed again, went into a coma, and died later that same day. The students who mistreated Bruce were put on trial and charged with causing his death.

Bruce's father wrote a letter to the administration, faculty, and student body. He didn't excuse the cruel injustice of what happened to his son, but he said: "I would like to take this opportunity to express the appreciation of my family for the great outpouring of concern and sympathy from Texas A&M University and the community over the loss of our son Bruce... We harbor no ill will... We know our God makes no mistakes... Bruce is now secure in his celestial home. When the question is asked, 'Why did this happen?' perhaps one answer will be, 'So that many will consider where they will spend eternity.'"

Trusting in the sovereignty of God can turn outrage into compassion and hatred into concern. HWR

*The Lord can turn a tragedy
Into an opportunity
To show us that eternity
Must never be ignored. —Sper*

No tragedy is beyond God's sovereignty.

Tough Trees

Read: Romans 5:1–5

*Tribulation produces perseverance; and perseverance,
character; and character, hope. Romans 5:3–4*

Bristlecone pines are the world's oldest living trees. Several are estimated to be 3,000 to 4,000 years old. In 1957, scientist Edmund Schulman found one he named "Methuselah." This ancient, gnarled pine is nearly 5,000 years old! It was an old tree when the Egyptians were building the pyramids.

Bristlecones grow atop the mountains of the western United States at elevations of 10,000 to 11,000 feet. They've been able to survive some of the harshest living conditions on earth: arctic temperatures, fierce winds, thin air, and little rainfall.

Their brutal environment is actually one of the reasons they've survived for millennia. Hardship has produced extraordinary strength and staying power.

Paul taught that "tribulation produces... character" (Romans 5:3–4). Adversity is part of the process that God uses to produce good results in our lives. Trouble, if it turns us to the Lord, could actually be the best thing for us. It leaves us wholly dependent on Him.

So we should pray not just for relief from our affliction, but for the grace to turn it into greater openness to God and to His will for us. Then we can be strong in calamity, and at peace in the place where God has planted us. DHR

THINKING IT OVER

*What trial in your life is making you wonder
why God is allowing it?*

God uses our difficulties to develop our character.

May 23

For Better or Worse?

Read: Ephesians 5:22–33

*Wives, submit to your own husbands, as to the
Lord. . . . Husbands, love your wives, just as Christ
also loved the church. Ephesians 5:22, 25*

Within a chip shot of our house is a golf course. When I stand
in my backyard, I see ponds waiting hungrily for my next
errant shot. At times I can imagine sand traps and trees joking about
my bad days.

I mention the sport with mixed feelings. I like to golf occasionally, but living so close to the course reminds me of my failures in
playing the game, which has its disadvantages.

A similar problem can occur in marriage. Sometimes a husband
and wife can lose sight of the hopes and dreams they once shared.
Then the very presence of the other becomes a source of irritation,
a reminder of past failures and disappointments.

When the apostle Paul wrote his letter to the Ephesians, he asked
husbands and wives to turn their thoughts to their relationship with
the Son of God (5:22–33). In Him we find undying love and forgiveness for our failures. In Him we find Someone who loves to
forget the worst and bring out the best. He reminds us not of what
we've lost but of what we have yet to find.

*"Forgive us, Father, for focusing on our flaws and failures rather than on
the love of Your Son, Jesus Christ. Help us to rediscover our spouse in the
light of our Lord's great love for us."*　　　　　　　　　　　MD

REFLECTING ON MARRIAGE

*As a couple, recall the hopes and dreams you had when
you were first married. Name some that have come true.
Share with each other your hopes for the future.*

Marriages may be made in heaven, but they have to be
worked out on earth.

Dealing with Self-Doubt

Read: Psalm 26

I will walk in my integrity; redeem me and be merciful to me.
My foot stands in an even place. Psalm 26:11–12

Sometimes, when I've been falsely accused, I have found myself questioning my sincerity. When I do, I follow the example of David in Psalm 26 as he responded to his critics.

Appealing directly to the Lord, he expressed his firm conviction that he had walked in "integrity" (the Hebrew word means *sincerity*, not *faultlessness*). He asked God to vindicate him, for he had renounced the ways of the wicked, declared his love for God's temple, and pleaded for deliverance from the fate of the ungodly (vv. 1–10). Finally, he reaffirmed his resolve to live with sincerity, humbly asked God to redeem him, and acknowledged his need for mercy (v. 11).

What happened next? God gave David the assurance that he stood in "an even place" (v. 12), a symbolic way of saying he was in a place of safety, accepted and protected by the Lord. As a result, he closed his psalm on a note of confidence and anticipation.

Have the painful barbs of critics or the accusations of your conscience filled you with fear and self-doubt? Talk to the Lord. If you need to confess sin, do it. Then put your hope and trust in God. He will replace your insecurity and doubt with His supernatural peace. He has done that for me. He will do the same for you.   HVL

When you live every hour by the grace of His power
And you know He will guide you aright,
Then day in and day out faith is stronger than doubt,
And faith puts your worries to flight. —Gilbert

Feeding your faith will starve your doubts.

How to Fail Successfully

Read: 1 John 1:5–2:2

If anyone sins, we have an Advocate with the Father,
Jesus Christ the righteous. 1 John 2:1

Inventor Charles Kettering has suggested that we must learn to fail intelligently. He said, "Once you've failed, analyze the problem and find out why, because each failure is one more step leading up to the cathedral of success."

Kettering gave these suggestions for turning failure into success: (1) Honestly face defeat; never fake success. (2) Exploit the failure; don't waste it. Learn all you can from it. (3) Never use failure as an excuse for not trying again.

Kettering's practical wisdom holds a deeper meaning for the Christian. The Holy Spirit is constantly working in us to accomplish "His good pleasure" (Philippians 2:13), so we know that failure is never final.

We can't reclaim lost time. And we can't always make things right, although we should try. Some consequences of our sins can never be reversed. But we can make a new start, because Jesus died to pay the penalty for all our sins and is our "Advocate with the Father" (1 John 2:1).

Knowing how to benefit from failure is the key to continued growth in grace. According to 1 John 1:9, we need to confess our sins—it's the first step in turning our failure into success.   DJD

Onward and upward your course plan today,
Seeking new heights as you walk Jesus' way;
Heed not past failures, but strive for the prize,
Aiming for goals fit for His holy eyes. —Brandt

Failure is never final for those who begin again with God.

May 26

Giving Away Happiness

Read: Proverbs 11:16–26

The generous soul will be made rich, and he who waters will also be watered himself. Proverbs 11:25

A U.S. News & World Report cover story explored the subject of happiness. According to the article, scientists have found that "strong marriages, family ties, and friendships predict happiness, as do spirituality and self-esteem. Hope is crucial, as is the feeling that life has meaning." But what if some of these elements are missing in our lives? Researchers say that "helping people be a little happier can jump-start a process that will lead to stronger relationships, renewed hope, and general upward spiraling of happiness."

What we give, more than what we get, produces joy in our lives. The Bible says, "There is one who scatters, yet increases more.... The generous soul will be made rich, and he who waters will also be watered himself" (Proverbs 11:24–25).

Is there some small way you can help someone else be happier today? Perhaps it's sending a card, making a phone call, or giving yourself in friendship. Hoarding never produces happiness. It comes as we seek the good of others and give away what God has given us.

The source of such an attitude is found in our relationship with Christ and His Spirit (Galatians 5:22–23). From Him grows the fruit of generosity, happiness, and love.

What will you give away today?   DCM

It is more blessed to give than to receive.

Battle Praise

Read: 2 Chronicles 20:1–22

When they began to sing and to praise, the Lord set ambushes against the people... who had come against Judah. 2 Chronicles 20:22

Visitors to the Military Museum in Istanbul, Turkey, can hear stirring music that dates back to the early years of the Ottoman Empire. Whenever their troops marched off to war, bands accompanied them.

Centuries earlier, worship singers led the people of Judah into battle, but there was a big difference. Whereas the Ottomans used music to instill self-confidence in their soldiers, the Jews used it to express their confidence in God.

Threatened by huge armies, King Jehoshaphat of Judah knew that his people were powerless to defend themselves. So he cried out to God for help (2 Chronicles 20:12). The Lord's answer came through Jahaziel, who said, "Do not be afraid nor dismayed... for the battle is not yours, but God's" (v. 15).

Jehoshaphat responded by worshiping and then by appointing singers to lead the army (vv. 18, 21). As the people sang, "Praise the Lord, for His mercy endures forever," God confused the invaders and they killed one another (vv. 22–24).

No matter what battles we may face today, the Lord will help us when we cry out to Him. Instead of retreating in fear, we can march ahead with confidence in God's power and sing praise to Him.   JAL

Praise is the voice of faith.

The Upside of Sorrow

Read: Ecclesiastes 7:1–14

*Sorrow is better than laughter, for by a sad countenance
the heart is made better. Ecclesiastes 7:3*

Sorrow can be good for the soul. It can uncover hidden depths in ourselves and in God.

Sorrow causes us to think earnestly about ourselves. It makes us ponder our motives, our intentions, our interests. We get to know ourselves as never before.

Sorrow also helps us to see God as we've never seen Him. Job said, out of his terrible grief, "I have heard of You by the hearing of the ear, but now my eye sees You" (Job 42:5).

Jesus, the perfect man, is described as "a man of sorrows," intimately acquainted with grief (Isaiah 53:3). It is hard to fathom, but even the incarnate Son of God learned and grew through the heartaches He suffered (Hebrews 5:8). As we think about His sorrow and His concern for our sorrow, we gain a better appreciation for what God is trying to accomplish in us through the grief we bear.

The author of Ecclesiastes wrote, "Sorrow is better than laughter, for by a sad countenance the heart is made better" (7:3). Those who don't let sorrow do its work, who deny it, trivialize it, or try to explain it away, remain shallow and indifferent. They never understand themselves or others very well. In fact, I think that before God can use us very much, we must first learn to mourn.   DHR

We can learn more from sorrow than from laughter.

What, Me Worry?

Read: Numbers 13:26–33

Be anxious for nothing, but in everything by prayer and supplication, with thanksgiving, let your requests be made known to God. Philippians 4:6

Whenever a preacher begins to talk about worry, I sense a pair of eyes staring at me. Without even turning my head, I know that my husband is looking at me to see if I'm paying attention.

I hate to admit it, but I'm a worrier. And precisely because there are a lot of people just like me, Jesus addressed this problem in Matthew 6:25–34 when He said: "Do not worry." Don't worry about the basic needs of life—food, clothing, shelter—and don't worry about tomorrow.

Worry may be a symptom of a bigger problem. Sometimes it's a lack of gratitude for the way God has cared for us in the past. Or perhaps it's a lack of faith that God really is trustworthy. Or it may be a refusal to depend on God instead of ourselves.

Some people expand the worry circle to their families, friends, and churches. They're a lot like the ten spies in Numbers 13:26–33 who spread their fear and doubt to everyone else. But those who put their trust in God alone can stand alongside Joshua and Caleb, the only ones in the group of twelve whom God allowed to enter the Promised Land.

Don't let worries hold you back from what God may be trying to teach you. He invites you to bring your anxious thoughts directly to Him (Philippians 4:6).　　　　　　　CHK

To be anxious about nothing, pray about everything.

Hope for the World

Read: Isaiah 2:1–5

We should [be] looking for the blessed hope and glorious appearing of our great God and Savior Jesus Christ. Titus 2:12–13

PEACE TALKS FALL APART AGAIN
UNEMPLOYMENT RATE RISES
TORNADO RIPS THROUGH TOWN

These newspaper headlines, selected at random, tend to lead us to despair. There just doesn't seem to be any hope for this world. And yet, according to the Scriptures, the dream of abolishing war is not merely wishful thinking. The idea of prosperity for all is more than a political gimmick. The Bible tells us that the eventual taming of nature is a certainty.

The hope for this world, however, is not to be found in human efforts but in the return of Jesus Christ. He alone can solve the problems that are baffling mankind.

The prophet Isaiah said that someday "nation shall not lift up sword against nation, neither shall they learn war anymore" (Isaiah 2:4). This glorious prospect will become a reality when the Lord Jesus himself returns as "King of kings and Lord of lords" (1 Timothy 6:15) to set up His kingdom of peace and righteousness. We are to be "looking for the blessed hope and glorious appearing of our great God and Savior Jesus Christ" (Titus 2:13). Because we have this hope, we can be optimistic even in the deepening gloom of this age.

Keep looking up! RDH

The only hope for world peace
is the coming of the Prince of Peace.

Hymns of Praise

Read: Psalm 149

*Sing to the Lord a new song, and His praise
in the assembly of saints. Psalm 149:1*

Music is one of those good things in life we take for granted. Yet, as is so often the case, sinful man has taken this good gift from God and used it to serve evil purposes. In our day we're especially aware of its misuse and of the shameful lyrics that so often are a part of it. Good music, however, is a blessing from the Lord. It's a soothing tonic for troubled hearts. It can motivate us to live for Christ, and through it we can lift our hearts in praise to the Lord. Without music, we would be greatly deprived.

An old Jewish legend says that after God had created the world He called the angels to himself and asked them what they thought of it. One of them said, "The only thing lacking is the sound of praise to the Creator." So God created music, and it was heard in the whisper of the wind and in the song of the birds. He also gave man the gift of song. And throughout all the ages, music has blessed multitudes of people.

Singing God's praises honors the Lord, edifies our brothers and sisters in Christ, and brings us joy. As we join with other Christians in singing, it should be with a renewed appreciation of music. So let us join voices with fellow believers and lift our hearts in hymns of praise whenever we have the privilege.   RDH

Hearts in tune with God will sing His praises.

June 1

A Ray of Hope

Read: 1 Thessalonians 4:13–18

I do not want you to be ignorant, brethren,
concerning those who have fallen asleep, lest you sorrow as
others who have no hope. 1 Thessalonians 4:13

It was to be an exciting summer for our family. We had many activities planned, including a trip to Florida to help our daughter Julie begin her teaching career.

Instead, the summer of 2002 began with tragedy. When our teenage daughter Melissa was killed in an automobile accident on the last day of school, our summer of hope turned into a nightmare.

Right away, I began to pray that the loss of our bright, athletic, friendly daughter could have a positive impact on teenagers—first among her friends and then in ever-widening ways.

Toward the end of the summer, we did take that Florida trip to get Julie started, heavy-hearted as we were. As she began teaching, Julie never forgot the desire to see Melissa's life change the lives of others. She told her classes about her sister and her faith.

One day, a student talked to Julie after class. "I'm scared," she said, "because I'm not a Christian like Melissa was." Julie then led her to faith in Jesus Christ. I imagined Melissa rejoicing in heaven.

The summer of 2002 didn't turn out as planned, but we were thankful to see some fruit of a life well-lived. Even in our sorrow, God gave us this ray of hope.   DB

Lord, give us grace to trust You when
Life's burdens seem too much to bear;
Dispel the darkness with new hope
And help us rise above despair. —Sper

Even in life's darkest hour, Christians have the brightest hope.

June 2

Fretting Is a Waste

Read: Psalm 90:10–17

*Teach us to number our days, that we may gain
a heart of wisdom. Psalm 90:12*

The older we get, the shorter life seems. Author Victor Hugo said, "Short as life is, we make it still shorter by the careless waste of time."

There's no sadder example of wasted time than a life dominated by fretting. Take, for example, an American woman whose dream of riding a train through the English countryside came true. After boarding the train she kept fretting about the windows and the temperature, complaining about her seat assignment, rearranging her luggage, and so on. To her shock, she suddenly reached her journey's end. With deep regret she said to the person meeting her, "If I'd known I was going to arrive so soon, I wouldn't have wasted my time fretting so much."

It's easy to get sidetracked by problems that won't matter at life's end—difficult neighbors, a tight budget, signs of aging, people who are wealthier than you. Moses acknowledged the brevity of life and prayed, "Teach us to number our days, that we may gain a heart of wisdom" (Psalm 90:12).

Instead of fretting, feed on God's Word and apply it to yourself. Strive to grow in God's wisdom every day. Stay focused on eternal values. Make it your goal to greet your waiting Savior one day with a heart of wisdom, rather than a heart of care.   JY

*Day by day and with each passing moment,
Strength I find to meet my trials here;
Trusting in my Father's wise bestowment,
I've no cause for worry or for fear.* —Berg

Worry casts a big shadow behind a small thing.

A Walk in the Woods

Read: Romans 6:11–14

Do not let sin reign in your mortal body, that you
should obey it in its lusts. Romans 6:12

A friend of mine wrote to me about certain "reservations" in his life—areas of secret sin that he reserved for himself and into which he frequently withdrew. These "reservations" are like the large tracts of wilderness in my home state of Idaho. It may sound exciting to wander around these untamed regions by oneself, but it's dangerous.

Each journey into sin takes its toll. We sacrifice our closeness with God, forfeiting His blessing (Psalm 24:1–5), and we lose our influence on others that comes from purity of mind and body (1 Timothy 4:12).

The wild areas in us may never be fully tamed, but we can set up perimeters that keep us from wandering into them. One perimeter is to remember that we are dead to sin's power (Romans 6:1–14). We do not have to give in to it.

The second perimeter is to resist temptation when it first attracts us. Initial temptation may not be strong, but if we entertain it, it will in time gain power and overwhelm us.

The third perimeter is accountability. Find a person who will commit to ask you each week, "Have you 'taken a hike in the wild'? Have you gone where you should not go?"

Impurity is ruinous, but if we long for holiness and ask God for help, He will give us victory. Press on! — DHR

O Lord, help us to recognize
When we begin to compromise;
And give us strength to follow through
With what we know is right and true. —Sper

Beware—the more you look at temptation, the better it looks!

God Is Good

Read: Genesis 3:1–7

Good and upright is the Lord; therefore
He teaches sinners in the way. Psalm 25:8

The phrase "God is good, all the time; all the time, God is good" is repeated by many Christians almost like a mantra. I often wonder if they really believe it or even think about what they're saying. I sometimes doubt God's goodness—especially when it feels as though God isn't hearing or answering my prayers. I assume that if others were more honest, they'd admit they feel the same way.

The serpent planted a doubt in Eve's mind about whether God had been good to her and had her best interest at heart. He said, "God knows that in the day you eat of [the fruit] your eyes will be opened, and you will be like God, knowing good and evil" (Genesis 3:5). Satan tried to convince her to believe that God was holding out on her and not giving her something really good—more knowledge.

Do you feel as though God isn't answering your prayers? Are you tempted to doubt His goodness? When I feel this way, I have to remind myself that my circumstances aren't the barometer of God's love and goodness—the cross is. He has shown how good He is by giving His only Son Jesus to die for our sin. We can't rely on our feelings. But day by day as we choose to trust Him more, we learn to believe with confidence that God is good—all the time.   AC

When you are tempted to deny
God's goodness, love, and grace,
Look to the cross of Calvary,
Where Jesus took your place. —Sper

Circumstances aren't the barometer of
God's love and goodness—the cross is.

A Nineteen-Mile Fall

Read: Deuteronomy 33:26–29

Underneath are the everlasting arms. Deuteronomy 33:27

On August 16, 1960, U.S. Air Force Captain Joseph Kittinger Jr. sat in a gondola suspended from a high-altitude balloon. When the balloon reached 102,800 feet above the surface of Earth (more than 19 miles), Kittinger jumped out. Four minutes and 36 seconds later his main parachute opened at 18,000 feet, but not before he had attained a velocity of 614 miles per hour! Kittinger carefully planned his record-setting descent.

In the spiritual realm, we're more likely to find that life is filled with unexpected free falls. The loss of a loved one, a broken relationship, or a terminated job can make us feel as if we're dropping into the unknown. For believers, however, there is a spiritual "parachute"—the loving arms of God.

Thousands of years ago, Moses wrote these words to the Israelites just before he died: "The eternal God is your refuge, and underneath are the everlasting arms" (Deuteronomy 33:27). The words "everlasting arms" refer to the protection and preservation of God's people. Despite the stressful circumstances they would surely face, they could rest in the assurance of God's watchful care.

Do you feel as if you're in a free fall? Take heart. God's loving arms are there to catch you.   DF

O the sweet unfailing refuge
Of the everlasting arms;
In their loving clasp enfolded
Nothing worries or alarms. —Hennessay

With God behind you and His arms beneath you,
you can face whatever lies ahead of you.

June 6

When People Pray

Read: Acts 4:23–31

*When they had prayed, the place where they were
assembled together was shaken. Acts 4:31*

Peter and John were in danger. The religious leaders in Jerusalem opposing the gospel had warned them to cease their missionary efforts (Acts 4:18). When the apostles reported this to the other believers, they immediately held a prayer meeting.

What happened next is thrilling. The believers first praised God. Then they asked for boldness that they might continue the work. The results were dramatic. The house shook, and the believers were filled with the Holy Spirit. They boldly witnessed, enjoyed spiritual unity, and gave unselfishly to those in need (vv. 31–37).

I've never felt a building shake at a prayer meeting, but I have seen God's power at work. When I've tried to help repair a broken marriage or a divided church, I've asked those involved to pray. Sometimes they refused. Other times, though, they mumbled carefully worded prayers. Those meetings failed.

But occasionally someone would pray in earnest. Almost immediately the atmosphere would change. Confession and forgiveness soon replaced charges and countercharges.

When we pray sincerely, praising God and seeking His glory, great things happen. Prayer must always come from the heart.

HVL

*Dissension's fuse is easy to ignite—
It fuels our anger, yet it dims the light;
Help us, we pray, to humbly seek Your Name,
And in pride's place restore the Spirit's flame.* —TLG

Sincere intercession is the key to God's intervention.

Promised Strength

Read: Isaiah 40:10–11, 28–31

To those who have no might [God]
increases strength. Isaiah 40:29

Jonah Sorrentino was deeply hurt at age six when his parents separated. As a result, he held a lot of anger and bitterness inside. At fifteen, Jonah learned of God's love for him and became a believer in Jesus Christ.

Jonah, also known as recording artist KJ-52, admits that he used to live like a victim of circumstances. In an interview with *Christianity Today*, he explained how he began to experience healing: "You definitely have to acknowledge that, no, you're not okay."

He added, "You also have to reach a point of saying, 'I'm not going to dwell on everything of the past . . . on anger or bitterness or hurt. I'm going to move forward because God is going to give me the strength to do that.'" God helped him to forgive his parents and to write song lyrics that encourage others.

If we've been hurt badly, we may wonder how we can live with a painful past. God could take away our pain instantly and forever if He chose to. Often, though, He heals us slowly and scars remain. He carries us and gently leads us as a shepherd cares for his flock (Isaiah 40:11).

We may not be healed completely in this life, but we can count on God's promises. He gives "power to the weak" and increases their strength (v. 29). AC

Those who wait on the Lord shall renew their strength.

Suffering: How Do We Respond?

Read: Job 16:6–17

*Man who is born of woman is of few days
and full of trouble. Job 14:1*

Why is there suffering? You might ask that question when you hear of hurricanes, mudslides, earthquakes, and other disasters taking people's lives. Job asked that question too.

Why is there so much pain in God's world? Consider these reasons:

We can't escape the laws that govern our universe. We need such things as gravity, weather, and fire to survive, but they can lead to tragedy (Matthew 5:45). Fire is good in your stove, but an out-of-control fire can kill.

We are a social race. Our lives are intertwined, so we sometimes suffer when the sin or foolishness of others spreads trouble (1 Corinthians 12:26).

Sin brought a curse on the earth and its people. This curse includes disease and death (Genesis 3:15–24).

Suffering awakens compassion. Jesus told us to care for those who suffer in poverty. We are His partners in helping others (Luke 10:33–35).

As Job discovered, God's world is a fallen place. When we see suffering, we can use it as an opportunity to serve God by helping others, to trust Him in spite of the difficulty, and to grow in our faith in Him.

When trouble hits, let our first reaction be to trust the Lord and care for the needs of others.   DB

Our response to suffering can either make us or break us.

What Now?

Read: 2 Chronicles 20:5–17

*We have no power against this great multitude that
is coming against us; nor do we know what to do,
but our eyes are upon You. 2 Chronicles 20:12*

During the years that I taught junior high students in an over-crowded school, I used to say (only slightly in jest) that my morning prayer was in 2 Chronicles 20:12—"O our God, will You not judge them? For we have no power against this great multitude that is coming against us; nor do we know what to do, but our eyes are upon You."

When Judah's King Jehoshaphat spoke those words, it was a matter of life and death. As a coalition of armies marched against Jerusalem, the people of Judah gathered to seek God's guidance and help (v. 13).

During threatening times of disruption and change, we need to ask, "Lord, what do You want to do with this moment?" And like King Jehoshaphat, we should begin our prayer with praise to our sovereign and powerful Father in heaven (vv. 5–9).

God told the king and his people: "Do not be afraid nor dismayed... for the battle is not yours, but God's. Tomorrow go down against them... for the Lord is with you" (vv. 15–17).

In stressful, confusing situations, we might ask a worried "What now?" But if we look to the Lord and trust in His care, our fear will be replaced with peace.   DCM

*O Lord, whenever we're afraid,
We'll put our trust in You
To lead, protect, and guide our way,
And help us make it through. —Sper*

Faith ends where worry begins,
and worry ends where faith begins.

He's Always Watching

Read: Psalm 34

The eye of the LORD is on those who fear Him,
on those who hope in His mercy. Psalm 33:18

Marcie (not her real name) had broken up with her boyfriend, and now he was harassing her. He followed her, stared at her, and intimidated her in subtle ways. She avoided him as much as she could.

One place she could not escape his gaze was at football games, because she was a cheerleader. During one game, he stood at field level right in front of the cheerleading squad and stared at her as she did her routines. Her mom and stepdad, sitting in the stands, saw him there and realized that she was getting more and more afraid.

At a break, she ran into the stands, her eyes filled with panic. "Do you see him over there?" she blurted out. "Yes, I do," her stepdad said. "I'm watching, and I will not take my eyes off you." Relieved that he saw what was going on and understood how she was feeling, Marcie calmed down and went back to her station.

One of the wonderful joys of being a believer in Jesus is knowing that our Father in heaven is always watching over us. The promise expressed by David in today's psalm applies to us wherever we go. Whatever confronts us, the "eyes of the Lord" are on us and His ears "are open to [our] cry" (Psalm 34:15).

We are never out of God's sight.   DCE

How wonderful to know that He
Who watches from above
Will always keep us sheltered in
His ever-present love. —*King*

His eye is on the sparrow, and I know He watches me.
—Martin

Life's Storm-Tossed Sea

Read: Mark 4:35–41

Casting all your care upon Him,
for He cares for you. 1 Peter 5:7

Emilie, wife of nineteenth-century German pastor Christoph Blumhardt, envied his ability to pray for his parishioners and then effortlessly fall asleep. So one night she pleaded, "Tell me your secret!"

He answered, "Is God so powerless that my worrying would help the well-being of our parish?" Then he added, "There comes a moment each day when we must simply drop what weighs on us and hand it over to God."

One evening Jesus and His disciples were crossing the Sea of Galilee. Weary after a long day of ministry, Jesus fell asleep in the stern of the boat. A fierce squall suddenly arose—so fierce that even the Lord's fishermen-turned-disciples were terrified. But Jesus continued to sleep serenely until His frightened followers woke Him, crying out, "Teacher, do You not care that we are perishing?" (Mark 4:38). You see, Jesus was in the habit of entrusting himself to His heavenly Father. Having made that commitment, He could sleep through the turbulent squall.

When worries begin to gnaw at our mind, let's surrender them to the Lord and not take them back again (1 Peter 5:7). That's the secret of soul-serenity when we're on life's storm-tossed sea.   VCG

Jesus knows the pain you feel,
He can save and He can heal—
Take your burden to the Lord
And leave it there. —Tindley

Drop what weighs you down by giving it to God.

Do Your Best and Leave the Rest

Read: 1 Thessalonians 5:14–24

He who calls you is faithful, who also will do it.
1 Thessalonians 5:24

Have you at some time found yourself under extreme pressure? Have there been episodes in your life when you were so burdened by tasks and responsibilities that there was simply no breathing space to prepare for your service to God?

That was the experience of a pastor by the name of A. J. Gossip. During one hectic week, he didn't have his customary amount of time to prepare his sermon. As he walked to his pulpit that Sunday morning, he felt guilty about the scanty sermon notes in his hand. It seemed that the Lord was asking him, "Is this the best you could do for Me this week?" And Gossip honestly replied, "Yes, Lord, it is my best." He told a friend later that Jesus took that ill-prepared piece of work and in His hands "it became a trumpet" to his congregation.

The apostle Paul encouraged the Thessalonians to give their all for God (1 Thessalonians 5:14–22). They were to exhort, warn, comfort, rejoice, pray, and express their gratitude to God—among other things. We too should always do our best in our Christian life and service. But when pressure-periods come and we just don't have the time we feel we need, we should do the best we can and then prayerfully trust God's faithfulness (v. 24). VCG

Give of your best to the Master,
Give Him first place in your heart;
Give Him first place in your service,
Consecrate every part. —*Grose*

Be faithful—and leave the results to God.

Angry Floods

Read: Psalm 93

The floods have lifted up their voice;
the floods lift up their waves. Psalm 93:3

Trouble comes our way, according to Psalm 93, in relentless waves that surge and pound against our souls and break upon them with furious force. "The floods have lifted up, O LORD, the floods have lifted up their voice," and they are deafening (v. 3).

Yet above the tempest we hear the psalmist's refrain: "The LORD on high is mightier than the noise of many waters, than the mighty waves of the sea" (v. 4).

Indeed, "the Lord reigns"! He is clothed with majesty and strength. He sits as King, exalted higher than the waves that rise above us, deeper than their immeasurable depths, greater than their strongest surge. The storm is in His all-powerful hands: "The world is established, so that it cannot be moved," for His rule over it was established long ago (v. 1). He rules the raging of the sea; the "wind and the sea obey Him" (Mark 4:37–41). He speaks and they are still.

The storm will not last forever. Yet while it rages, you can cling to the Lord's promises of love and faithfulness, for His "testimonies are very sure" (Psalm 93:5). Waves of trouble and grief may sweep over you, but you will not be swept away. He "is able to keep you from stumbling" (Jude 24). Our Father in heaven is holding your hand.   DHR

When overwhelmed with problems,
When weak or tired or ill,
When storms are fierce and raging
Just hear His "Peace, be still." —Jarvis

When adversity is ready to strike us, then God is most ready
to strengthen us.

Never Alone

Read: Psalm 139:7–18

*You comprehend my path and my lying down, and are
acquainted with all my ways. Psalm 139:3*

In today's world of inexpensive, high-tech spying devices, total
privacy has become a rare and precious thing. A special agent for
the Georgia Bureau of Investigation says, "Don't assume that you
are alone, not ever."

Cameras are used to monitor people in public places like banks
and shopping malls. In addition, tiny wireless video cameras that
sell for less than one hundred dollars are being used by ordinary
people for less-than-honorable purposes.

It might seem odd, therefore, to hear someone celebrate a complete lack of privacy, until we realize that the One watching his
every move was Almighty God. After stating that God knew each
thought, word, and action before it happened, David said, "Such
knowledge is too wonderful for me; it is high, I cannot attain it"
(Psalm 139:6).

No place was beyond the presence, guidance, and protection of
God (vv. 7–10). The deepest darkness became flooded with light
because God was there (vv. 11–12). From the womb to the tomb,
every day of David's life was known to his Creator (vv. 13–16). And
the number of times God thought about him could not be counted
(vv. 17–18).

We are completely known and never alone in our relationship
with God. What a comfort!   DCM

I never walk alone, Christ walks beside me,
He is the dearest Friend I've ever known;
With such a Friend to comfort and to guide me,
I never, no, I never walk alone. —Ackley

He is not alone who is alone with Jesus.

Not Fair

Read: Psalm 19:7–14

He is the Rock, His work is perfect; for all His
ways are justice. Deuteronomy 32:4

When I was coaching high school freshman girls' basketball in the fall of 2005, I was surprised at how many times I heard, "That's not fair!"

The girls' motivation seemed to depend on whether or not they thought what I asked them to do was fair. If I asked some girls to do a defensive drill while others shot free throws, I heard, "Not fair." If I allowed one group to play offense longer than another group, I heard, "Not fair."

So many situations in life shout, "Not fair!" I observe Christian couples who struggle to have babies while others are blessed with children and then abuse them. I look at families whose children are all alive and well, while I go through life without one of mine. I see friends who long to serve God but can't because of health issues.

It's then that I must go back to a basic truth. We are not the arbiters of fairness. God is, and He knows far more than we do about His plans and purposes. The question isn't about fairness. In the end, it's about trust in a faithful God who knows what He is doing. "He is the Rock, His work is perfect; for all His ways are justice" (Deuteronomy 32:4).

Life will never look fair. But when we trust God, we always know that He is faithful. DB

If you feel that blessings pass you by,
And for you life seems a bit unfair,
Just remember, Christ was born to die,
And in His great salvation you can share. —Hess

Life is not always fair, but God is always faithful.

The Maker of Mountains

Read: Psalm 102:3–12

As the mountains surround Jerusalem, so the Lord surrounds His people. Psalm 125:2

The Bible uses vivid imagery to express the brevity of our life on earth. Job said that his days were "swifter than a runner" and "they pass by like swift ships" (Job 9:25–26).

I recall preaching at the funeral service of a young mother. From where I stood I could see the Rocky Mountains towering over the western horizon. The scene prompted me to consider how I will one day follow that friend through the valley of the shadow of death, and yet those peaks will still be thrusting themselves skyward. Eventually they will crumble into dust, but the God who made them will exist forever in undiminished glory. I also remember thinking that my deceased friend and I will, by God's grace, live with Him forever and ever.

Whenever we are troubled by the shortness of life and the impermanence of everything in this world, let's remember the Maker of the mountains. He has always been and will always be. As the psalmist said, "You, O Lord, shall endure forever" (102:12).

That truth inspires us with hope. If by faith we belong to Jesus Christ the Savior, who is from everlasting to everlasting, we will one day rejoice in heaven in unending praise to Him. VCG

Immortal, invisible, God only wise,
In light inaccessible hid from our eyes;
Most blessed, most glorious, the Ancient of Days,
Almighty, victorious, Thy great Name we praise. —Smith

To see God's hand in everything makes life a great adventure.

Does God Forget?

Read: Hebrews 8:6–13

Their sins and their lawless deeds I will remember no more.
Hebrews 8:12

God longs to forgive sinners! But in the minds of many people, this thought seems too good to be true. Countless sermons have been preached to convince guilt-ridden individuals that it *is* true. Many of these sermons emphasize that God not only forgives the sinner but also forgets the sin. I've often said it myself, never doubting its soundness.

Then one Sunday I heard a sermon that revolutionized my thinking. The speaker caught my attention when he said, "The idea that God forgets my sins isn't very reassuring to me. After all, what if He suddenly remembered? In any case, only imperfection can forget, and God is perfect."

As I was questioning the biblical basis for such statements, the pastor read Hebrews 8:12, "Their sins and their lawless deeds I will remember no more." Then he said, "God doesn't say He'll forget our sins—He says He'll remember them no more! His promise not to remember them ever again is stronger than saying He'll forget them. Now that reassures me!"

Do you worry that there are certain sins you'll be punished for someday? Because Christ died for all our sins (1 Corinthians 15:3), God promises to forgive us and never bring up our sin again (Psalm 103:12).   JY

God, whose every way is perfect,
Said in justice and in grace
That our sins He'll not remember,
And our fears He will erase. —Hess

To enjoy the future, accept God's forgiveness for the past.

Impaired Vision

Read: 1 Corinthians 13:8–13

Now we see in a mirror, dimly.
1 Corinthians 13:12

When I was a child, I had to wear glasses. Interestingly, my vision improved, and from high school until age forty I didn't need them. Prior to that landmark age, my vision was better than 20/20. Now, because of the natural degeneration of the eyes, I wear bifocals. Without glasses, my vision is impaired.

About our "spiritual vision" the apostle Paul said, "Now we see in a mirror, dimly, but then face to face" (1 Corinthians 13:12). The word *dimly* (*enigma* in Greek) implies that our current spiritual perceptions in our earthly state are impaired, at best.

In the ancient world, they didn't have the clear glass mirrors we have today. Instead, mirrors were made of polished metal and provided a reflection that was dim and distorted. What was seen in a mirror was only an imperfect representation of what would be clear if it could be seen directly.

If you have questions about what God is doing in your life, continue to trust Him and to seek clarity through prayer and His Word.

For now, our understanding is limited (1 Corinthians 13:9). Our current spiritual vision is impaired, but in eternity we will see clearly. We will see Jesus "face to face." DF

We now see Jesus in the Bible, but then, face to face.

June 19

Remembering

Read: Psalm 103:1–5

Bless the Lord, O my soul, and forget not
all His benefits. Psalm 103:2

Some days we awaken with aching joints and dull spirits and wonder how we can shake off our lethargy and make it through the day.

Here's an idea: Like David, try lifting up your thanks to God. Use mind and memory to rekindle thankfulness for all God's "benefits" (Psalm 103:2). Gratefulness will lead to joy.

Thank God for His forgiveness. He "forgives all your iniquities" (v. 3), and "has cast all our sins into the depths of the sea" (Micah 7:19).

Thank Him for healing your diseases (v. 3). God uses infirmity and disorders to draw you more deeply into His love and care. And, one day when your Lord comes for you, He will heal all of your diseases.

Thank Him for redeeming your life from destruction (v. 4). This is more than rescue from a premature death. It is redemption from death itself.

Thank Him for crowning your life "with lovingkindness and tender mercies" (v. 4).

Thank the One who satisfies your desires (v. 5). He is your satisfaction. Each day, He renews your strength and vigor. Then your spirit can rise up and soar like the eagle.

"Bless the Lord, O my soul, and forget not all His benefits" (v. 2).

DHR

Give me a spirit of thankfulness, Lord,
For numberless blessings given;
Blessings that daily come to me
Like dewdrops falling from heaven. —Dawe

Gratitude is the memory of a glad heart.

June 20

Slow Down and Live

Read: Psalm 1

His delight is in the law of the Lord, and in His law
he meditates day and night. Psalm 1:2

Many of our New Year's resolutions may actually accelerate our pace of life instead of helping us to slow down. In a quest for greater productivity and efficiency, we overschedule our days, then rush through meals, drive impatiently, and wonder why the joy of living eludes us.

Carol Odell, who writes a business advice column, says that slowing down can positively affect our lives at work and at home. She believes that rushing can cloud our judgment and cause us to overlook important things and valuable people. Carol encourages everyone to slow down, and even suggests the radical idea of welcoming red traffic lights and using the waiting time to meditate.

In Psalm 1 there is no hint of a frenzied pace. It describes a person who enjoys the blessing of God. Instead of thinking and acting like those who rarely consider spiritual matters, "His delight is in the law of the Lord, and in His law he meditates day and night" (v. 2). The result is a fruitful life and a well-nourished soul (v. 3).

Isaiah wrote, "You will keep him in perfect peace, whose mind is stayed on You, because he trusts in You" (Isaiah 26:3). Just for today, try thinking about that verse whenever you have to wait. Isn't it time for all of us to slow down and live?   DCM

If you're working hard to make a living,
Never taking time to smell the roses,
Now's the time to heed the Bible's wisdom:
Find true joy before your life's day closes. —Hess

Come apart and rest awhile or you may just plain come apart!
—Havner

Existing or Truly Living?

Read: John 10:1–11

I have come that they may have life, and that they may
have it more abundantly. John 10:10

On a family visit to Disneyland, I pondered the sign over the entrance arch that read, "Welcome to the happiest place on earth." The rest of the day I looked at the faces of the people and was impressed by the small number who were actually smiling during their visit to "the happiest place on earth." I roamed the park with divided attention—trying to make sure my kids had a good time and wondering why so few adults seemed to be enjoying themselves.

As I think of that day, I am reminded of a line from an old song that says, "Life goes on, long after the thrill of living is gone." So it seems.

To live life to the fullest is qualitatively different than merely existing. In fact, Jesus said that part of His mission was to enable us to live life to the fullest: "I have come that they may have life, and that they may have it more abundantly" (John 10:10). He came so that we could experience life to the full—not according to the standards of a fallen world, but life as it was intended to be. It is life according to the designs and desires of the Creator of life.

By coming to provide forgiveness for rebellious, broken people, Jesus has made it possible for us to live a life of joy and hope in a world of despair. BC

Jesus came to bring us life—
Abundant living, full and free;
Trusting Him to save and keep us
Gives us joy the world can see. —Sper

To know God puts a song in your heart
and a smile on your face.

June 22

Noon

Read: Psalm 23

*He makes me to lie down in green pastures; He leads me
beside the still waters. Psalm 23:2*

Our office is a busy place where things sometimes feel like they are moving at breakneck speed. This often involves meeting after meeting, hallway conferences, and an avalanche of e-mail.

In the midst of this extreme busyness, I sometimes feel the need to escape, to decompress. My response? To create a quiet place. On those days when I have no lunch meeting, I retreat to the quiet of my car. I grab some lunch and sit in my car, where I can read, listen to music, think, pray—and be refreshed.

I think this is the essence of what the shepherd-psalmist points to in Psalm 23:2. He sees the Good Shepherd bringing him to "still waters"—that is, waters to rest by. It pictures a quiet place, a retreat from the pressures of life, where you can rest in the presence of the Shepherd of your heart and be strengthened for what lies ahead. Even Jesus withdrew to a solitary place to pray and commune with His Father (Mark 1:35).

We all need retreats in our lives, not only because of the overwhelming nature of life, but because of our dependence on the resources of the Master. In our fast-paced days, it is essential to find a place of solitude, "a place of quiet rest, near to the heart of God." Where's yours? BC

*There is a place of quiet rest,
Near to the heart of God,
A place where sin cannot molest,
Near to the heart of God. —McAfee*

When we draw near to God our minds are refreshed and our
strength is renewed!

Stagecoach Prayer

Read: John 15:7–14

Whatever you ask in My name, that I will do, that the Father may be glorified in the Son. John 14:13

Five-year-old Randy wanted a toy stagecoach for Christmas. While shopping with Mom, he found just the one he wanted. It was about six inches long and had cool wheels and dark brown plastic horses pulling it. "Mommy, I want this one. Pleeeease!" he begged. As young children sometimes do, he threw a tantrum, insisting that he get that stagecoach for Christmas. Mom said, "We'll see," and took him home.

Randy was sure he'd get what he asked for. Christmas morning came, and he opened the package confidently. Sure enough, it was the stagecoach he had begged for. He was so pleased. But then his older brother said, "You really did a dumb thing to insist on getting *that* coach. Mom bought you a much bigger one, but when you begged for that little one, she exchanged it!" Suddenly the small stagecoach didn't seem so appealing.

Sometimes we're like that with God. We pray about a specific need and tell Him how He ought to answer. We beg and plead— and God may even give us exactly what we ask for. But He may have had something better in mind.

Phillips Brooks once said, "Pray the largest prayers. You cannot think a prayer so large that God, in answering it, will not wish you had made it larger." AC

Do not presume to know what's best
When you begin to pray;
But say to God, "Your will be done,"
Then trust His perfect way. —Sper

Large asking results in large receiving.

Celebrating Disappointment

Read: Psalm 30

You have turned for me my mourning into dancing.
Psalm 30:11

After receiving his second Academy Award, Denzel Washington said to his family, "I told you, if I lost tonight, I'd come home and we'd celebrate. And if I won tonight, I'd come home and we'd celebrate." Denzel, a Christian, was trusting God, whether in blessing or in disappointment.

A Christian couple I know were inspired to follow Denzel's example. The woman was applying for a dream job that had just opened up where she worked. The interview went well, but she knew she might not get the position. Her husband suggested, "Let's make reservations at our favorite restaurant this Friday to celebrate—no matter what the outcome."

Soon the news came that someone else was offered the job. But that Friday the disappointed couple still celebrated. While eating a delicious meal, they were able to count their blessings and renew their faith in the God who holds tomorrow's opportunities in His hand.

When the psalmist counted his blessings, he was lifted out of his despair and praised God, saying, "You have turned for me my mourning into dancing" (Psalm 30:11).

Are you facing a situation in which you could be disappointed? Why not plan a celebration to count your blessings no matter what the outcome? DF

Thank God in your disappointment,
Celebrate His grace and love;
Know that He will never leave you
And will bless you from above. —DJD

The pain of disappointment is soothed by a heart of gratitude.

An Age-Old Question

Read: Job 2:1–10

Shall we indeed accept good from God, and shall
we not accept adversity? Job 2:10

When Jeremy was seventeen, he struggled with a question that theologians have wrestled with for centuries. For him the problem was not theoretical but practical. He was trying to understand why his mother had to have brain surgery. He asked, "Why do good people suffer, Mom?"

She told him, "Suffering is part of living in a sin-cursed world, and good people suffer like anybody else. That's why I'm glad we have Jesus. If I die, I'll go to a better place, and I'll long for the day when I can see you again." She then said that she could understand his frustration, but she told him not to put the blame on God.

If you and I are baffled by the suffering of good people, we can put the question squarely before God, argue with Him if we must, and struggle with our doubts. But let's not blame Him.

God didn't explain to Job what He was doing but said that He could be trusted to do what is right (Job 38–42). And He has assured us in His Word that Jesus suffered on our behalf, rose from the dead, and is now preparing a suffering-free place for us.

These may not be the answers we want, but they are the answers we need to help us live with that age-old and often unanswerable question of suffering. —DJD

Why must I bear this pain? I cannot tell;
I only know my Lord does all things well.
And so I trust in God, my all in all,
For He will bring me through, whate'er befall. —Smith

God is not obligated to give us answers,
but He promises us His grace.

Still Small Voice

Read: 1 Kings 19:11–18

*Be still, and know that I am God; I will be exalted among
the nations, I will be exalted in the earth! Psalm 46:10*

When God spoke to Elijah on Mount Horeb, He could have
done so in the wind, earthquake, or fire. But He didn't. He
spoke with a "still small voice" (1 Kings 19:12). God asked, "What
are you doing here, Elijah?" (v. 13) as he hid from Jezebel, who had
threatened to kill him.

Elijah's reply revealed what God already knew—the depth of his
fear and discouragement. He said, in effect, "Lord, I have been most
zealous when others have forsaken You. What do I get for being the
only one standing up for You?" (see v. 14).

Was Elijah really the only one serving God? No. God had "seven
thousand in Israel... whose knees have not bowed to Baal" (v. 18).

In the depths of our fear or despair, we too may think we're the
only one serving God. That may happen right after the height of
a success, as it did for Elijah. Psalm 46:10 reminds us to "be still,
and know" that He is God. The sooner we focus on Him and His
power, the quicker we will see relief from our fear and self-pity.

Both the clashing cymbals of our failures and the loud trumpet-
ing of our successes can drown out God's still small voice. It's time
for us to quiet our hearts to listen for Him as we meditate on His
Word.   AL

Keep listening for the "still small voice"
If you are weary on life's road;
The Lord will make your heart rejoice
If you will let Him take your load. —Hess

To tune in to God's voice we must tune out this world's noise.

June 27

In Every Bad Experience

Read: 2 Kings 5:1–15

Now I know that there is no God in all the earth,
except in Israel. 2 Kings 5:15

When I rear-ended a truck with my nearly new car, positive thoughts did not immediately come to mind. I was thinking primarily of the cost, the inconvenience, and the injury to my ego. But I did find some hope in this thought, which I often share with other writers: "In every bad experience there's a good illustration."

Finding the good can be a challenge, but Scripture confirms that God uses bad circumstances for good purposes.

In 2 Kings 5, we find two people who had bad things happen to them. First is a young girl from Israel who was taken captive by the Syrian army. Second is Naaman, the commander of the army, who had leprosy. Even though the girl had good reason to desire bad things for her captors, she offered help instead. Israel's prophet Elisha, she said, could heal Naaman. Eager to be cured, Naaman went to Israel. However, he was reluctant to follow Elisha's humiliating directions. When he finally did, he was healed, which caused him to proclaim that Israel's God is the only God (v. 15).

God used two bad things—a kidnapping and a deadly disease—to change Israel's enemy into a friend. Even when we don't know why something bad has happened, we know that God has the power to use it for good. JAL

His purposes will ripen fast,
Unfolding every hour;
The bad may have a bitter taste
But sweet will be the flower. —Cowper

God is the master of turning burdens into blessings.

His Part and Our Part

Read: Joshua 1:1–9

Arise, go over this Jordan. . . . I will not leave you
nor forsake you. Joshua 1:2, 5

Whenever the Lord assigns us a difficult task, He gives us what we need to carry it out. John Wesley wrote, "Among the many difficulties of our early ministry, my brother Charles often said, 'If the Lord would give me wings, I'd fly.' I used to answer, 'If God bids me fly, I will trust Him for the wings.'"

Today's Scripture tells us that Joshua was thrust into a position of great responsibility. No doubt the enormity of the challenge before him made him tremble with fear. How could he ever follow such a great leader as Moses? In his own strength it would be impossible to lead the people into the Promised Land. But along with the marching orders, the Lord gave him an assuring promise: "I will not leave you nor forsake you" (Joshua 1:5). Then He said, "Have I not commanded you? Be strong and of good courage; do not be afraid, nor be dismayed, for the Lord your God is with you wherever you go" (v. 9). Such reassurances were the backing Joshua needed.

If God has given you some special work to do that frightens you, it's your responsibility to jump at it. It's up to the Lord to see you through. As you faithfully do your part, He will do His part.

RDH

I'll go where You want me to go, dear Lord,
O'er mountain or plain or sea;
I'll say what You want me to say, dear Lord,
I'll be what You want me to be. —Brown

Where God guides, God provides!

God Remembers

Read: Genesis 8:1–17

God remembered Noah, and every living thing, and all the animals that were with him in the ark. Genesis 8:1

A Chinese festival called Qing Ming is a time to express grief for lost relatives. Customs include grooming gravesites and taking walks with loved ones in the countryside. Legend has it that it began when a youth's rude and foolish behavior resulted in the death of his mother. So he decided that henceforth he would visit her grave every year to remember what she had done for him. Sadly, it was only after her death that he remembered her.

How differently God deals with us! In Genesis, we read how the flood destroyed the world. Only those who were with Noah in the ark remained alive. But God remembered them (8:1) and sent a wind to dry the waters so that they could leave the ark.

God also remembered Hannah when she prayed for a son (1 Samuel 1:19). He gave her a child, Samuel.

Jesus remembered the dying thief who said, "Lord, remember me when You come into Your kingdom." Jesus replied, "Today You will be with Me in Paradise" (Luke 23:42–43).

God remembers us wherever we are. Our concerns are His concerns. Our pain is His pain. Commit your challenges and difficulties to Him. He is the all-seeing God who remembers us as a mother remembers her children, and He waits to meet our needs.

CPH

There is an Arm that never tires
When human strength gives way;
There is a Love that never fails
When earthly loves decay. —Wallace

To know that God sees us brings both conviction and comfort.

The Bus Driver

Read: 1 John 4:7–12

Be imitators of God . . . and walk in love.
Ephesians 5:1–2

In the middle of carting seventy pieces of luggage, an electronic piano, and other equipment through airports and on and off a tour bus, it's easy to wonder, "Why are we doing this?"

Taking twenty-eight teenagers on an eleven-day ministry trip to a land across the ocean is not easy. But at the end of the trip our bus driver, who had carted us all over England and Scotland, grabbed the bus microphone and in tears thanked the kids for how wonderful they had been. Then after we got home, he e-mailed us to say how much he appreciated the thank-you cards the kids had written to him—many of which contained the gospel.

Although the students ministered to hundreds through song during the trip, perhaps it was the bus driver who most benefited from their Christlikeness. In Ephesians we are told to be imitators of God and to walk in love (Ephesians 5:1–2). Others see God in us when we show love to one another (1 John 4:12). The bus driver saw Jesus in the students and told them that they might just convert him to faith in Christ. Maybe it was for this man that we took that trip.

Why do you do what you do? Whose life are you affecting? Sometimes it's not our target audience that we impact most. Sometimes it's the bus drivers of the world. DB

Lord, may I be a shining light
For all the world to see
Your goodness and Your love displayed
As You reach out through me. —Sper

Witnessing is not just something a Christian says,
but what he is.

The Best Eraser

Read: Luke 16:19–31

I have blotted out, like a thick cloud,
your transgressions. Isaiah 44:22

What is memory? What is this faculty that enables us to recall past feelings, sights, sounds, and experiences? By what process are events recorded, stored, and preserved in our brain to be brought back again and again? Much is still mystery.

We do know that memories can be blessings—full of comfort, assurance, and joy. Old age can be happy and satisfying if we have stored up memories of purity, faith, fellowship, and love. If a saint looks back on a life of Christian service and remembers the faithfulness of Him who promised: "I will never leave you nor forsake you" (Hebrews 13:5), his or her sunset years can be the sweetest of all.

But memory can also be a curse and a tormentor. Many people as they approach the end of life would give all they possess to erase from their minds the past sins that haunt them. What can a person do who is plagued by such remembrances? Just one thing. He can take them to the One who is able to forgive them and blot them out forever. He's the One who said, "Their sins and their lawless deeds I will remember no more" (Hebrews 10:17).

You may not be able to forget your past. But the Lord offers to blot out, "like a thick cloud, your transgressions" (Isaiah 44:22).

MRD

The deep remorse that's in the soul
No human eye may trace;
But Jesus sees the broken heart,
And can its woes erase. —Bosch

The best eraser is honest confession to God.

The Father's Faithfulness

Read: Psalm 107:1–16

Through the Lord's mercies we are not consumed, because His compassions fail not.... Great is Your faithfulness. Lamentations 3:22–23

Hudson Taylor, the humble servant of God to China, demonstrated extraordinary trust in God's faithfulness. In his journal he wrote:

"Our heavenly Father is a very experienced One. He knows very well that His children wake up with a good appetite every morning... He sustained three million Israelites in the wilderness for forty years. We do not expect He will send three million missionaries to China; but if He did, He would have ample means to sustain them all... Depend on it, God's work done in God's way will never lack God's supply."

We may be faint and weary, but our heavenly Father is all-powerful. Our feelings may fluctuate, but He is unchangeable. Even creation itself is a record of His steadfastness. That's why we can sing these words from the hymn "Great Is Thy Faithfulness" by Thomas Chisholm: "All I have needed Thy hand hath provided."

What an encouragement to live for Him! Our strength for the present and hope for the future are not based on the stability of our own perseverance but on the fidelity of God. No matter what our need, we can count on the Father's faithfulness.　　　　PVG

He who abandons himself to God will never
be abandoned by God.

I Will Never Leave You

Read: Deuteronomy 31:1–8

I am with you always, even to the end of the age.
Matthew 28:20

One of my earliest memories of hearing good music was when a male quartet rehearsed at our home. I was about ten years old, and I was especially attentive to my dad, who sang first tenor. One of the quartet's favorites was titled "I Am with You." Even at that tender age, I not only appreciated the music but I "got the message."

Those words of Jesus to His disciples just before He ascended—"I am with you always"—became precious to me as the quartet sang, "In the sunlight, in the shadow, I am with you where you go."

One of the first references to God's unfailing presence was spoken by Moses in Deuteronomy 31:6–8, when he instructed his successor about leading God's people into the "land of promise." And Joshua himself heard the same word from the Lord, "As I was with Moses, so I will be with you. I will not leave you nor forsake you" (Joshua 1:5).

That promise is repeated in the New Testament, where the writer of Hebrews gave this assurance: "He Himself has said, 'I will never leave you nor forsake you'" (13:5).

Wherever you may be today, you are not alone. If you've placed your trust in Jesus for your eternal salvation, you can be certain that He will never leave you.   ODB

Jesus whispers "I am with you"
In the hour of deepest need;
When the way is dark and lonesome,
"I am with you, I will lead." —Morris

First make sure you are with Him, then you can be sure
He'll be with you.

Thunderstorm Thoughts

Read: Matthew 8:23–27

The God of peace will be with you.
Philippians 4:9

I laugh every time I hear the radio commercial that has a woman shouting to her friend in conversation. She's trying to talk above the sounds of the thunderstorm in her own head. Ever since a storm damaged part of her home, that's all she hears because her insurance company isn't taking care of her claims.

I've heard thunderstorms in my head, and maybe you have too. It happens when a tragedy occurs—to us, to someone close to us, or to someone we hear about in the news. Our minds become a tempest of "what if" questions. We focus on all the possible bad outcomes. Our fear, worry, and trust in God fluctuate as we wait, we pray, we grieve, and we wonder what the Lord will do.

It's natural for us to be fearful in a storm (literal or figurative). The disciples had Jesus right there in the boat with them, yet they were afraid (Matthew 8:23–27). He used the calming of the storm as a lesson to show them who He was—a powerful God who also cares for them.

We wish that Jesus would always calm the storms of our life as He calmed the storm for the disciples that day. But we can find moments of peace when we're anchored to the truth that He's in the boat with us and He cares.   AC

Fierce drives the storm, but wind and waves
Within His hand are held,
And trusting His omnipotence
My fears are sweetly quelled. —Brown

To realize the worth of the anchor, we need to feel the stress
of the storm.

July 5

In All Kinds of Weather

Read: Acts 18:9–11

Lo, I am with you always, even to the end of the age.
Matthew 28:20

When Jesus sent His disciples out, He gave them this promise: "I am with you always, even to the end of the age" (Matthew 28:20). Literally, the word *always* means "all the days," according to Greek scholars Jamieson, Fausset, and Brown.

Jesus didn't simply say, "always," but "all the days." That takes into account all our various activities, the good and bad circumstances surrounding us, the varied responsibilities we have through the course of our days, the storm clouds and the sunshine.

Our Lord is present with us no matter what each day brings. It may be a day of joy or of sadness, of sickness or of health, of success or of failure. No matter what happens to us today, our Lord is walking beside us, strengthening us, loving us, filling us with faith, hope, and love. As He envelops us with quiet serenity and security, our foes, fears, afflictions, and doubts begin to recede. We can bear up in any setting and circumstance because we know the Lord is at hand, just as He told Paul in Acts 18:10, "I am with you."

Practice God's presence, stopping in the midst of your busy day to say to yourself, "The Lord is here." And pray that you will see Him who is invisible—and see Him everywhere. DHR

God's unseen presence comforts me,
I know He's always near;
And when life's storms besiege my soul,
He says, "My child, I'm here." —DJD

Seek the Lord while He may be found, call
upon Him while He is near. —Isaiah 55:6

July 6

Faithfulness in Everything

Read: Colossians 3:12–17

Whatever you do in word or deed, do all in the name
of the Lord Jesus. Colossians 3:17

In August 2007, a major bridge in Minneapolis collapsed into the Mississippi River, killing thirteen people. In the weeks that followed, it was difficult for me not to think about that tragedy whenever crossing a bridge over a body of water.

Some time later, I was watching an episode of *Dirty Jobs* on the Discovery Channel. Host Mike Rowe was talking to an industrial painter whose work he was trying to duplicate. "There's really no glory in what you do," he said. "No," the painter agreed, "but it's a job that needs to be done."

You see, that man paints the inside of the Mackinac Bridge towers in Northern Michigan. His unnoticed job is done to ensure that the steel of the magnificent suspended structure won't rust from the inside out, compromising the integrity of the bridge. Most of the twelve thousand people who cross the Straits of Mackinac each day aren't even aware that they are depending on workers like this painter to faithfully do their jobs well.

God also sees our faithfulness in the things we do. Though we may think our deeds—big and small—sometimes go unnoticed, they are being observed by the One who matters most. Whatever our task today, let's "do all in the name of the Lord Jesus" (Colossians 3:17). CHK

Whatever task you find to do,
Regardless if it's big or small,
Perform it well, with all your might,
Because there's One who sees it all. —Sper

Daily work takes on eternal value when it is done for God.

July 7

Does God Care?

Read: Mark 14:32–42

[Jesus] began to be troubled and deeply distressed. Then He said to them, "My soul is exceedingly sorrowful, even to death." Mark 14:33–34

One dreadful year, three of my friends died in quick succession. My experience of the first two deaths did nothing to prepare me for the third. I could do little but cry.

I find it strangely comforting that when Jesus faced pain, He responded much as I do. It comforts me that He cried when His friend Lazarus died (John 11:32–36). That gives a startling clue into how God must have felt about my friends, whom He also loved.

And in the garden the night before His crucifixion, Jesus did not pray, "Oh, Lord, I am so grateful that You have chosen Me to suffer on Your behalf." No, He experienced sorrow, fear, abandonment, even desperation. Hebrews tells us that Jesus appealed with "vehement cries and tears to Him who was able to save Him from death" (5:7). But He was not saved from death.

Is it too much to say that Jesus himself asked the question that haunts us: *Does God care?* What else can be the meaning of His quotation from that dark psalm: "My God, My God, why have You forsaken Me?" (Psalm 22:1; Mark 15:34).

Jesus endured in His pain because He knew that His Father is a God of love who can be trusted regardless of how things appear to be. He demonstrated faith that the ultimate answer to the question *Does God care?* is a resounding *Yes!*   PY

The aching void, the loneliness,
And all the thornclad way,
To Thee I turn with faith undimmed
And 'mid the darkness pray. —O. J. Smith

When we know that God's hand is in everything,
we can leave everything in God's hand.

What Are We Holding On To?

Read: 1 Timothy 6:11–16

*Fight the good fight of faith, lay hold
on eternal life. 1 Timothy 6:12*

Tolkien's classic *The Lord of the Rings* trilogy came to life in recent years on film. In the second epic story, the hero, Frodo, reached a point of despair and wearily confided to his friend, "I can't do this, Sam." As a good friend, Sam gave a rousing speech: "It's like in the great stories… Full of darkness and danger they were… Folk in those stories had lots of chances of turning back, only they didn't. They kept going. Because they were holding on to something." Which prompted Frodo to ask: "What are we holding on to, Sam?"

It's a significant question, one that we all need to ask ourselves. Living in a fallen, broken world, it's no wonder that sometimes we feel overwhelmed by the powers of darkness. When we are at the point of despair, ready to throw in the towel, we do well to follow Paul's advice to Timothy: "Fight the good fight of faith, lay hold on eternal life" (1 Timothy 6:12).

In life's battles, let's hold on to the fact that good will triumph over evil in the end, that one day we will see our Master and Leader face-to-face, and we will reign with Him forever. You can be part of this great story, knowing that if you have trusted Jesus for salvation you are guaranteed a victorious ending!   JS

*Though weak and helpless in life's fray,
God's mighty power shall be my stay;
Without, within, He gives to me
The strength to gain the victory.* —DJD

The trials of earth are small compared with the triumphs of heaven.

July 9

You Are Not Forgotten

Read: Hebrews 11:24–40

God is not unjust to forget your work and labor of love
which you have showed toward His name, in that you
have ministered to the saints. Hebrews 6:10

When Britain's oldest man turned 111, vintage aircraft did a flyover, and the Band of the Royal Marines played "Happy Birthday." According to the *Daily Mirror*, Henry Allingham was amazed by all of the attention. Until six years earlier, he had for eighty-six years kept secret the horrific memories of what happened in the trenches of World War I. Only when tracked down by the World War I Veteran's Association did this old man, who had been shelled, bombed, and shot, receive honor for what he had endured on behalf of his country.

The story of the Bible gives us parallels to Henry's story. The Scriptures show that those who fight the battles of God often end up wounded, imprisoned, and even killed as a result of their service.

The cynic might observe such lives and conclude with a sigh that no good deed goes unpunished. But the author of Hebrews sees a bigger picture. He reminds us that everything and anything we have done in faith and love will one day be honored by God (6:10).

Are you discouraged today? Do you feel insignificant? Do you feel forgotten after trying to serve God? Be assured that God will not forget anything you have done in your service to Him or others.

MD

Does the place you're called to labor
Seem so small and little known?
It is great if God is in it,
And He'll not forget His own. —Suffield

God remembers the good we forget.

July 10

To Be or Not to Be

Read: 2 Corinthians 1:3–11

We were burdened beyond measure, . . . so that we
despaired even of life. 2 Corinthians 1:8

When I was a child, kids on the playground jokingly quoted Shakespeare's famous line: "To be or not to be—that is the question!" But we really didn't understand what it meant. Later I learned that Shakespeare's character Hamlet, who speaks these lines, is a melancholy prince who learns that his uncle has killed his father and married his mother. The horror of this realization is so disturbing that he contemplates suicide. The question for him was: "to be" (to go on living) or "not to be" (to take his own life).

At times, life's pain can become so overwhelming that we are tempted to despair. The apostle Paul told the church at Corinth that his persecution in Asia was so intense he "despaired even of life" (2 Corinthians 1:8). Yet by shifting his focus to his life-sustaining God, he became resilient instead of overwhelmed, and learned "that we should not trust in ourselves but in God" (v. 9).

Trials can make life seem not worth living. Focusing on ourselves can lead to despair. But putting our trust in God gives us an entirely different perspective. As long as we live in this world, we can be certain that our all-sufficient God will sustain us. And as His followers, we will always have a divine purpose "to be."   DF

Lord, give us grace to trust You when
Life's burdens seem too much to bear;
Dispel the darkness with new hope
And help us rise above despair. —Sper

Trials make us think; thinking makes us wise; wisdom makes life profitable.

How to Be Happy

Read: Psalm 146

Happy is he who has the God of Jacob for his help. Psalm 146:5

Everyone wants to be happy. But many fail in their quest to find that elusive prize because they are looking in the wrong places.

Proverbs 16:20 tells us, "Whoever trusts in the Lord, happy is he." The foundation for happiness is a proper relationship with the Lord. But to fully experience that happiness, we must build on that foundation in practical ways, as we find in this list of "Ten Rules for Happier Living":

Give something away.
Do a kindness.
Give thanks always.
Work with vim and vigor.
Visit the elderly and learn from their experience.
Look intently into the face of a baby and marvel.
Laugh often—it's life's lubricant.
Pray to know God's way.
Plan as though you will live forever—you will.
Live as though today is your last day on earth.

These are excellent ideas for living a happy life. Undergird each of these rules with praise, and your happiness will be complete. "Praise the Lord, O my soul! While I live I will praise the Lord" (Psalm 146:1–2). RDH

Trusting and obeying the Lord brings true happiness.

Deep Water

Read: Psalm 69:13–18

Let not the floodwater overflow me, nor let the
deep swallow me up. Psalm 69:15

The builders of sport utility vehicles (SUVs) like to show us their products in mind-boggling situations. High on a mountain crag, where no truck could seemingly go. Or in a swamp so impassable you'd need a hovercraft to negotiate it. We're supposed to think that SUVs are invincible.

That's why I found unintended humor in the disclaimer in a recent ad for a four-wheel-drive SUV. A photo showed the vehicle up to its headlights in water as it forged across a foreboding river. The disclaimer said: "Traversing deep water can cause damage, which voids the vehicle warranty."

Deep water is a problem not only for cars but also for us. As we travel the roadways of life, we often find ourselves surrounded with oceans of grief or crashing waves of broken relationships. We need help.

The writers of the Psalms told of that needed assistance. They said God is "a refuge in times of trouble" (9:9), and that "in the time of trouble He shall . . . set me high upon a rock" (27:5). No disclaimers here. Traversing deep water won't affect our spiritual warranty. God will always be there to guarantee His support.

Are you in deep water? Reach up and grab God's hand of mercy. —DB

When you're passing through the waters
Of deep sorrow and despair
And you get no help from others,
Just remember, Christ is there. —Elliott

When trouble overtakes you, let God take over.

Undeserved Blessings

Read: Habakkuk 3:17–19

God . . . has blessed us with every spiritual blessing
in the heavenly places in Christ. Ephesians 1:3

Tennis superstar Arthur Ashe died of AIDS, which he contracted from a blood transfusion during heart surgery. More than a great athlete, Ashe was a gentleman who inspired and encouraged many with his exemplary behavior on and off the court.

Ashe could have become embittered and self-pitying in the face of his disease, but he maintained a grateful attitude. He explained, "If I asked, 'Why me?' about my troubles, I would have to ask, 'Why me?' about my blessings. Why my winning Wimbledon? Why my marrying a beautiful, gifted woman and having a wonderful child?"

Ashe's attitude rebukes those of us who often grumble, "Why me? Why is God allowing this to happen?" Even if we're suffering acutely, we must not forget the mercies God pours into our lives— such things as food, shelter, and friends—blessings that many are deprived of.

And what about spiritual blessings? We can hold the very Word of God in our hands and read it. We have the knowledge of His saving grace, the comfort of His Spirit, and the joyful assurance of life everlasting with Jesus.

Think about God's blessings and ask, "Why me?" Then your grumbling will give way to praise. —VCG

Are you ever burdened with a load of care?
Does the cross seem heavy you are called to bear?
Count your many blessings, every doubt will fly,
And you will be singing as the days go by. —Oatman

With unwanted burdens come undeserved blessings.

Panic Prayers

Read: Psalm 37:1–8

Commit your way to the Lord, trust also in Him,
and He shall bring it to pass. Psalm 37:5

In her book *Beyond Our Selves*, Catherine Marshall wrote about learning to surrender her entire life to God through a "prayer of relinquishment." When she encountered situations she feared, she often panicked and exhibited a demanding spirit in prayer: "God, I must have thus and so." God seemed remote. But when she surrendered the dreaded situation to Him to do with it exactly as He pleased, fear left and peace returned. From that moment on, God began working things out.

In Psalm 37, David talked about both commitment and surrender: "Commit your way to the Lord," he said, "trust also in Him" (v. 5). Committed believers are those who sincerely follow and serve the Lord, and it's appropriate to urge people to have greater commitment. But committing ourselves to God and trusting Him imply surrendering every area of our lives to His wise control, especially when fear and panic overtake us. The promised result of such wholehearted commitment and trust is that God will do what is best for us.

Instead of trying to quell your fears with panic prayers, surrender yourself to God through a prayer of relinquishment, and see what He will do.   JY

Lord, take my life and make it wholly Thine;
Fill my poor heart with Thy great love divine.
Take all my will, my passion, self, and pride;
I now surrender, Lord—in me abide. —Orr

Prayer is the bridge between panic and peace.

What's the Point?

Read: Ecclesiastes 1:1–11; 12:13–14

Fear God and keep His commandments,
for this is man's all. Ecclesiastes 12:13

What's the point? This question came to mind as I watched my grandsons' dog fetch a ball for me again and again.

What's the point? That's what the writer of Ecclesiastes asked as he thought about the monotonous cycle he observed in nature and in life—the same things happening year after year, generation after generation.

What's the point? That's what a retired businessman was asking, in effect, when he told me he would just as soon die as live any longer. He had seen and done everything he had wanted to do. Now he had reached the place where life held more pain for him than pleasure.

What's the point? Here it is. A few years before a friend of mine died, he said, "Life is a wonderful experience. It's marvelous to see that God keeps nature going in its pattern. It's wonderful to know that we're here to love God above everything and to love our neighbor as ourselves. It's comforting to believe that all our sins are forgiven because of what Christ did on the cross. And it's exciting to think about the eternity God has for us. It sure is great to be alive."

Life can be depressing when God is left out. But how exciting it is when He is at the center! HVL

When we focus on Christ, everything else becomes clear.

July 16

Raku

Read: James 1:2–4

Rejoicing in hope, patient in tribulation. Romans 12:12

Some friends gave us a piece of Raku pottery. "Each pot is hand-formed," the tag explained, "a process that allows the spirit of the artist to speak through the finished work with particular directness and intimacy."

Once the clay has been shaped by the potter it is fired in a kiln. Then, glowing red hot, it is thrust into a smoldering sawdust pile where it remains until finished. The result is a unique product—"one of a kind," the tag on our piece insists.

So it is with us. We bear the imprint of the Potter's hand. He too has spoken through His work "with particular directness and intimacy." Each of us is formed in a unique way for a unique work: "We are His workmanship, created in Christ Jesus for good works, which God prepared beforehand that we should walk in them" (Ephesians 2:10).

But though we are created for good works, we're not yet finished. We must experience the kiln of affliction. Aching hearts, weary spirits, aging bodies are the processes God uses to finish the work He has begun.

Don't fear the furnace that surrounds you. Be "patient in tribulation" and await the finished product. "Let patience have its perfect work, that you may be perfect and complete, lacking nothing" (James 1:4).   DHR

He who has begun a good work in you will complete it
until the day of Jesus Christ. —Philippians 1:6

Frightened by a Boxer

Read: Psalm 91:1–11

Fear not, for I am with you; be not dismayed,
for I am your God. Isaiah 41:10

On a bright Sunday morning one of my boys, who was just a little fellow, was walking to church with me. Soon the sights and sounds of a new day invited him to skip on ahead. Suddenly his carefree progress came to an end. A few yards away was a boxer dog looking at him. Stopping abruptly, my son turned and rushed to my side. Only when his hand was securely in mine and he knew I was right beside him was he able to walk undisturbed past the boxer.

What a picture of our pilgrimage through this world! From time to time the fierce-looking obstacles of illness, money problems, or personal conflicts appear before us, striking fear into our hearts. At first we are bewildered and life seems to be at a dead end. But then by faith we make our way to the Savior, realizing we dare not go forward without the assurance of His presence. As we completely trust in Him, He helps us face the future by walking with us each step of the way.

If anxiety and dread are lurking on the threshold of your tomorrow, remember God's wonderful promise in Isaiah 41:10, "Fear not, for I am with you; be not dismayed, for I am your God. I will strengthen you, yes, I will help you, I will uphold you with My righteous right hand."   DJD

Though there are dangers untold and stern
Confronting me in the way,
Willingly still would I go, nor turn,
But trust You for grace each day. —Tovey

If you can't find a way out, look up.

What God Can Do

Read: 2 Corinthians 1:3–11

[God] delivered us from so great a death, and does deliver us; in whom
we trust that He will still deliver us. 2 Corinthians 1:10

They were called the "lost boys" of Sudan. Thousands of them fled the civil war in that country and sought refuge from the chaos and killing. Many had been taught the gospel in churches founded by missionaries, but they knew little of the world beyond their villages.

A *National Geographic* article profiled one of these "lost boys" who is now resettled in the United States. He told a church congregation that he is grateful for the comforts of the U.S., but also for the faith he learned through hardship. "Americans believe in God," he told them, "but they don't know what God can do."

In the crucible of testing, we move from theory to reality as we experience God's power. When there seems to be no hope, we may share Paul's feeling of being "burdened beyond measure, above strength, so that we [despair] even of life" (2 Corinthians 1:8). But we can also learn, as Paul did, that in the darkest times "we should not trust in ourselves but in God who raises the dead" (v. 9).

If God has allowed you to be in a desperate situation today, why not reconsider all that the Almighty has done and can still do. By trusting God in hardship we learn what He can do in our lives.

DCM

Though weak and helpless in life's fray,
God's mighty power shall be my stay;
Without, within, He gives to me
The strength to gain the victory. —DJD

God is the only ally we can always count on.

July 19

A Reason for Optimism

Read: John 16:16–33

A merry heart does good, like medicine. Proverbs 17:22

The Bible isn't a psychology textbook, but it gives us the wisest counsel for experiencing happiness here and now. Proverbs 17:22, for example, assures us that "a merry heart does good, like medicine, but a broken spirit dries the bones."

That simple statement was recently corroborated by the extensive research of Dr. Daniel Mark, a heart specialist at Duke University. *The New York Times* article that reported his findings carried this headline: "Optimism Can Mean Life for Heart Patients and Pessimism Death." The article begins with these words: "A healthy outlook helps heal the heart."

But Dr. Nancy Frasure-Smith, a heart specialist who has studied the effect of depression, anxiety, and anger, admitted, "We don't know how to change negative emotions."

Faith in God, however, can produce that change. People who look beyond their present difficulty and put their trust in God's goodness cannot help but be joyful.

It's significant that our Savior said on several occasions, "Be of good cheer" (Matthew 9:2, 22; 14:27; Acts 23:11). Knowing that life is filled with many crises, He encourages us with this word of reassurance: "Be of good cheer, I have overcome the world" (John 16:33). VCG

All your anxiety, all your care
Bring to the mercy seat, leave it there;
Never a burden He cannot bear,
Never a friend like Jesus. —Joy

No matter what happens, you can find joy in the Lord.

Sing of Your Love

Read: Revelation 5:8–14

I will sing of the mercies of the Lord forever. Psalm 89:1

I was driving to work and listening to a local Christian radio station. Amid the usual morning banter came the song "I Could Sing of Your Love Forever."

I have no idea what came over me. As soon as this uplifting praise song began, I felt tears running down my face. There I was, almost at work, and I could hardly see to drive because of a song. What was going on?

I sat in my car after I arrived at my destination, trying to figure it out. Then it struck me. The song reminded me that while another day of normal activity was beginning here on earth, my daughter Melissa was fulfilling the ultimate hope of that song in heaven. I pictured her brightly singing of God's love—getting a head start on the rest of us in that forever song. It was a bittersweet moment of understanding Melissa's joy while being reminded again of our sadness in not having her with us.

Much of life is like that. Joys and sorrows intermingle—making reminders of God's glory so vital. We need those glimpses of a promising praise-filled future in our Savior's presence. In the sadnesses of life, we need the anticipation of joy—the joy that comes from singing of God's love and enjoying His presence forever. DB

The saints of all ages in heaven sing praise
With voices and harps to the Ancient of Days;
No music on earth with that sound can compare,
Yet in that vast chorus our voices will share. —DJD

Those who know Christ now will sing His praises forever.

Well-Known

Read: Psalm 139:1–12

The Lord knows those who are His. 2 Timothy 2:19

Arctic sea birds called guillemots live on rocky coastal cliffs, where thousands of them come together in small areas. Because of the crowded conditions, the females lay their eggs side by side in a long row. It's incredible that a mother bird can identify the eggs that belong to her. Studies show that even when one is moved some distance away, she finds it and carries it back to its original location.

Our heavenly Father is far more intimately acquainted with each of His children. He is aware of every thought, emotion, and decision we make. From morning till night He gives personal attention to our daily affairs. Overwhelmed by this glorious reality, the psalmist exclaimed in amazement, "Such knowledge is too wonderful for me; it is high, I cannot attain it" (Psalm 139:6).

Not only does this evoke our praise, but it should also bring great comfort to our hearts. Jesus told His disciples that the Father knows when a single sparrow falls to the ground. Because people are of so much greater value than the birds, God's children can be assured of His constant care.

How wonderful it is to be such a well-loved, "well-known" person!   MD

With God, you're never lost in a crowd.

Little by Little!

Read: Exodus 23:20–33

*Little by little I will drive them out from before you, until you have
increased, and you inherit the land. Exodus 23:30*

When I was a little girl, my mother gave me her prized
"reader" to help me learn, just as it had helped her years
earlier. I loved one particular story, never dreaming how much it
would affect me years later.

It was about a little boy with a small shovel. He was trying
to clear a pathway through deep, new-fallen snow in front of his
house. A man paused to observe the child's enormous task. "Little
boy," he inquired, "how can someone as small as you expect to finish a task as big as this?" The boy looked up and replied confidently,
"Little by little, that's how!" And he continued shoveling.

God awakened in me the seed of that story at a time when I was
recovering from a breakdown. I remember how my "adult" self
taunted the weak "child" within me: "How can someone as inadequate as you expect to surmount so great a mountain as this?" That
little boy's reply became my reply: "Little by little, that's how!" And
I did overcome—by depending on God. But it was one small victory after another.

The obstacles facing Israel as they considered claiming the land
God had promised them must have seemed insurmountable. But He
didn't ask them to do it all at once.

"Little by little" is the strategy for victory.   JY

He does not lead me year by year,
Nor even day by day;
But step by step my path unfolds—
My Lord directs my way. —Ryberg

Trust God to move your mountain, but keep on climbing.

Where to Look

Read: Romans 8:35–39

Let us run . . . , looking unto Jesus. Hebrews 12:1–2

Let's see. What is the crisis of the day? It could be terrorism and its random threat. Or the economy and the fear that we will run out of money before we run out of time. Maybe it's a personal crisis with no foreseeable solution—a tragedy or a failure too great to bear.

Before we fall under the weight of our accumulated fears, we would do well to look back to a twentieth-century woman who bore sadness, pain, and heartache with grace.

Corrie ten Boom lived through the hellish life of Nazi concentration camps—a place where hope was lost for most people. She survived to tell her story of unfaltering faith and tight-fisted hope in God.

She saw the face of evil up close and personal. She saw some of the most inhumane acts man can do to man. And when she came out of it all, she said this: "If you look at the world, you'll be distressed. If you look within, you'll be depressed. But if you look at Christ, you'll be at rest."

Where are you looking? Are you focusing on the world and its dangers? Are you gazing at yourself, hoping to find your own answers? Or are you looking to Jesus, the author and finisher of your faith? (Hebrews 12:1–2). In an uncertain world, we must keep looking to Him. DB

When your world is falling apart,
trust Jesus to hold it together.

Say "Mercy!"

Read: Philippians 4:1–7

Be anxious for nothing, but in everything by prayer... let
your requests be made known to God. Philippians 4:6

You may have played the game when you were a child. You interlace your fingers with someone else's and try to bend the other's hands back until one or the other cries "Mercy!" The winner is the one who gets the other person to surrender.

Sometimes we try to play "Mercy" with God when we pray. We have a request that we desperately want answered in a certain way, so we try to "bend His fingers back" and get Him to give in. When it seems we aren't winning, we try a little harder to convince Him by begging or bargaining. We may even give up grudgingly and say, "Lord, You always win! That's not fair!"

God does want honesty of heart. But occasionally in our honesty a demanding spirit comes out. Deep down we know that prayer is not meant to be a contest with God that we try to win. In our wiser moments, we make our requests known to our Lord, surrender them to Him, rely on His grace, and wait for His answers (Philippians 4:6–7). Author Hannah Whitall Smith said, "Be glad and eager to throw yourself unreservedly into His loving arms, and to hand over the reins of government to Him."

Instead of praying with grudging resignation, "Lord, You always win," surrender to Him. Say "Mercy!"   AC

In Jesus' name we voice our prayers—
The Bible tells us to;
But may we never use that name
To tell God what to do. —DJD

Prayer isn't a time to give orders but to report for duty!

July 25

Boring?

Read: Numbers 11:1–9

*Our whole being is dried up; there is nothing at all except
this manna before our eyes! Numbers 11:6*

Many of our recurring complaints focus not on what we
don't have, but on what we do have and find uninterest-
ing. Whether it's our work, our church, our house, or our spouse,
boredom grumbles that it's not what we want or need. This frustration with sameness has been true of the human spirit since the
beginning.

Notice the protest of God's people about their menu in the wilderness. Recalling the variety of food they ate as slaves in Egypt,
they despised the monotony of God's current provision: "Our
whole being is dried up; there is nothing at all except this manna
before our eyes!" (Numbers 11:6).

God provided exactly what they needed each day, but they
wanted something more exciting. Are we tempted to do the same?
Oswald Chambers said: "Drudgery is the touchstone of character.
There are times when there is no illumination and no thrill, but just
the daily round, the common task. Routine is God's way of saving
us between our times of inspiration. Do not expect God always to
give you His thrilling minutes, but learn to live in the domain of
drudgery by the power of God."

During the boring times of life, God is working to instill His
character in us. Drudgery is our opportunity to experience the
presence of the Lord. DCM

Steadfast, then, in our endeavor,
Heavenly Father, may we be;
And forever, and forever,
We will give the praise to Thee. —*MacKellar*

Blessing is found along the pathway of duty.

The Storm Will Pass

Read: Exodus 5:1–14, 22–23

*He who trusts in his own heart is a fool, but whoever walks
wisely will be delivered. Proverbs 28:26*

The local TV meteorologist occasionally points to a map and
says something like this: "I'm afraid that things are going to
get worse before they get better."

Such a forecast could very well have applied to Israel when God
sent Moses to free His people from slavery in Egypt. The barometer
of events was falling rapidly, and the dark, ominous sky of oppression would soon break forth into a churning, flashing storm of cruelty unleashed by Pharaoh.

Moses had appealed to Pharaoh to let the Hebrews go into the
desert to worship God, but the king accused them of loafing on the
job (Exodus 5:1, 17). So he multiplied their workload, and the situation went from bad to horrible (v. 18). Moses cried out in bitterness to the Lord for an explanation (vv. 22–23). He found it hard to
believe that a glorious exodus could be just around the corner.

The plans of the Lord were not being frustrated, however. Before
conditions would get better for His children, God tested them by
allowing their suffering to increase.

Even when we are obedient to the Lord, the skies of adversity
may not always clear immediately. Circumstances may get worse
before they improve. But praise God, His grace will sustain us, and
the storm will pass.   MDH

It's always darkest before the dawn.

July 27

Stars and Sand

Read: Psalm 147:1–11

*He counts the number of the stars; He calls
them all by name. Psalm 147:4*

A team led by an Australian astronomer calculated the number of stars in the known universe to be seventy sextillion— seven followed by twenty-two zeros. That unfathomable number is said to be more than the grains of sand in every beach and every desert on earth. The calculation was the by-product of research on the development of galaxies. One team member said, "Finding the number of stars is not really the research we were doing, but it was a nice result to play around with."

Having an estimate of the number of stars can help us praise God with greater awe and wonder. Psalm 147 says: "It is good to sing praises to our God; for it is pleasant, and praise is beautiful... He counts the number of the stars; He calls them all by name. Great is our Lord, and mighty in power; His understanding is infinite" (vv. 1, 4–5).

This psalm not only presents God's majesty, but it also affirms His personal concern for each of us. He "heals the brokenhearted" (v. 3), "lifts up the humble" (v. 6), and "takes pleasure in those who fear Him, in those who hope in His mercy" (v. 11).

Let's praise the great God of stars and sand who knows and cares for each one of us. DCM

The God who made the firmament,
Who made the deepest sea,
The God who put the stars in place
Is the God who cares for me. —Berg

All creation points to the almighty Creator.

Dots and Doughnut Holes

Read: Psalm 104:1–15

Bless the Lord, O my soul, and forget not
all His benefits. Psalm 103:2

As a minister was addressing a group of men, he took a large piece of paper and made a black dot in the center of it. Then he held up the paper and asked them what they saw.

One person replied, "I see a black mark." "Right," the preacher said. "What else?" Complete silence prevailed. "I'm really surprised," the speaker commented. "You have completely overlooked the most important thing of all—the sheet of paper."

We are often distracted by small, dot-like disappointments, and we are prone to forget the innumerable blessings we receive from the Lord. But like the sheet of paper, the good things are far more important than the adversities that monopolize our attention.

This reminds me of a whimsical bit of verse that expresses good practical advice. "As you travel down life's pathway, may this ever be your goal: Keep your eye upon the doughnut, and not upon the hole!"

Yes, rather than concentrating on the trials of life, we should fix our attention on its blessings. Let's say with the psalmist, "Blessed be the Lord, who daily loads us with benefits" (Psalm 68:19).

Let's keep praising Him so we won't be distracted by dots and doughnut holes. RDH

So amid the conflict, whether great or small,
Do not be discouraged—God is over all;
Count your many blessings—angels will attend,
Help and comfort give you to your journey's end. —Oatman

Spend your time counting your blessings—
not airing your complaints.

Riding a Roller Coaster

Read: Galatians 6:1–10

*Let us not grow weary while doing good, for in due season
we shall reap if we do not lose heart. Galatians 6:9*

If you love someone who struggles with a substance-abuse problem, you know that your emotions and his can be like riding a roller coaster—up and down. Today he wants help; tomorrow he's drinking or is high on drugs again. Today she's being honest; tomorrow she's running from the truth.

The Holy Spirit helps us learn how to love people like that, even in their sins and struggles. Here are a few principles we can put into practice:

Treat the person with respect. Be gentle when trying to restore him (Galatians 6:1). But don't do for him what he should do for himself. Don't get in the way of the consequences that God can use to bring change.

Remember that you do not have the power to change another person. Instead, ask God to help you become the person He wants you to be (vv. 4–5).

Reach out in love. Seek God's wisdom in what to say and do in each encounter (James 1:5). Then rebuke or be silent—in love.

Depend on God. You will make mistakes. But anchor yourself in God's Word and continually commit yourself and your loved one to the Lord in prayer (Philippians 4:6).

Making some of these choices can help to slow down the roller coaster ride of changing emotions. AC

Love helps people even when it hurts.

July 30

A Bumpy Road

Read: Philippians 1:27–30

To you it has been granted on behalf of Christ, not only to believe in Him, but also to suffer for His sake. Philippians 1:29

When people tell me life is hard, I always reply, "Of course it is." I find that answer more satisfying than anything else I can say. Writer Charles Williams said, "The world is painful in any case; but it is quite unbearable if anybody gives us the idea that we are meant to be liking it."

The path by which God takes us often seems to lead away from what we perceive as our good, causing us to believe we've missed a turn and taken the wrong road. That's because most of us have been taught to believe that if we're on the right track God's goodness will always translate into a life free of trouble.

But that's a pipe dream far removed from the biblical perspective. God's love often leads us down roads where earthly comforts fail us. Paul said, "To you it has been granted on behalf of Christ, not only to believe in Him, but also to suffer for His sake" (Philippians 1:29). When we come to the end of all our dark valleys, we'll understand that every circumstance has been allowed for our ultimate good.

"No other route would have been as safe and as certain as the one by which we came," Bible teacher F. B. Meyer said. "If only we could see the path as God has always seen it, we would have selected it as well." DHR

If some darker lot be good,
Lord, teach us to endure
The sorrow, pain, or solitude
That makes the spirit pure. —Irons

No trial would cause us to despair
if we knew God's reason for allowing it.

July 31

Broken Things

Read: Psalm 31:9–24

I am like a broken vessel. Psalm 31:12

Few unbroken lives in this world are useful to God. Few men and women can fulfill their hopes and plans without some interruption and disappointment along the way.

But man's disappointments are often God's appointments, and the things we believe are tragedies may be the very opportunities through which God chooses to exhibit His love and grace. We have but to follow these lives to the end to see that people who have been broken become better and more effective Christians than if they had carried out all their own plans and purposes.

Are you, my friend, being broken today? Has the dearest thing in your life been torn away? Then remember that if you could see the purpose of it all from God's standpoint, you would praise the Lord.

The best things that come to us are not those that accrue from having our way, but by letting God have His way. Though the way of testing and trial and sorrow often seems hard and cruel, it is the way of God's love and in the end will be the best for us.

Remember, we have the Lord's promise: "No good thing will He withhold from those who walk uprightly" (Psalm 84:11).

MD

Then trust in God through all thy days;
Fear not, for He doth hold thy hand;
Though dark thy way, still sing and praise,
Sometime, sometime, we'll understand. —Cornelius

For a Christian, wholeness always comes after brokenness.

August 1

Are You Struggling?

Read: Hebrews 12:1–7

Consider Him who endured such hostility . . . , lest you become weary and discouraged in your souls. Hebrews 12:3

I was in my second year of widowhood and I was struggling. Morning after morning my prayer life consisted of one daily sigh: "Lord, I shouldn't be struggling like this!" "And why not?" His still, small voice asked me from within one morning.

Then the answer came—unrecognized pride! Somehow I had thought that a person of my spiritual maturity should be beyond such struggle. What a ridiculous thought! I had never been a widow before and needed the freedom to be a true learner—even a struggling learner.

At the same time, I was reminded of the story of a man who took home a cocoon so he could watch the emperor moth emerge. As the moth struggled to get through the tiny opening, the man enlarged it with a snip of his scissors. The moth emerged easily—but its wings were shriveled. The struggle through the narrow opening is God's way to force fluid from its body into its wings. The "merciful" snip, in reality, was cruel.

Hebrews 12 describes the Christian life as a race that involves endurance, discipline, and correction. We never get beyond the need of a holy striving against self and sin. Sometimes the struggle is exactly what we need to become what God intends us to be.

JY

When God allows His chastening hand
To give us little rest,
His only purpose is our good—
He wants for us His best. —DJD

We experience God's strength in the strain of our struggle.

Get Rid of the Grubs

Read: Proverbs 3:19–26

Keep sound wisdom and discretion... Then you will walk safely in your way. Proverbs 3:21, 23

A frustrated homeowner had a yard full of moles. He tried everything he knew to defeat his underground enemy, but he was losing the battle. Finally a friend informed him that he was trying to solve his problem the wrong way. The moles weren't the true culprits. The real problem was the grubs that the moles were feeding on. Get rid of them and the moles would have no reason to stay.

The third chapter of Proverbs gives us a parallel situation. Instead of moles, the problem is fear—the kind of fear that robs us of strength during the day and sleep at night (vv. 24–25).

What is also evident from this chapter is that we can eliminate our fears only by attacking the "grubs" that attract it. We must go after our self-sufficiency and irreverence (vv. 5–8). We have to treat our evil and foolish ways with a strong application of divine wisdom and understanding (vv. 13–18). Then and only then will fear lose its grip.

What's important is to know the real problem so that we can work on it. When it comes to fear, we must make wise decisions based on God's Word and build a love-trust relationship with Christ. That's what it takes to get rid of the "grubs."   MD

*When you are deeply troubled
By fear and inward doubt,
Strive to do what pleases God,
And He will lead you out. —Lloyd*

Keep your eyes on God and you'll soon lose sight
of your fears.

A God of Absolutes

Read: Malachi 3:6–12

I am the Lord, I do not change. Malachi 3:6

I am dubious about the accuracy of our bathroom scale. So I've learned to manipulate it in a self-satisfying manner. The little adjustment knob serves to vary the register, and if that becomes too much bother, I just lean a certain way. The idea is to get a favorable reading—hopefully one that is a few pounds less.

We live in an age when many people believe there are no absolutes. Self-serving behavior is rampant and tramples the moral law given for the protection of society. Our culture prides itself on "freedom" that is actually slavery to sin (Romans 6:16–17).

But there is a God of absolutes whose scales never lose their adjustment. With Him, a pound is a pound, right is right, and wrong is wrong. He says, "I am the Lord, I do not change" (Malachi 3:6).

For us as believers, this puts steel into our spiritual backbone. We gain confidence in the face of difficulty and are assured of the fulfillment of every divine promise.

If God were easily moved by every whim or notion, our eternal destiny would be in constant jeopardy. But because He is the Unchanging One, we "are not consumed" (v. 6). "His compassions fail not. They are new every morning" (Lamentations 3:22-23).

PVG

Unchanging God who reigns above,
His truth remains forever;
And from this faithful God of love
No earthly trial can sever. —DJD

Earth changes, but thy soul and God stand sure.
—Browning

Hurting and Hearing

Read: Exodus 6:1-9

I have surely seen the oppression of My people who are in Egypt,
and have heard their cry. Exodus 3:7

When we are experiencing deep sorrow or difficult circumstances, we may feel offended if someone suggests that
something good can emerge from our adversity. A well-meaning
person who tries to encourage us to trust God's promises may be
perceived as insensitive or even unrealistic.

That happened to the children of Israel when God was working
for their deliverance from Egypt. As Pharaoh hardened his heart
toward the Lord's command to let His people go, he increased the
Hebrew slaves' workload by forcing them to gather the straw they
needed to make bricks (Exodus 5:10-11). They became so discouraged, they couldn't accept Moses's assurance that God had heard
their cries and promised to take them to a land of their own (6:9).

There are times when our hurts and fears can close our ears to
the hopeful words of God. But the Lord doesn't stop speaking to us
when it's hard for us to hear. He continues working on our behalf
just as He did in delivering His people from Egypt.

As we experience God's compassion and His loving care, we can
begin to hear again even as the hurt continues to heal.   DCM

O yes, He cares—I know He cares!
His heart is touched with my grief;
When the days are weary, the long nights dreary,
I know my Savior cares. —Graeff

Even when we don't sense God's presence,
His loving care is all around us.

Rough Going

Read: John 16:19–33

In the world you will have tribulation; but be of good cheer,
I have overcome the world. John 16:33

There's a lake near our home in the mountains that is known for good fishing. To get there, I had to hike two miles up a steep ridge—a hard climb for an old-timer like me. But then I discovered that it's possible to drive within a half-mile of the lake. I spent most of a day driving several mountain roads until I found the one that got me the closest. Then I carefully mapped the road so I could find it again.

Several months later, I drove the road again. I came to a section that was much worse than I remembered—rocky, rutted, and steep. I wondered if I had missed a turn, so I stopped and checked my map. There, penciled alongside the stretch on which I was driving, were the words: "Rough and steep. Hard going." I was on the right road.

Jesus said that our life's journey will be rough going if we choose to follow Him. "In the world you will have tribulation" (John 16:33). So we shouldn't be surprised if our path becomes difficult, nor should we believe we've taken a wrong turn. We can "be of good cheer" because Jesus also said that in Him we can have peace, for He has "overcome the world" (v. 33).

If you're following Christ and experiencing some bumpy times, take heart—you're on the right road!   DHR

Following Jesus is always right—but not always easy.

From Worms to Wars

Read: Judges 6:11–16, 33–40

*The Lord said to [Gideon], "Peace be with you;
do not fear." Judges 6:23*

It was ten-year-old Cleotis's first time fishing, and as he looked into the container of bait he seemed hesitant to get started. Finally he said to my husband, "Help me, I-S-O-W!" When my husband asked him what the problem was, Cleotis responded, "I-S-O-W! I'm Scared of Worms!" His fear had made him unable to act.

Fear can paralyze grown men too. Gideon must have been afraid when the angel of the Lord came to him as he was threshing wheat in secret, hiding from his Midianite enemies (Judges 6:11). The angel told him he had been chosen by God to lead His people in battle (vv. 12–14).

Gideon's response? "O my Lord, how can I save Israel? Indeed my clan is the weakest in Manasseh, and I am the least in my father's house" (v. 15). After being assured of the Lord's presence, Gideon still seemed fearful and asked Him for signs that He would use him to save Israel as He promised (vv. 36–40). And God responded to Gideon's requests. The Israelites were successful in battle and then enjoyed peace for forty years.

We all have fears of various kinds—from worms to wars. Gideon's story teaches us that we can be confident of this: If God asks us to do something, He'll give us the strength and power to do it.

AC

*When you're afraid of what's ahead,
Remember, God is near;
He'll give you strength and joy and hope
And calm your inner fear. —Sper*

To take the fear out of living, put your faith in the living God.

Don't Be Afraid

Read: Isaiah 12

*God is my salvation, I will trust and
not be afraid. Isaiah 12:2*

I have an ancient leaf blower that I use to clean up our patio. It sputters, rattles, smokes, emits irritating fumes, and is considered by my wife (and probably by my neighbors) to be excessively noisy.

But our old dog is utterly indifferent to the racket. When I start up the blower, she doesn't even raise her head, and only reluctantly moves when I blow leaves or dirt in her direction. That's because she trusts me.

A young man who occasionally mows our yard uses a similar blower, but his is *not* tolerated by our dog. Years ago, when she was a puppy, he teased her with the machine and she has never forgotten. Now, when the man enters the backyard, we have to put her in the house, because she growls, barks, and snarls at him. Same set of circumstances, but the hands that use the blower make all the difference.

So it is with us. Frightening circumstances are less troublesome if we trust the hands that control them. If our world and our lives were governed by a thoughtless and indifferent force, we would have good reason to fear. But the hands that control the universe— God's hands—are wise and compassionate. We can trust them in spite of our circumstances and not be afraid.   DHR

*When fear and worry test your faith
And anxious thoughts assail,
Remember, God is in control,
And He will never fail. —Sper*

God is in control, so we have nothing to fear.

The Answer Is No

Read: 2 Samuel 12:13–23

*David arose from the ground, . . . and he went into the house
of the Lord and worshiped. 2 Samuel 12:20*

C hildren are so lovable and innocent—until their parents say
no to their demands. When that happens, some kids scream
uncontrollably, insisting on what they want.

When our children were little, my wife and I thought it was
important for them to learn to accept no for an answer. We felt this
would help them to handle the disappointments of life more effectively. We prayed that it would also help them submit to God's will.

Today's Bible reading records King David's admission of guilt
when confronted by Nathan. David was forgiven, but God let the
consequence of his sin fall on the baby conceived out of wedlock.
David fasted and prayed to the Lord day and night for his son's healing. In spite of his sincere petitions, the baby died.

Instead of behaving like a demanding child and being angry
with God, David got up, washed, changed his clothes, "went into
the house of the Lord and worshiped" (2 Samuel 12:20). His actions
teach us an important lesson: Sometimes we must accept no from
God as the answer to our pleas.

In times of difficulty or loss, we should seek God's help and
deliverance. But we must still trust Him if He does not answer our
prayers the way we want Him to.

Have we learned to take no for an answer?   AL

Our weakness is a blessing when we lean on God's strength.

In the Car Wash

Read: Isaiah 43:1–13

When you pass through the waters,
I will be with you. Isaiah 43:2

I'll never forget my first experience using an automatic car wash. Approaching it with the dread of going to the dentist, I pushed the money into the slot, nervously checked and rechecked my windows, eased the car up to the line, and waited. Powers beyond my control began moving my car forward as if on a conveyor belt. There I was, cocooned inside, when a thunderous rush of water, soap, and brushes hit my car from all directions. *What if I get stuck in here or water crashes in?* I thought irrationally. Suddenly the waters ceased. After a blow-dry, my car was propelled into the outside world again, clean and polished.

In the midst of all this, I remembered stormy times in my life when it seemed I was on a conveyor belt, a victim of forces beyond my control. "Car-wash experiences," I now call them. I remembered that whenever I passed through deep waters my Redeemer had been with me, sheltering me against the rising tide (Isaiah 43:2). When I came out on the other side, which I always did, I was able to say with joy and confidence, "He is a faithful God!"

Are you in the middle of a car-wash experience? Trust God to bring you through to the other side. You'll then be a shining testimony of His keeping power. — JY

How wonderful to know that He
Who watches from above
Will always keep us sheltered in
His ever-present love! —King

A tunnel of testing can produce a shining testimony.

August 10

More Than Wishing

Read: Matthew 6:5–15

*Your Father knows the things you have need of
before you ask Him. Matthew 6:8*

As a child, C. S. Lewis enjoyed reading the books of E. Nesbit, especially *Five Children and It*. In this book, brothers and sisters on a summer holiday discover an ancient sand fairy who grants them one wish each day. But every wish brings the children more trouble than happiness because they can't foresee the results of getting everything they ask for.

The Bible tells us to make our requests known to God (Philippians 4:6). But prayer is much more than telling God what we want Him to do for us. When Jesus taught His disciples how to pray, He began by reminding them, "Your Father knows the things you have need of before you ask Him" (Matthew 6:8).

What we call the Lord's Prayer is more about living in a growing, trusting relationship with our heavenly Father than about getting what we want from Him. As we grow in faith, our prayers will become less of a wish list and more of an intimate conversation with the Lord.

Toward the end of his life, C. S. Lewis wrote, "If God had granted all the silly prayers I've made in my life, where should I be now?"

Prayer is placing ourselves in the presence of God to receive from Him what we really need.   DCM

We grasp but a thread of the garment of prayer;
We reel at the thought of His infinite care;
We cannot conceive of a God who will say:
"Be careful for nothing; in everything pray." —Farrell

Our highest privilege is to talk to God;
our highest duty is to listen to Him.

August 11

Our Living Hope

Read: John 6:39–54

*God . . . has begotten us again to a living hope through the
resurrection of Jesus Christ from the dead. 1 Peter 1:3*

The morning after my mother died, I was reading the Bible and
talking to the Lord about my sadness. The Bible-in-One-Year
reading for that day was John 6.

When I came to verse 39, the Lord whispered comfort to my
sad heart: "This is the will of the Father who sent Me, that of all He
has given Me I should lose nothing, but should raise it up at the last
day." Mom's spirit was with the Lord already, but I knew that one
day she would be raised and given a new body.

As I continued reading, I noticed three other times in John 6
that Jesus said He will raise His people from the dead at the last day.
He was repeating this truth to those who were listening long ago as
well as to my heart that day.

Our hope of resurrection will be realized when Jesus returns. "In
a moment, in the twinkling of an eye, at the last trumpet. For the
trumpet will sound, and the dead will be raised incorruptible, and
we shall be changed" (1 Corinthians 15:52). After the resurrection,
believers in Jesus will receive their new bodies and rewards for their
faithful service (1 Corinthians 3:12–15; 2 Corinthians 5:9–11).

The resurrection is the living hope of the Christian. Do you
have that hope?   AC

Jesus arose and conquered death;
He robbed it of its fear and power;
And one day He'll return to earth,
Though we know not the day nor hour. —DJD

The risen Christ will come from heaven to take
His own to heaven.

Recovery

Read: Jeremiah 33:1–9

I will heal them and reveal to them the abundance
of peace and truth. Jeremiah 33:6

Over thirty-five years ago, May 18, 1980, Mount St. Helens erupted in one of the greatest natural disasters of modern times. The top of the mountain was blown into the atmosphere and became a dark plume of pulverized rock eleven miles high. At the same time, avalanches of rock, mud, and ice swept down the mountain—destroying everything in their path, clogging rivers, and stopping ships.

During the past few decades, the U.S. government has spent over one billion dollars on Mount St. Helens's recovery and long-term improvements of the area. Much of the engineering and construction work done by the U.S. Army Corps of Engineers is unseen because "it takes the form of floods that will not happen, homes and communities that will not be destroyed, [and] river traffic that will flow smoothly."

In this process of recovery, I see a picture of God's forgiveness and healing for the disastrous results of our disobedience. When God allowed His people to be taken captive by the Chaldeans, He promised: "I will heal them and reveal to them the abundance of peace and truth" (Jeremiah 33:6).

True spiritual recovery often takes time. But as we allow the Lord to clean up our lives, He can safeguard us against future failures. —DCM

Events may sometimes touch our lives
With change and dire destruction,
But God by grace can heal, restore,
And bring us reconstruction. —Hess

Christ's cleansing power can remove
the most stubborn stain of sin.

Doing Our Part

Read: 2 Kings 20:1–7

I have heard your prayer . . . ; surely I will heal you. On the third day you shall go up to the house of the Lord. 2 Kings 20:5

A runner at a school track meet crossed the finish line just ahead of his nearest rival. A bystander, noticing that the winner's lips were moving during the last couple of laps, wondered what he was saying. So he asked him about it. "I was praying," the runner answered. Pointing to his feet, he said, "I was saying, 'You pick 'em up, Lord, and I'll put 'em down.'" That athlete prayed for God's help, but he also did what he could to answer his own prayer.

When we ask God for help, we must be willing to do whatever we can, using whatever means He gives. When Hezekiah heard that he was going to die, he prayed for a miracle, and God promised to extend his life fifteen years. Then Isaiah gave instructions to place a lump of figs on the troublesome boil (2 Kings 20:5–7). God did the healing, but He used human effort and natural means.

A couple of children were walking to school one morning when it suddenly dawned on them that unless they really hurried they were going to be late. One of them suggested that they stop and pray that they wouldn't be tardy. "No," the other replied, "let's pray while we run as fast as we can."

When we ask the Lord to do something, we must also be ready to do our part. RDH

POINTS TO PONDER

How does the truth of today's reading apply to illness?

To receiving a job promotion? To social evils?

To final exams? To increasing faith?

Pray as if everything depends on God;
work as if everything depends on you.

Short and Full of Trouble

Read: Genesis 47:1–10

*Jacob said to Pharaoh, ". . . Few and evil have been
the days of the years of my life." Genesis 47:9*

J acob's life was full of trials. And as it was for the old patriarch,
so it is for us. Life buffets and restricts us, makes demands on us
that we do not want to bear. Yet even the most unjust, undeserved, and pointless suffering is an opportunity for us to respond in
such a way that our Lord can turn us into His own likeness. We can
take joy in our trials, because we know that adversity is working
to make us "perfect and complete, lacking nothing" (James 1:3–4).
But this takes time.

We want the quick fix, but there are no shortcuts that can
accomplish God's ultimate purpose for us. The only way to grow
into Christ's likeness is to submit each day to the conditions God
brings into our lives. As we accept His will and submit to His ways,
His holiness becomes ours. Gradually but inexorably, God's Spirit
begins to turn us into kinder, gentler men and women—sturdier,
stronger, more secure and sensible. The process is mysterious and
inexplicable, but it is God's way of endowing us with grace and
beauty. Progress is inevitable.

As Ruth Bell Graham puts it, may God give us grace "to bear
the heat of cleansing flame, not bitter at our lot, but mete to bear
our share of suffering and keep sweet, in Jesus' name."   DHR

Give me, Father, a purpose deep,
In joy or sorrow Thy trust to keep;
And so through trouble, care, and strife,
Glorify Thee in my daily life. —Bell

God often empties our hands to fill our hearts.

Touching Bottom

Read: Revelation 1:10–18

Jesus . . . has abolished death and brought life and immortality to light through the gospel. 2 Timothy 1:10

Crowds gathered each week to hear the soul-stirring sermons of Joseph Parker, the famous pastor of London's City Temple in the late nineteenth century. Then a crisis hit him hard. His wife died after an agonizing illness. Parker later said he would not have allowed a dog to suffer as she did. A heartbroken husband whose prayers had gone unanswered, he confessed publicly that for a week he had even denied that God existed.

But Parker's loss of faith was only temporary. From that experience he gained a stronger personal trust in Jesus's death-destroying resurrection and began to testify: "I have touched the bottom, and it is sound."

Listen to this exclamation of triumph from the risen Christ as He proclaims His victory over the grave: "Do not be afraid; I am the First and the Last. I am He who lives, and was dead, and behold, I am alive forevermore" (Revelation 1:17–18).

Death is our most venomous enemy, robbing us of joy and hope—unless the triumph of Christ's resurrection reverberates in our heart. As we believe in the mighty Victor over death, doubt is banished and light drives away the darkness.

Hold fast to that triumphant trust as you struggle through life's worst crises. VCG

Some through the waters, some through the flood,
Some through the fire, but all through the blood;
Some through great sorrow, but God gives a song
In the night season and all the day long. —Young

Because of Christ's empty tomb, we can be full of hope.

God Said That

Read: Psalm 23

You are with me; Your rod and Your staff,
they comfort me. Psalm 23:4

When my eight-year-old grandson Jacob visited me in the hospital, he came with his own custom-made "Get Well" card. It was an 8 1/2" x 11" piece of stiff white paper folded in half. On the front he had written, "Hope you feel better soon." On the inside, in large block letters, was this message:

I will be with you wherever you go.

There was no Scripture reference, so Jacob added these words: "God said that." He wanted to be sure I didn't expect *him* to be at my side during my entire hospital stay.

That added note conveyed an unintended and deeper truth that brought a smile to my face and comfort to my heart. A hospital can be a lonely place. It's a world of unfamiliar faces, first-time medical procedures, and uncertain diagnoses. But it's in just such a setting that God can quiet an anxious heart and give assurance that He'll go with you down every hall, through every new door, into any unknown future—yes, even through "the valley of the shadow of death" (Psalm 23:4).

Maybe you have had an unexpected setback or loss. Your future is unknown. Trusting Jesus as your Savior and Lord, you can be sure of this: He will go with you wherever you go. You can believe it. God said that! DJD

Whenever I feel that Christ is near,
All cares and sorrows flee;
He is my strength, my hope, my life,
He's all in all to me. —Lewis

No danger can come so near the Christian
that God is not nearer.

Have a Great Day!

Read: Psalm 118

*This is the day the Lord has made; we will rejoice
and be glad in it. Psalm 118:24*

I was in a convenience store one day, standing in line behind a man paying for his groceries. When he was finished, the clerk sent him off with a cheery "Have a great day!"

To the clerk's surprise (and mine) the man exploded in anger. "This is one of the worst days of my life," he shouted. "How can I have a great day?" And with that he stormed out of the store.

I understand the man's frustration; I too have "bad" days over which I have no control. *How can I have a great day,* I ask myself, *when it's beyond my control?* Then I remember these words: "This is the day the Lord has made" (Psalm 118:24).

The Lord has made every day, and my Father will show himself strong on my behalf today. He has control over everything in it— even the hard things that will come my way. All events have been screened through His wisdom and love, and they are opportunities for me to grow in faith. "His mercy endures forever" (v. 1). "The Lord is on my side; I will not fear" (v. 6).

Now, when people give me the parting admonition to have a great day, I reply, "That's beyond my control, but I can be grateful for whatever comes my way, and rejoice—for this is the day the Lord has made."   DHR

*When dawn announces each new day,
Before you rise up out of bed,
Rejoice—be glad and give God praise,
And thank Him for what lies ahead. —Sper*

A smile is a curve that can set things straight.

August 18

Look at the Birds

Read: Matthew 6:25–34

Look at the birds of the air. . . . Are you not
of more value than they? Matthew 6:26

When you shift your mind into neutral and just let it idle, where do your thoughts go? Do you worry about money? We are to be careful with money, but Jesus taught that we are not to be full of care about it. If you have put your faith in the Lord, you don't have to worry about life's necessities. God himself has assumed responsibility for your food and clothing—and all your needs.

When Jesus spoke of our need for food, He pointed to the birds and said, "They neither sow nor reap nor gather into barns; yet your heavenly Father feeds them. Are you not of more value than they?" (Matthew 6:26). That doesn't mean we get what we need by doing nothing. Birds must scratch and search for food. The point is, they don't worry about it.

Jesus instructed us to center our lives on God's kingdom. Then clothing, food, and drink will be ours as well. Look at it this way: Whether or not you live only for money, you'll ultimately leave it or it will leave you. But if you focus your life on God and doing His will, all these other things will be provided.

Does your concern for making money and keeping it overshadow your concern for doing God's will? If so, stop and look at the birds.   HWR

Children of the heavenly Father
Safely in His bosom gather;
Nestling bird nor star in heaven
Such a refuge e'er was given. —Berg

Poverty of purpose is far worse than poverty of purse.

No Bad News

Read: Esther 1:1–9

Come to Me, all you who labor and are heavy laden,
and I will give you rest. Matthew 11:28

The unwillingness to listen to bad news has been blamed for everything from space shuttle disasters to corporate collapses to the spread of terrorism. Lengthy studies aren't needed to determine why this happens. Bad news reveals problems; problems require solutions; solutions cost time, money, and energy we would rather spend celebrating past successes.

This isn't new to our century. In the fifth century BC, King Ahasuerus of Persia refused to allow mourners to enter his gates (Esther 4:1–2). One commentator suggests that he preferred to surround himself with people who were awed by his wealth and were eager to attend his lavish parties (1:4). His reluctance to be bothered by bad news nearly resulted in the annihilation of the Jewish people.

Contrast the leadership of Ahasuerus with that of Jesus, who said, "Come to Me, all you who labor and are heavy laden, and I will give you rest" (Matthew 11:28). Ahasuerus ruled his kingdom by allowing only happy people to enter his presence. Jesus builds His kingdom by welcoming the burdened and sorrowful into His presence. What's more, Jesus not only invites us to tell Him our bad news, He has the willingness and the power to turn our most troubling circumstances into a celebration of praise.　　　JAL

I walked life's path with worry,
Disturbed and quite unblest,
Until I trusted Jesus;
Now faith has giv'n me rest. —Bosch

The gospel is bad news to those who reject it and good news
to those who receive it.

A Brilliant Idea

Read: 2 Chronicles 16:1–13

Help us, O Lord our God, for we rest on You.
2 Chronicles 14:11

An ancient Indonesian fable tells of a turtle that could fly. He would hold on to a stick with his mouth as it was carried by geese. When the turtle heard the onlookers on the ground saying, "Aren't those geese brilliant!" his pride was so hurt that he shouted, "It was *my* idea!" Of course he lost his grip. His pride became his downfall.

For forty-one years, Asa was a strong and humble king. He brought peace and prosperity to the kingdom of Judah. During the early years of Asa's reign he prayed, "Lord, it is nothing for You to help, whether with many or with those who have no power; help us, O Lord our God, for we rest on You" (2 Chronicles 14:11).

But toward the end of his reign, when the army of the northern kingdom of Israel confronted him, Asa sought help from the king of Syria instead of from God. Because of his foolishness, his rule weakened and his nation experienced wars. What went wrong? Proud of past achievements, Asa had forgotten to depend on the Lord, so the Lord was no longer showing "himself strong" on Asa's behalf (16:9).

God is still looking for those who will allow Him to show himself strong in their lives. Living a humble, God-dependent life is truly a brilliant idea!   AL

We must depend upon our God
With deep humility,
Lest pride should rob us of His strength
And bring futility. —DJD

No one is stronger than the one who depends on God.

August 21

Wounded Oysters

Read: Genesis 41:46–57

*God has caused me to be fruitful in the land
of my affliction. Genesis 41:52*

When seemingly needless suffering invades our lives, we often ask ourselves, "Who needs all this grief?" But consider, for a moment, the origin of pearls.

Each pearl is formed by an oyster's internal response to a wound caused by an irritant, such as a grain of sand. Resources of repair rush to the injured area. The final result is a lustrous pearl. Something beautiful is created that would have been impossible without the wound.

In today's Bible reading, we see Joseph in a position of influence, a position God soon used to feed surrounding nations and Joseph's family during famine. But how did he become influential? It began with a wound—being sold into slavery (Genesis 39)—which produced a pearl of usefulness. Because Joseph drew on God's resources when humiliated, he became better, not bitter. He named his second son Ephraim, which means "twice fruitful," and he said, "God has caused me to be fruitful in the land of my affliction" (41:52).

Author Paul E. Billheimer says of Joseph, "If human pity could have rescued him from the sad part of his life, the glorious part that followed would have been lost." So if you're suffering, remember: No wounds, no pearls!   JY

If we accept adversity,
Enduring every pain,
Then we will learn what we should know;
Our grief will turn to gain. —Sper

Adversities are often blessings in disguise.

August 22

The Day the Sun Didn't Shine

Read: Psalm 103

*Bless the Lord, O my soul, and forget not
all His benefits. Psalm 103:2*

We often take God's blessings for granted until they are taken
from us. Then we recognize how important even the most
common gifts of God really are.

There's a legend about a day the sun didn't rise. At six in the
morning it was dark. At seven it was still night. Noon came and it
was like midnight. By four in the afternoon, people flocked to the
churches to beg God for the sun.

The next morning, huge crowds gathered outdoors to face the
eastern sky. When the first rays of sunlight pushed open the door
of the morning, the people burst into cheers and praised God for
the sun.

The psalmist knew he couldn't possibly remember all of God's
benefits to him. He was distressed that he might forget them all, so
he took his sluggish soul in hand, shook it, and urged it to consider
at least some of the good gifts God gave to him.

Because God's goodness is as constant as the sun, we are in danger of forgetting what He showers on us each day. If we count our
blessings one by one, we'll never get finished. But if we jot down
a list of ten or twenty gifts God gives us each day, something will
happen to our hearts.

Let's try it and find out for ourselves. HWR

If you want to be rich, count all the things you have that
money can't buy.

Source of Hope

Read: Lamentations 3:19–41

Through the Lord's mercies we are not consumed.
Lamentations 3:22

What good is faith when all seems lost? I've asked that penetrating question in my life, and not long ago I received a letter from a mom who has asked it as well.

She told me that she and her husband set out in their marriage to seek God's will for their lives and entrust their future to Him. Then their second son was born with Down syndrome. Their initial response was "grief, shock, and disbelief." Yet the same day he was born, God used Philippians 4:6–7 to put peace in their hearts and give them an undying love for their precious son. It says: "Let your requests be made known to God; and the peace of God, which surpasses all understanding, will guard your hearts."

But their days in the desert were not over. Nine years later, their fourth son was diagnosed with cancer. Before he reached his third birthday, he was gone. Shock, pain, and sadness again broke into their world. And again, they found help from God and His Word. "When the grief overwhelms us," says this mom, "we turn to God's Word and His gift of eternal life through Jesus Christ."

When life's troubles hit us like a tidal wave, we can remember that God's compassions never fail (Lamentations 3:22). He can give us the hope we need.   DB

Feeling hopeless reminds us that we are helpless without God.

The Worry Box

Read: Philippians 4:1–9

Do not worry about your life. Matthew 6:25

I heard about a woman who kept a box in her kitchen that she called her Worry Box. Every time something troubled her, she would write it down on a piece of paper and put it in the box. She resolved not to think about her problems as long as they were in the box. This enabled the woman to put her troubles completely out of mind. She knew they could be dealt with later.

Occasionally she would take out a slip of paper and review the concern written on it. Because she had not been drained by anxiety, she was relaxed and better able to find the solution to her problem. Many times she discovered that a specific worry no longer existed.

Writing your worries on paper and putting them in a box may be helpful, but how much better it is to place them in the hands of God. Worry robs us of joy, drains us of energy, stunts our spiritual growth, and dishonors God. Jesus said, "Do not worry about tomorrow, for tomorrow will worry about its own things. Sufficient for the day is its own trouble" (Matthew 6:34).

Let's believe the Lord's promises and trust Him to meet our needs. Placing our problems in His hands is far better than putting them in a worry box. RDH

Never a trial that He is not there,
Never a burden that He does not bear;
Never a sorrow that He does not share—
Moment by moment, I'm under His care. —Whittle

When we put our cares in God's hands,
He puts His peace in our heart.

What We Cannot Lose

Read: Psalm 92:12–15

Even to your old age, I am He, and even to gray hairs
I will carry you! I have made, and I will bear; even
I will carry, and will deliver you. Isaiah 46:4

Years ago I heard about an elderly gentleman who was suffering from the first stages of dementia. He lamented the fact that he often forgot about God. "Don't you worry," said a good friend, "He will never forget you."

Growing old is perhaps the hardest task we have to face in this life. As the saying goes, "Getting old is not for sissies."

Mainly, growing old is about losses. We devote most of our early life to acquiring things, but they are merely things we will lose as we age. We lose our strength, our looks, our friends, our job. We may lose our wealth, our home, our health, our spouse, our independence, and perhaps the greatest loss of all, our sense of dignity and self-worth.

But there is one thing that you and I will never lose—the love of God. "Even to your old age, I am He," God said to the prophet, "and even to gray hairs I will carry you! I have made, and I will bear; even I will carry, and will deliver you" (Isaiah 46:4).

"The righteous shall flourish like a palm tree," wrote the songwriter (Psalm 92:12). "Those who are planted in the house of the Lord shall flourish in the courts of our God. They shall still bear fruit in old age" (vv. 13–14).   DHR

Jesus loves me, this I know,
Though my hair is white as snow;
Though my sight is growing dim,
Still He bids me trust in Him. —Warner

God's love never grows old.

Count It All Joy

Read: James 1:2–12

Blessed is the man who endures temptation; for when he has been
approved, he will receive the crown of life. James 1:12

A pastor placed this sign on his door: "If you have problems, come in and tell me all about them. If you don't have any problems, come in and tell me how you avoid them."

What do we do when problems come unannounced and with great intensity? James told us to "count it all joy," because trials do not happen without a reason. He said, "The testing of your faith produces patience. But let patience have its perfect work, that you may be perfect and complete" (James 1:3–4). Armed with this understanding, our prayer changes from asking God "why" to thanking Him for what He is doing.

Having endured many trials and facing a new struggle with cancer, *Our Daily Bread* author Joanie Yoder shared her thoughts in a letter: "I have relinquished my destiny to God's will. Nothing, praise God, not even cancer, can thwart His will. I may have cancer, but cancer doesn't have me—God alone has me. So in this light, I would value your prayers that Christ may be magnified in my body, whether by life or by death."

Trials are unavoidable and unpredictable, and they come in an unimaginable variety. Knowing that our sovereign God will walk with us and use trials to deepen our maturity, we can count them "all joy." AL

Heavenly peace, divinest comfort,
Here by faith in Him to dwell!
For I know, whatever befall me,
Jesus doeth all things well. —Crosby

We can endure trials in this life because of the joys
in the life to come.

Walking Away

Read: Exodus 33:12–23

*My Presence will go with you, and I will
give you rest. Exodus 33:14*

After winning a bronze medal in the 2004 Olympics in Athens, wrestler Rulon Gardner took off his shoes, placed them in the center of the mat, and walked away in tears. Through that symbolic act, Gardner announced his retirement from the sport which had defined his life for many years.

Times of walking away come to all of us, and they can be emotionally wrenching. A loved one "walks away" in death. A child moves away from home. We leave a job or a community and it feels as if we've left everything behind. But when we know the Lord, we never have to walk into an unknown future alone.

It's worth pausing to reflect on how much the children of Israel walked away from when Moses led them out of Egypt. They left the heavy burden of slavery, but they also left everything stable and predictable they had ever known. Later, when the Lord told Moses, "My Presence will go with you, and I will give you rest" (Exodus 33:14), Moses replied, "If Your Presence does not go with us, do not bring us up from here" (v. 15).

During our most difficult times, our stability comes from the presence and peace of God. Because He goes with us, we can walk into the future with confidence.   DCM

Every loss leaves a space that only God's presence can fill.

August 28

Facing Your Enemies

Read: Psalm 27

Though an army may encamp against me,
my heart shall not fear. Psalm 27:3

During the U.S. Civil War, fierce fighting was taking place near Moorefield, West Virginia. Because the town was close to enemy lines, it would be controlled one day by Union troops, and the next by Confederates.

In the heart of the town lived an old woman. According to the testimony of a Presbyterian minister, one morning several enemy soldiers knocked on her door and demanded breakfast. She asked them in and said she would prepare something for them.

When the food was ready, she said, "It's my custom to read the Bible and pray before breakfast. I hope you won't mind." They consented, so she took her Bible, opened it at random, and began to read Psalm 27. "The Lord is my light and my salvation; whom shall I fear? The Lord is the strength of my life; of whom shall I be afraid?" (v. 1). She read on through the last verse: "Wait on the Lord; be of good courage, and He shall strengthen your heart" (v. 14). When she finished reading, she said, "Let us pray." While she was praying, she heard sounds of the men moving around in the room. When she said "amen" and looked up, the soldiers were gone.

Meditate on Psalm 27. If you are facing enemies, God will use His Word to help you.   HWR

When you know the Lord is near,
Face the enemy without fear;
Though an army may surround you,
You are safe—God's arms around you. —Hess

Let your fears drive you to your heavenly Father.

Rock Bottom

Read: Psalm 119:65–72

*It is good for me that I have been afflicted,
that I may learn Your statutes. Psalm 119:71*

I was in my early thirties, a dedicated wife and mother, a Christian worker at my husband's side. Yet inwardly I found myself on a trip nobody wants to take—the trip downward. I was heading for that certain sort of breakdown that most of us resist, the breakdown of my stubborn self-sufficiency.

Finally I experienced the odd relief of hitting rock bottom, where I made an unexpected discovery: The rock on which I had been thrown was none other than Christ himself. Cast on Him alone, I was in a position to rebuild the rest of my life, this time as a God-dependent person rather than the self-dependent person I had been. My rock-bottom experience became a turning point and one of the most vital spiritual developments of my life.

Most people feel anything but spiritual when they hit bottom. Their misery is often reinforced by Christians who take a very shortsighted view of what the sufferer is going through, and why. But our heavenly Father is well pleased with what He intends to bring out of such a painful process.

A person who knows the secret of the God-dependent life can say, "It is good for me that I have been afflicted, that I may learn Your statutes" (Psalm 119:71). JY

When a Christian hits rock bottom,
he finds that Christ is a firm foundation.

August 30

Why Me?

Read: Luke 17:11–19

One of them, when he saw that he was healed, returned,
and with a loud voice glorified God. Luke 17:15

A few years ago, an unkempt, poorly adjusted youth named Tim (not his real name) was converted to Christ in an evangelistic crusade. Several days later, still unkempt but bathed in the love of Christ, he was sent to my home so that I could help him find a good church. And so it was that he began attending with me.

Though Tim needed and received much loving help in personal grooming and basic social graces, one characteristic has remained unchanged—his untamed love for his Savior.

One Sunday after church Tim rushed to my side, looking somewhat perplexed. He exclaimed, "Why me? I keep asking myself, why me?" Oh, no, I thought, he's become another complaining Christian. Then with arms outstretched, he went on to say, "Out of all the people in the world who are greater and smarter than I am, why did God choose me?" With that he joyfully clapped his hands.

Over the years I've heard many Christians, including myself, ask "Why me?" during tough times. But Tim is the first one I've heard ask that question when talking about God's blessings. Many were converted the same night as Tim, but I wonder how many among them have humbly asked, "Why me?" May we ask it often.   JY

I know not why God's wondrous grace
To me He hath made known;
Nor why, unworthy, Christ in love
Redeemed me for His own. —Whittle

Gratitude should be a continuous attitude.

August 31

Sing to the Lord

Read: Psalm 30

*Weeping may endure for a night, but joy
comes in the morning. Psalm 30:5*

It's as though a sinister stranger comes knocking on your door.
You must let him in, for he knocks insistently and will not go
away. He is sorrow personified.

You believe no one sees your tears and you feel all alone—but
God sees them and He understands. "All night I make my bed
swim; I drench my couch with my tears," David said in Psalm 6.
"The Lord has heard the voice of my weeping" (vv. 6, 8). "You
number my wanderings; put my tears into Your bottle; are they not
in Your book?" (56:8). Though "weeping may endure for a night,"
it is a transient houseguest, for "joy comes in the morning" (30:5).

We remember, as David did, that God's love and favor last for a
lifetime. He has promised never to leave us nor forsake us. When
God's love comes into our thoughts, our feelings of sorrow and
dread flee. Our mourning is turned into dancing, our garments
of sackcloth and sorrow are stripped away and we are girded with
gladness. We can rise to greet the day with shouts of ringing praise
for His mercy, guidance, and protection. We rejoice in His holy
name (30:11–12).

No matter our circumstances, let's sing to the Lord once again!

DHR

*Come, Thou Fount of every blessing,
Tune my heart to sing Thy grace;
Streams of mercy, never ceasing,
Call for songs of loudest praise. —Robinson*

Praise is the voice of a soul set free.

September 1

Fleeting Success

Read: Ecclesiastes 4:13–16

*Set your mind on things above, not on things
on the earth. Colossians 3:2*

Having many friends and being rich are great blessings, but popularity and success do not guarantee a happy life. To make this point, Solomon called attention to an elderly king who ignored the wishes of his subjects and was replaced. His young successor was popular at first, but he also fell into disfavor. Solomon concluded, "Surely this also is vanity and grasping for the wind" (Ecclesiastes 4:16).

Life at the top is fleeting. Presidents and prime ministers may have extremely high approval ratings for a while, but they don't last. About twenty years ago I knew several top executives who were highly successful because of their winning personalities and outstanding abilities. Yet they lost their high-salaried positions because they could not keep up with the rapid changes their jobs demanded. Today, because of company mergers and corporate downsizing, many of their replacements have also lost their positions.

How we view popularity and success depends on what we value most. If we set our hearts on earthly things, we will eventually be disappointed. But if we set our hearts on Christ and live for Him, we will find that He is faithful to provide for our every need. Many have made this discovery. Have you? HVL

The master key to success is knowing the Master.

September 2

An Eternal Perspective

Read: Colossians 3:1–7

Set your mind on things above, not on things on the earth.
Colossians 3:2

In the movie *Gladiator*, General Maximus Decimus Meridius seeks to stir his cavalry to fight well in the imminent battle against Germania. Addressing his troops, he challenges them to give their very best. He makes this profound statement: "What we do in life echoes in eternity."

These words from a fictional military leader convey a powerful concept that is of particular significance to believers in Christ. We are not just taking up time and space on a rock that's floating in the universe. We are here with the opportunity to make an eternal difference with our lives.

Jesus himself said, "Lay up for yourselves treasures in heaven, where neither moth nor rust destroys and where thieves do not break in and steal" (Matthew 6:20). Having the perspective of living for eternity can make all the difference in this world.

How can we learn to set our minds "on things above"? (Colossians 3:2). A good way to begin is to discover what our eternal God values. Throughout the pages of the Bible, He reminds us that He values people above possessions and our character above our performance. Those are the truths that last forever. Embracing them can bring an eternal perspective to our daily living.   BC

FOR FURTHER THOUGHT

What is your purpose for living?

What we do in this life echoes in eternity.

Mailbox Faith

Read: Hebrews 11:1–6

Faith is the substance of things hoped for, the evidence of things not seen. Hebrews 11:1

Whenever I mail a letter, it's an exercise of trust. Let me explain what I mean. When I write to a distant friend, it's impossible to deliver the letter myself. I need the help of the postal service. But for them to do their part, I have to drop my letter in the mailbox first. I can't hang on to it. I have to place it in the mail slot and let go. Then I must trust the postal service to take over until my letter is delivered to my friend's home. Although I can't see what happens to it, my faith in the postal service assures me that my letter is as good as there!

Likewise, whenever we're faced with a problem, our faith is challenged. Knowing that it's impossible to resolve the difficulty ourselves, we recognize our need of God's help. First, though, we must go to Him in prayer. Until that moment, we're still holding on to our problem. We know the situation won't get resolved until we let go and commit it into God's hands. Once we let go, we then must trust God to take over until the problem is resolved in His way. Although we can't see what He's doing, our faith is "the evidence of things not seen" (Hebrews 11:1), the assurance that His work is as good as done!

Have you exercised trust in Him today?   JY

Help us, Lord, to give our burdens
To Your tender, loving care;
Grant us faith to trust You fully,
Knowing that each one You bear. —DJD

Trusting God turns problems into opportunities.

Let Up on the Throttle

Read: Mark 6:30–32

Come aside by yourselves to a deserted place
and rest a while. Mark 6:31

The Red Baron and his counterparts in World War I flew planes that were not equipped with throttles for slowing down or speeding up. As you can imagine, constant full speed took its toll on the life of the engines, and takeoffs and landings were always an adventure. Veteran missionary pilot Bob Griffin described those WWI aircraft in his book *Cleared for Takeoff.*

In contrast to those planes, Bob flew an aircraft with a throttle and a tough Lycoming engine that came with these instructions: "Takeoff power (full power) may be used for only a maximum of five minutes." The pilot was instructed to back off from full power as soon as possible. Trouble was ahead for those who ignored the warning.

God did not create us to run at full speed all the time. We may race for a while with open throttle through our Christian lives, packing our time with one activity after another, but if we don't slow down occasionally we are headed for burnout or a crash landing.

During an especially busy time, Jesus urged His disciples to "come aside... and rest a while" (Mark 6:31). We too need times of rest not only for physical renewal but also for spiritual refreshment through reflection, Bible reading, and prayer.

Are you running at full speed? Let up on the throttle.   DCE

If our body, soul, and spirit
Are to function at their best,
Time is needed for renewal—
Time for leisure, time for rest. —DJD

Come to Me, all you who labor and are heavy laden, and I
will give you rest. —Matthew 11:28

Guided Tour

Read: Genesis 24:10–27

*In all your ways acknowledge Him, and He
shall direct your paths. Proverbs 3:6*

Former college basketball coach Don Callan decided to venture
off on his own in Nepal—but he found he wasn't really alone.

Don and a missions leader were in Nepal to look for ways to
assist the people of that land. While his colleague took care of some
business in Katmandu, Don flew to Pokhara to investigate that
beautiful city in the heart of Nepal. He was praying for God's guidance as he went.

Don had been given the name of a man in Pokhara who could
serve as a guide, but no one knew he would be visiting there. Not
knowing the city, he randomly chose a hotel and took a taxi from
the airport to its location. When he arrived, he walked into the
hotel lobby feeling unsure of himself. He didn't know anyone and
couldn't speak the language. A group of men were standing at the
front desk, so Don ventured over to them and said, "I'm looking for
Jeevan." What a surprise when one of the men said, "I'm Jeevan."
Obviously, God had directed Don's path.

We do not always see God's guidance so clearly, but this story
reassures us that He does direct our lives. He led Isaac to Rebekah
(Genesis 24), and He leads us as well. As we walk by faith on our
earthly journey, we can trust God because He is our guide.   DB

I may not see the path ahead,
Or find my way with ease,
But Jesus leads me by the hand—
He knows the way, He sees. —Adams

God does not ask you to go where He does not lead.

A Test of Faith

Read: Genesis 22:1–14

God will provide for Himself the lamb. Genesis 22:8

When I was a boy, I disliked the story of Abraham going to Mount Moriah to sacrifice his son Isaac. Why would God tell Abraham to do such a thing? I was an only son, and I didn't want that happening to me! My parents assured me that God was testing Abraham's faith. And he passed that test. Even with the knife in his hand, Abraham believed God (Genesis 22:8–10). He had learned that the Lord could be trusted.

It is easy to make a profession of faith. But the real test comes when God asks us to lay our dearest treasures on the line. As with Abraham, the issue becomes one of obedience. A businesswoman lost a high-paying job because she wouldn't compromise her standards. And a pastor was driven from his church when he obeyed God's Word and spoke out against racism in his congregation.

Shouldn't these people have been rewarded when they did the right thing? Faith meets its toughest test when we feel that the Lord has not rewarded our faithfulness.

You may be faced with giving back to God something you feel He has given you. Learn to see this test as an opportunity to demonstrate your faith in the One who always keeps His promises— even when you don't understand. HWR

Be still, my soul—the Lord is on thy side!
Bear patiently the cross of grief or pain;
Leave to thy God to order and provide—
In every change He faithful will remain. —von Schlegel

Faith is the ability to see God in the dark.

The Gloom Index

Read: Acts 16:16–25

*At midnight Paul and Silas were praying and
singing hymns to God. Acts 16:25*

Gray skies and blue moods—the two seem to go together. In fact, some weather forecasters describe the amount of cloudy days a region can expect during its winter season as "the gloom index."

Other factors might be figured into a gloom index. Think, for instance, of what Paul and Silas, those two first-century coworkers for Christ, endured (Acts 16). Any one of their troubles was enough to ruin the sunniest day.

Try to imagine the frustration of dealing with greedy profiteers who had turned a demon-possessed girl into a sideshow (vv. 16–17). Think about the pain of confronting an angry mob and furious judges (v. 22), of receiving a whipping and imprisonment (v. 23), and of having your feet locked in stocks (v. 24). How's that for a gloomy atmosphere?

Paul and Silas were able, though, to rise above their circumstances (v. 25) because they were motivated by a desire to obey God and spread the message of Christ.

We too can rise above the gray skies of discouraging circumstances by relying on the Holy Spirit. We can find encouragement and hope in God's Son, our Lord and Savior, Jesus Christ. We can overcome the gloom index. —MD

*God, give us wings to rise above
The clouds of trial that block the sun,
To soar above gray skies and see
The love and goodness of Your Son. —Sper*

No day is dark when you live in the light of God's Son.

When Trouble Works for Us

Read: 2 Corinthians 4:7–18

Our light affliction . . . is working for us a far more exceeding and eternal weight of glory. 2 Corinthians 4:17

Is there something that seems to be working against you today—time, health, money, opportunity, people? Sometimes it's easy to feel that everything and everyone is against us. We know we're supposed to trust God, but it's hard to understand why He would allow our circumstances to become so difficult and confusing.

A friend of mine who has experienced many setbacks offered a fresh look at the role of our difficulties. He emphasized a single word in a familiar passage: "Our light affliction, which is but for a moment, is working *for* us a far more exceeding and eternal weight of glory" (2 Corinthians 4:17, emphasis added).

"We think our afflictions are working *against* us," my friend said, "but God says they are working *for* us. They're producing a glory that will last forever. Compared to our trials, the glory is always greater. That's why we don't lose heart."

From God's perspective, our deepest disappointments and sorrows are "but for a moment." It's difficult for us to accept this while we are in the midst of our trials, but we can trust the word of our kind and loving Father.

It's amazing to know that God can take the things that seem to be *against* us and cause them to work *for* us. By faith, we can embrace His perspective today.   DCM

God can weave the thorns of life into a crown of glory.

September 9

Consider Your Ways!

Read: Haggai 1:1–11

Thus says the Lord of hosts: "Consider your ways!" Haggai 1:7

How long has it been since you read Haggai? If you're like me, it's been a while. Why not take a few minutes and read all 38 verses of this book. Look for the word *consider*. It occurs four times (1:5, 7; 2:15, 18).

God spoke through Haggai to the Israelites who had returned from exile. He said, in effect, "Think about it. You don't have enough to eat. Your clothes don't keep you warm. You're not prospering. I have commanded you to rebuild My house. When you obey, My blessing will return."

That message applies to us as well. When everything seems to be going wrong, the first step in solving our problems may be to consider our ways. Let me illustrate.

During one semester in college, my grades dropped dramatically, I got in trouble in the dorm, and I was called into the dean's office. I went back to my room and thought seriously about my situation. The problem was not schoolwork or the guys in the dorm. I was the problem. When I changed my attitude and my behavior, things began to go better.

Not all our troubles are of our own making. But when difficulties arise, it's wise to consider our ways. Like the people of Haggai's day, we may find that our disobedience is blocking God's blessing.

DCE

So many problems come our way
Because down deep inside
Rebellion, envy, selfishness
Are what we try to hide. —DJD

The way of obedience is the only way of blessing.

Who's in Control?

Read: Romans 8:1–14

As many as are led by the Spirit of God,
these are sons of God. Romans 8:14

By nature we all have a desire to control our world. From infancy we turn to our own independent way, trying to control circumstances, the future, people—and even God if we could. Since we can't, we end up frustrated, hostile, and critical.

Our need to be in control is rooted in excessive self-love. For example, when people we love are sick, we often want them to get well so we can get some rest and not have to worry about them. "Boil it down to this," a Bible teacher once said, "we are madly in love with ourselves!"

In Romans 8, the apostle Paul called this self-centeredness "the flesh." By nature we live as if we owe the flesh our obedience. Paul reminded us in verse 12 that this isn't so. He then offered an effective alternative: We can be led and controlled by God's Spirit (v. 14). We may be afraid to give up control of our lives to God, but we needn't be. Human control shackles us; God's control gives us freedom. Human control insists on immediate results; God's control allows for a lifelong process of change.

Are you "madly in love" with yourself? Why not turn the controls of your life over to God? Ask Him to change you and help you to love Him and others. JY

The Spirit wants to fill us with
His blessing and His grace
If we will let Him take control
And have His rightful place. —Sherbert

To be under Christ's control is to have true freedom.

Carry Me!

Read: Deuteronomy 1:26–33

You saw how the Lord your God carried you,
as a man carries his son. Deuteronomy 1:31

Kelsey's daddy was reading to her, just as he did nearly every night before she went to sleep. She had picked the zoo book, and to her active imagination it was as if she and Daddy were there. She looked happily at the pages with the giraffes, zebras, and elephants. But when they got to the page with the grizzly bears, she said, "You would have to carry me." She said the same thing when she saw the gorillas on the next page. Curious, her dad asked her why he would have to carry her. "Because I'd be scared," came her straightforward reply.

When the Israelites saw that the fierce Amorites and Anakim were in the land ahead of them, they were afraid. So Moses, reminding them of how God helped them in the wilderness, said, "You saw how the Lord your God carried you." He would carry them again.

We can be certain that the Lord will do the same for us when we are afraid. When the scary times come, when we are called on to do the hard things life demands, God will lift us up and carry us along. He gives us His strength in Christ.

Is there something frightening in your life? Are there some difficult things you know you have to do? Ask your heavenly Father to see you through. He will hold you in His loving arms and carry you.   DCE

Beneath His watchful eye
His saints securely dwell;
That hand which bears all nature up
Shall guard His children well. —Doddridge

With God's arms beneath us, we need not fear
what lies before us.

The First Step

Read: Deuteronomy 2:16–25

I have begun to give Sihon and his land over to you.
Begin to possess it. Deuteronomy 2:31

There are many ways to handle an overwhelming task. We may keep putting it off, hoping that God will miraculously take care of it. Or we can take the first step in the right direction.

After forty years in the wilderness, Moses was told that it was time for the people to take possession of the land God had promised them. The first order of business was to decide what to do about a king named Sihon who stood between the Israelites and the land of Canaan. God's command was, "Begin to possess it, and engage him in battle" (Deuteronomy 2:24). God certainly could have eliminated Sihon without anyone's help, but He commanded His people to take the first step.

The same is often true with us. Difficult circumstances or broken relationships seem to defy solution. When they persist for months or years, we may feel that nothing we do will make a difference. But the Lord says, "Begin." We must make the first move—speak a kind word, ask forgiveness, pay some of what we owe. We must be the initiators.

Joy lies not only in attaining some distant goal but also in walking with our loving God, who says, "I have begun to give... Begin to possess it" (v. 31).

Is there a first step you should take today?   DCM

Nothing can be accomplished until we take the first step.

Turning Evil into Good

Read: 1 Thessalonians 2:13–18

We wanted to come to you . . . but Satan hindered us.
1 Thessalonians 2:18

The apostle Paul told the believers at Thessalonica that he and his coworkers wanted to visit them but Satan hindered them (1 Thessalonians 2:18).

Does it disturb you to read that a child of God can be blocked by the devil from doing what he believes to be the will of God? If it does, remember that nothing happens without God's knowledge, nor apart from His direct or permissive will. The Lord can take any deed, whether of Satan or man, and turn it around for His own purposes and glory. The devil's hindering of Paul, for example, resulted in great benefit to Christians! Because the apostle couldn't speak to the Thessalonians personally, he wrote them a letter. This portion of the Bible has been a source of rich blessing and comfort to believers down through the centuries.

I'm reminded of Joseph's response to his brothers who had sold him into slavery. They feared that he would seek revenge, but he said, "You meant evil against me; but God meant it for good" (Genesis 50:20).

What a comfort to know that nothing happens apart from the will of our heavenly Father! He is all-wise, all-knowing, all-powerful. Under God's sovereign control, evil can be turned around to accomplish His good purposes. RDH

God can bring showers of blessing out of storms of adversity.

September 14

What's Ahead?

Read: 1 Thessalonians 4:13–18

God will wipe away every tear from their eyes. Revelation 21:4

If we consider what people thought years ago about life in the future, we realize how hard it is to know what's ahead. For instance, what if everyone had believed the patent office worker who, in 1899, said, "Everything that can be invented has been invented"? Or what if folks in the nineteenth century had believed this memo from Western Union: "The telephone has too many shortcomings to be seriously considered as a means of communication"?

Predictions about the future are usually bad guesses. When I was a kid, I read science magazines that said that by the end of the twentieth century we would all be flying around in air-cars and living in domed houses.

One source for what's ahead, however, is never wrong. It's God's Word! The Bible has reassuring words for those who "believe that Jesus died and rose again" (1 Thessalonians 4:14). The apostle Paul gave us the comforting words that "the Lord Himself will descend from heaven with a shout" (v. 16). Christ will return to gather together all those, both living and dead, who have placed their faith in Him. "And thus we shall always be with the Lord," wrote Paul (v. 17). No matter what's ahead for us, we may with certainty "comfort one another with these words" (v. 18). DB

We can trust our all-knowing God for the unknown future.

An Answer for Everything

Read: Philippians 4:15–20

*My God shall supply all your need according to His riches
in glory by Christ Jesus. Philippians 4:19*

D ad, can I have ten dollars?" "Dad, can you help me with my
math?" "Dad, what's the capital of Maine?" "Dad, why can't
we get another car?" "Dad, I didn't make the team."

The questions and requests and needs of my children seem endless. Whether they are in junior high, in high school, in college, or
married, they never stop needing help.

Often I can provide the help they need, but sometimes I am
unable to come up with the answer or the solution. As much as I
would like to, I don't have an answer or the resources for everything. But I know who does. I know that God supplies all of our
needs (Philippians 4:19). And He knows when our requests are gen-
uine needs, or when He must redirect our thinking instead.

Consider this: When we think we are too tired to go on, Jesus
says, "I will give you rest" (Matthew 11:28). When we think no
one cares, Jesus says He loves us (John 15:12–13). When we can't
figure things out, God says He will guide us (Psalm 48:14). When
we need forgiveness, God says He will forgive us if we confess our
sins (1 John 1:9).

God is our heavenly Father, who wants us to come to Him with
our requests. He wants us to listen to Him speak through His Word.
He has an answer for everything.   DB

For answered prayer we thank You, Lord,
We know You're always there
To hear us when we call on You;
We're grateful for Your care. —DB

God never tires of our asking.

Frustrated or Content?

Read: Ecclesiastes 2:17–26

*I hated all my labor in which I had toiled
under the sun. Ecclesiastes 2:18*

King Solomon, who had studied diligently and worked hard for worthwhile earthly goals, realized that at his death his fortune would go to people who had not worked for it and might misuse it. This caused him to become resentful because of all the "sorrowful" days and sleepless nights (2:23) he had invested. He's not alone in feeling this way.

A highly successful lawyer told me he often wonders why he works so hard. He said his sons and daughters had been misusing his money and making a mess of their lives. He knows they will probably waste everything he leaves them. Another man who had worked hard and managed his money well said sadly, "All my hard work! And my kids can hardly wait for me to die."

Solomon, however, did not remain in this dejected state. He found meaning and satisfaction through faith in God. He said that inner contentment is a gift of God to His children. This enables them to enjoy the fruit of their labor (v. 24). God replaces frustration with contentment!

The more room we give to God in our lives, the more we will have "wisdom and knowledge and joy" (v. 26). Paul summed it up this way: "Godliness with contentment is great gain" (1 Timothy 6:6).

HVL

*O Lord, help us to be content
With all that we possess;
And may we show our gratitude
With heartfelt thankfulness. —Sper*

Contentment is the soil in which true joy thrives.

Be All There

Read: Jeremiah 29:4–14

Whatever you do, do it heartily,
as to the Lord. Colossians 3:23

A friend of mine has a view of life that is summed up in one of his favorite sayings: "Wherever you are, be all there." That is, whatever your situation, be the very best you can be.

During his college years, my friend got a job one summer at a resort. He expected it to be exciting, but when he arrived he was told that he would be washing dishes. He could see only two options—leave and be happy, or stay and be miserable. But a friend encouraged him to consider a third option: Stay and maintain the right attitude, then watch for positive results.

He decided to stay and be the best dishwasher he could be, concluding that he was really working for the Lord (Colossians 3:22–23). As a result, even in washing dishes, he was "all there."

In today's Scripture reading, God told the people of Israel, who were captive in Babylon, to "seek the peace of the city," and to "pray to the Lord for it; for in its peace you will have peace" (Jeremiah 29:7). Instead of sitting around lamenting their fate and wishing they were somewhere else, they were told by the Lord to be faithful where He had sent them.

We can't always choose our circumstances in life. We may not be able to change our job or location. Our situation may be difficult. But we can "be all there."　　　　　　　　　　　　　DCM

Your work for God will always count,
Although it may be small;
For He marks well your faithfulness
When you have given all. —DJD

Wherever you are, be all there for God.

What Is Your "Set Point"?

Read: Psalm 4:1–8

You have put gladness in my heart. Psalm 4:7

David Lykken, emeritus professor at the University of Minnesota, has developed what he calls a "set point" theory of happiness. He contends that most people return to their previous level of happiness within six months to a year after dramatic events like the sorrow of losing a loved one or the thrill of moving into a dream home. He calls that original reference point of happiness their "set point."

The Christian, however, has a different kind of "set point"— one that does not depend on the normal highs and lows of human experience. The Bible tells us to find our joy and sense of well being in the unchanging God rather than in our changing circumstances. The psalmist David praised the Lord, saying, "You have put gladness in my heart, more than in the season that their grain and wine increased" (4:7). He had a source of joy that was not tied to economic prosperity. In fact, the gladness God gave him was greater than that from any financial windfall.

We will have the same experience as the psalmist when we stop saying, "I would be happier if…" and begin affirming, "I am thankful to God because . . ." Joy that is centered in our unchanging God, no matter what our circumstances, should be the Christian's "set point." DCM

Now none but Christ can satisfy,
None other name for me;
There's love and life and lasting joy,
Lord Jesus, found in Thee. —McGranahan

To know lasting happiness, we must get to know Jesus.

When Life Goes Bad

Read: 1 Samuel 30:1–6

David strengthened himself in the Lord his God. 1 Samuel 30:6

Everything looked bleak to David and his men when they arrived at Ziklag (1 Samuel 30:1–6). The Amalekites had attacked the city and taken their wives and children captive. The men were so discouraged that they wept until they had no more energy. And David, their leader, was "greatly distressed" because the people were contemplating stoning him (v. 6).

In the end, David's army rescued their families and defeated the Amalekites. But the story takes a great turn even before that when "David strengthened himself in the Lord his God" (v. 6). Other translations use the words *encouraged* or *refreshed*.

The text doesn't say exactly how David did this. But it makes me wonder, *In what ways can we strengthen, encourage, or refresh ourselves in the Lord when we're feeling discouraged?*

First, we can remember what God has done. We can list the ways He has cared for us in the past, and how He has provided for us or answered a prayer request.

Second, we can remember what God has promised. "Be strong and of good courage; . . . for the Lord your God is with you wherever you go" (Joshua 1:9).

Like David, let's learn to strengthen ourselves in the Lord, and then let's leave the rest with Him.   AC

Our greatest strength is often shown in our ability to stand still and trust God.

True Satisfaction

Read: Ecclesiastes 5:8–12

*By humility and the fear of the Lord are riches
and honor and life. Proverbs 22:4*

Becoming rich and famous does not guarantee contentment. If it did, multimillionaire athletes would not jeopardize their careers by using illicit drugs. If it did, a wealthy lawyer would not have tearfully told me that he would gladly trade everything he had for a change in the behavior of his sons. If it did, the occurrence of multiple marriages among celebrities would not be commonplace. Obviously, contentment must come from a source other than wealth and fame.

In Ecclesiastes 5, Solomon said that because sinful people rule the world, we shouldn't be surprised when the poor are oppressed and when justice and righteousness are denied (vv. 8–9). The life of those who love money is not as rosy as it seems. They are never satisfied with what they have, and they face the emptiness of watching other people consume their riches (vv. 10–11). The humble laborer, content with little, can sleep soundly, while the rich man lies awake at night worrying about his money (v. 12).

How about you? Are you frustrated or satisfied? Paul wrote that we are "not to be haughty, nor to trust in uncertain riches but in the living God, who gives us richly all things to enjoy" (1 Timothy 6:17). Only when we trust in the Lord will we find true and lasting satisfaction.   HVL

Discontentment makes rich men poor;
contentment makes poor men rich!

I Have Everything

Read: Philippians 3:1–12

*I also count all things loss for the excellence of the knowledge
of Christ Jesus my Lord. Philippians 3:8*

The airline had mangled Debbie's luggage. Then her purse disappeared. Instead of entering the airport through an enclosed corridor, she stumbled off the plane in the pouring rain. She was drenched, far from home with no money, no identification, and no dry clothes.

Under normal conditions Debbie would have been furious, but that night it didn't matter. She had just survived the crash of Flight 1420 in Little Rock, Arkansas. "When I walked off that plane," Debbie said, "I walked off with nothing, then I stopped and thought, *I have everything.*" She had suddenly realized that her life was more important than all she had lost.

It sometimes takes a dramatic turn of events to alter our perspective. That was true for Saul of Tarsus. He had treasured his hard-earned reputation for "righteousness" more than anything in the world (Philippians 3:4–6). But when he met Christ on the Damascus road (Acts 9:1–6), his whole outlook changed. Later he wrote, "What things were gain to me, these I have counted loss for Christ" (Philippians 3:7).

Yielding our sinful pride and self-sufficiency to the Lord may seem as if we are losing everything. But only then will we discover that to have life in Christ is to have everything.   DCM

*We think we have what matters most
Of what this life can give;
But when we yield it all to Christ,
We've just begun to live. —DJD*

When we have nothing left but Christ,
we find that Christ is enough.

An Untroubled Heart

Read: John 13:31–14:1

*Let not your heart be troubled; you believe in God,
believe also in Me. John 14:1*

Noted British preacher J. H. Jowett believed that inner peace comes not from tranquil circumstances but from an untroubled heart. He said: "If we were to hear one hundred people repeating the sentence, 'Let not your heart be troubled,' we should find that ninety-nine of them put the emphasis upon the word *troubled*... I feel led to believe that the purposed emphasis is on the word *heart*... The heart is to be clothed in serene regality even when hell is knocking and rioting at its very gates."

Jowett's perceptive words caused me to wonder if I'm spending more energy trying to avoid difficulties than on letting them help me get to know Christ better. If so, I'm headed for nothing but frustration and failure.

Jesus told His disciples, "Let not your heart be troubled" (John 14:1). This was to prepare them for the dark day of His crucifixion. He knew they could weather the storm only by trusting Him in spite of the apparent triumph of evil.

Today, we can focus on the trouble in the world and in our lives, or we can focus on the victory we have in Christ because His death was followed by His resurrection. This wonderful fact gives new meaning to His words, "In the world you will have tribulation; but be of good cheer, I have overcome the world" (16:33).   DCM

*A troubled heart, a wearied mind
Are burdens hard to bear;
A lack of peace, a heavy load
Are lifted by God's care.* —Fitzhugh

When we keep our mind on God, God gives us peace of mind.

Flyleaf Wisdom

Read: 2 Samuel 12:1–23

He who trusts in the Lord, mercy shall
surround him. Psalm 32:10

All right, Mary, I confess. While I was a guest at your home in Manila, I used your Bible one day for my devotions. When I opened it, I saw these words written on the flyleaf: *Acknowledgment. Acceptance. Adjustment.*

Those words express the steps that believers in Christ need to take when they receive bad news. I see these actions illustrated in the life of David.

Acknowledgment. When David was confronted by Nathan about his sin, he admitted his guilt (2 Samuel 12:13). When we are faced with a problem, whether it's the result of our sin or not, it's futile to run from the truth.

Acceptance. When his infant son died as punishment for his sin with Bathsheba, David accepted it as God's will (vv. 19–23) and learned from it. We too need to see difficulties as opportunities to trust God and to grow spiritually (James 1:2–4).

Adjustment. David turned to the Lord for forgiveness and help, and he later wrote about what he had learned (Psalm 32). For us, we may need to ask the Lord for the ability to make a lifestyle change or to take some specific action.

Have you been hit hard by bad news? These steps from Mary's Bible can help you to handle it in a way that will please the Lord and result in good. — DCE

Day by day and with each passing moment,
Strength I find to meet my trials here;
Trusting in my Father's wise bestowment,
I've no cause for worry or for fear. —Berg

God takes us into His darkroom to develop our character.

The Folly of Worry

Read: Matthew 6:25–34

Do not worry about tomorrow, for tomorrow will worry about its own things. Matthew 6:34

Ralph Easter had driven many times from Calgary, the foothills city of Alberta, to Banff, high in the Canadian Rockies. But it was his first trip that left an indelible impression on him. He said that as the road wound westward from Calgary over rolling hills, there always loomed before him in the distance a range of snow-capped peaks that seemed to block the highway. He recalls wondering how he would ever pass over such an insurmountable barrier, but he drove steadily on.

Finally as he reached the point where it had looked as if the road would stop, he came to a sharp bend and the highway stretched on as before. Many such turns kept him progressing upward and forward until he came to the other side of the range.

As we travel the road of life, obstacles often loom up before us, filling us with apprehension. Illness, surgery, financial reversal, or loss of a job threaten to keep us from reaching our goals. But as we keep on by faith, God opens a new way before us. Most of what we worry about never comes to pass. But even when trouble comes, God is there to show us a new course. We can avoid the folly of worry by trusting Him today for all our tomorrows.   RDH

Worry is a burden that God never meant for us to bear.

September 25

God's Tears

Read: John 11:28–37

Jesus wept. John 11:35

In C. S. Lewis's story *The Magician's Nephew*, Digory recalled his terminally ill mother and how his hopes were all dying away. With a lump in his throat and tears in his eyes, he blurted out to Aslan, the great lion who represents Christ, "Please, please—won't you—can't you give me something that will cure Mother?"

Then, in his despair, Digory looked up at Aslan's face. "Great shining tears stood in the Lion's eyes. They were such big, bright tears compared with Digory's own that for a moment he felt as if the Lion must really be sorrier about his Mother than he was himself. 'My son, my son,' said Aslan. 'I know. Grief is great. Only you and I in this land know that yet. Let us be good to one another.'"

I think of Jesus's tears at Lazarus's grave (John 11:35). I believe He wept for Lazarus as well as for Mary and Martha and their grief. Later, Jesus wept over Jerusalem (Luke 19:41–44). And He knows and shares our grief today. But as He promised, we will see Him again in the place He's preparing for us (John 14:3). In heaven, our grief will end. "God will wipe away every tear from [our] eyes; there shall be no more death, nor sorrow, nor crying" (Revelation 21:4).

Until then, know that God weeps with you.   DHR

He knows our burdens and our crosses,
Those things that hurt, our trials and losses,
He cares for every soul that cries,
God wipes the tears from weeping eyes. —Brandt

If you doubt that Jesus cares, remember His tears.

Persistent Prayer

Read: Luke 18:1–8

*Men always ought to pray and
not lose heart. Luke 18:1*

A friend of mine has been a woman of prayer for many years. She has received countless answers from God, but sometimes she is disheartened because certain prayers for loved ones remain unanswered. Yet she keeps on praying, encouraged by the parable in Luke 18. This story features a widow who badgered a heartless judge for help and finally got it.

Jesus ended His parable with a question: If an unrighteous and disrespectful judge finally answers a pestering widow's pleas for help, shall not God answer His own children who cry to Him day and night? (vv. 7–8). The expected answer: "Of course He will!"

George Müller (1805–1898), pastor and orphanage director, was known for his faith and persistent prayer. Whenever he prayed for specific needs for his orphanage, God sent exactly what was required. Yet for more than forty years he also prayed for the conversion of a friend and his friend's son. When Müller died, these men were still unconverted. God answered those prayers, however, in His own time. The friend was converted while attending Müller's funeral, and the son a week later!

Do you have a special burden or request? Keep on praying! Trust your loving heavenly Father to answer according to His wisdom and timing. God honors persistent prayer! JY

*Don't think that you are finished,
Just trust God's love and care;
Delays are not denials;
Persist in faith and prayer. —Jarvis*

Failure to pray is the line of least persistence.

He Always Answers

Read: Daniel 9:3–23

While I was speaking in prayer, the man
Gabriel... reached me. Daniel 9:21

Daniel was determined to pray regularly, and it got him thrown into the lions' den (Daniel 6). But have you ever noticed how God answered his prayers?

In Daniel 9, we learn that Daniel had been reading Jeremiah's prophecy that the exile of the Israelites was supposed to end after seventy years. So Daniel prayed that God would not delay the end of the captivity. He confessed Israel's sin and asked for God's intervention.

Then, while Daniel was still praying, God not only sent an answer but He also sent His angel Gabriel to deliver it. Daniel said, "While I was speaking in prayer, the man Gabriel,... being caused to fly swiftly, reached me" (v. 21). In other words, before Daniel had even finished his prayer, God heard it and immediately sent Gabriel with the answer (vv. 22–23).

Yet, on another occasion when Daniel prayed, Scripture tells us that the messenger God sent with the answer took three weeks to arrive (10:12–13).

We can learn important lessons from Daniel about how God answers our prayers today. Sometimes God sends the answer immediately. Sometimes the answer is delayed. Either way, He always answers.   DB

It matters not what tongue we speak,
Nor where life's pathway leads;
God hears the cries His children raise
And always meets our needs. —DJD

There are three possible answers to prayer: Yes, No, or Wait.

September 28

Why Good People Suffer

Read: Job 1:6–22

*The Lord said to Satan, "Have you considered
My servant Job?" Job 1:8*

My Sunday school class has been studying one book of the
Bible each week. Beginning with Genesis, we are looking
at the theme, structure, and uniqueness of each book. Little did I
realize that two women in my class were eager to get to the book
of Job. They are nurses who daily confront the problem of human
suffering, and they are often asked hard questions about God's role
in it.

All too often the explanation for suffering is similar to that
expressed by Job's three friends who came to sit with him. One
after another, Eliphaz, Bildad, and Zophar told Job that he deserved
the suffering because of his sin. The young observer Elihu came
along and told Job the same thing.

The real reason Job was suffering was that Satan, the leader of
the fallen angels, was trying to get him to turn from God. Because
Satan cannot dethrone the Lord, he opposes Him by attacking His
followers (1 Peter 5:8). He strikes at God by tempting us to sin.

One reason for suffering, therefore, is that it's part of a larger,
cosmic struggle. During hard times, we face the choice to trust
God or to turn from Him. If we endure suffering with our trust in
the Lord unshaken, we will thwart Satan's efforts and glorify our
God.   DCE

*How oft in the conflict, when pressed by the foe,
I have fled to my Refuge and breathed out my woe;
How often, when trials like sea billows roll,
Have I hidden in Thee, O Thou Rock of my soul. —Cushing*

When your world is shaking, run to the Rock.

September 29

Our Prayer and God's Power

Read: James 5:13–20

Pray for one another, that you may be healed. The effective,
fervent prayer of a righteous man avails much. James 5:16

When we pray for others, we become partners with God in His work of salvation, healing, comfort, and justice. God can accomplish those things without us, but in His plan He gives us the privilege of being involved with Him through prayer.

When we intercede for a grandson in trouble, a mother having surgery, a neighbor who needs Christ, or a pastor who needs strength, we are asking God to provide for that person what we can't provide. We are acting as go-betweens, asking God to direct His power in a specific direction.

In his classic book titled *Prayer*, Ole Hallesby described how it works: "This power is so rich and so mobile that all we have to do when we pray is point to the person or thing to which we desire to have [God's] power applied, and He, the Lord of this power, will direct the necessary power to the desired place."

This assumes, of course, that we are praying "according to [God's] will" (1 John 5:14). Prayer is not a magic wand for satisfying our own wishes, but it's an opportunity to work with the Lord in accomplishing His purposes.

James told us that "the effective, fervent prayer of a righteous man avails much" (James 5:16). So let's humbly and earnestly pray for one another. DCE

As we attempt to live like Christ
In actions, words, and deeds,
We'll follow His design for prayer
And pray for others' needs. —DB

The most powerful position on earth is kneeling before the Lord of the universe.

A Neglected Remedy

Read: 1 Kings 19:1–18

He gives His beloved sleep. Psalm 127:2

I am often asked to speak on the subject of stress. I'm not an expert on stress, just an experienced sufferer! I simply share counsel from God's Word that helps me live less stressfully and more restfully. Many listeners are desperate for any new insight I might offer. What blank looks I sometimes get when I make this particular recommendation: "Get more sleep!" In their longing to deepen their experience of God's peace, they were hoping for something more spiritual than that.

But I'm not alone in linking spirituality to sleep. A godly Bible teacher was asked to share the key ingredient in his own life for walking in the Spirit. He studied the Bible and prayed regularly, but his surprising reply was this: "Get eight hours of sleep each night."

This reply is less surprising in light of God's initial remedy for Elijah's stress and depression (1 Kings 19:1–18). Twice God gave him food and undisturbed sleep before gently confronting him at Mount Horeb with his error.

Psalm 4:8 says, "I will both lie down in peace, and sleep; for You alone, O Lord, make me dwell in safety." Sleep is not the full remedy for stress, but other solutions can become clearer to people who get adequate rest.   JY

When life is so busy and hectic and humming,
You're uptight and frazzled and stressed;
Slow down for a while and spend time with the Savior,
And be sure to get adequate rest. —Fitzhugh

We can sleep in peace when we remember that God is awake.

The Timeless Name

Read: Revelation 1:8–18

I am the Alpha and the Omega, the Beginning
and the End. Revelation 1:8

Whether the company is Twentieth Century Fox in Hollywood or Twentieth Century Data in Dallas, time has caught up with these companies and they're a century behind. Should they change their names? Consultant Frank Delano says, "You can't do business in the twenty-first century with a twentieth-century name. You need a name that is really universal with no limitations."

Through the ages, Christians have known and worshiped a Savior who is not bound by time. His name? In Revelation 1:8, Jesus Christ identified himself by saying, "I am the Alpha and the Omega, the Beginning and the End,... who is and who was and who is to come, the Almighty." He called himself "the First and the Last" (vv. 11, 17). And in verse 18, "I am He who lives, and was dead, and behold, I am alive forevermore."

Do clocks and calendars leave you exhausted? Jesus Christ is the Master of time. Has death brought the pain of separation? Jesus Christ is Lord of eternity. Are you facing unwanted changes? Jesus Christ is "the same yesterday, today, and forever" (Hebrews 13:8). Have failures filled you with despair? Jesus Christ is risen, the Victor over death and the grave!

It's true. In every century His name is universal, without limitation. Jesus Christ is the timeless name. DCM

Jesus Christ—a wonderful name,
Eternal, unchanging, always the same;
He's the beginning and He's the end,
He's my Savior, my Lord, and my Friend. —Fitzhugh

Jesus is the Lord of time and eternity.

October 2

No Explanation Required

Read: Job 42:1–17

I have uttered what I did not understand, things too wonderful
for me, which I did not know. Job 42:3

A Christian who believed God had led him to take a daring step of faith remarked, "If God doesn't give me success in this matter, He'll certainly have a lot of explaining to do!"

It's easy to judge this man's words, but have you ever said, "When I get to heaven, I certainly expect God to explain why some of my prayers were not answered and why tragedies were not always prevented!"

In Romans 8:28, Paul didn't promise that all circumstances and events would be explained—if, indeed, we could comprehend the explanation! Instead, he promised that "all things work together for good to those who love God, to those who are the called according to His purpose."

The story of Job reassures us that questioning God is common to human experience. Yet, when Job demanded that God justify His lack of intervention in his trials, He didn't comply. Instead, He bombarded Job with His own searching questions (Job 38–41). The Almighty does not have to explain himself, nor is He required to reveal His grand design. He reveals himself and His plans in His way and in His time.

Thoroughly humbled, Job admitted, "I have uttered what I did not understand, things . . . which I did not know." Like Job, will you now trust God—no explanation required? JY

What God is doing you may not know now,
Hereafter He may tell you why;
Questions that taunt you and trouble your mind
Will someday have heaven's reply. —Hess

When we trust God's promises,
we won't demand explanations.

Legacy of Affliction

Read: Psalm 119:65-80

*It is good for me that I have been afflicted, that I may
learn Your statutes. Psalm 119:71*

Lieutenant Paul Galanti, a U.S. Navy pilot, spent six and a half
years as a prisoner of war in North Vietnam. The experience
has given him a heightened sense of ordinary privileges that most of
us take for granted. Speaking of his life today, nearly three decades
after being released, Galanti says, "There's no such thing as a bad
day when there's a doorknob on the inside of the door."

After 2,300 straight days in a locked cell, you might consider the
privilege of walking outside whenever you please to be one of life's
greatest luxuries.

The writer of Psalm 119 makes the startling statement, "It is good
for me that I have been afflicted, that I may learn Your statutes"
(v. 71). From a time of suffering, the psalmist gained a greater love
for God and an increased appreciation for His commands. "Before I
was afflicted I went astray, but now I keep Your word" (v. 67).

Perhaps you can identify with the words of the psalmist. You've
"been there" and you know what he means. Or you may be in the
middle of a great hardship today. When the days are dark and relief
is out of sight, we need to cling to what we know to be true about
the goodness and faithfulness of God. And then, when He brings us
out into the light, we too will see the results and thank God for the
legacy of affliction.   DCM

In times of greatest trouble,
I've learned to trust God's Word;
For through the Spirit's teaching
My Savior's voice I've heard. —Fitzhugh

Tough times teach trust.

October 4

Give God a Chance

Read: Mark 6:1–6

*He could do no mighty work there ... And He marveled
because of their unbelief. Mark 6:5–6*

A child once asked, "What does God do all day?" If the answer to that question depended on how much we allow God to do in our individual lives, some of us would have to reply, "Not much!" In difficult situations, it's easy to say we trust God and yet try to handle things ourselves without turning to Him and His Word. This is masked unbelief. Although God is constantly working, He allows us to set a limit on the degree of work He does on our behalf.

We see this truth demonstrated in Mark 6 when Jesus tried to do mighty things in His hometown. Because the people saw Him merely as a carpenter's son and not as God's Son, they limited what He could do for them (v. 5). So Jesus moved on to other towns.

During my younger years, I tried hard to be a strong Christian, seldom revealing my weaknesses. Then, through a rock-bottom experience, I made this dynamic discovery: Strong Christians are those who unashamedly admit their weaknesses and draw on Christ's power. The more I learned to depend on God, the more opportunity this gave Him to be active in my life. Now, whenever I face a daunting task, I say, "Joanie and Jesus can do it!" So can you and Jesus. — JY

I am trusting Thee, Lord Jesus;
Never let me fall;
I am trusting Thee forever,
And for all. —Havergal

We must admit our weakness to experience God's strength.

October 5

People of Courage

Read: Acts 21:7–14

God has not given us a spirit of fear, but of power and of love
and of a sound mind. 2 Timothy 1:7

Police found it hard to believe, but an unarmed housewife captured three burglars single-handedly. The woman had come home and found three men loading household items into their car parked in her driveway. She pulled her van behind their car and then ordered the men to carry her belongings back into the house and sit on the couch until the police arrived. Later, when asked why they didn't escape, she replied, "The Lord was with me... I wasn't going to move my van so they could get away. What was I to do? Run away?"

The apostle Paul also showed unusual courage. His friends probably thought he was being reckless when he insisted on going to Jerusalem after he had been warned of the danger that awaited him (Acts 21:11–13). A strong argument could be made for him to delay his trip. After all, on another occasion he had escaped from danger (9:23–25). Yet Paul knew what he had to do. With unwavering determination he courageously headed for Jerusalem.

It's not easy to know when such boldness is wise or foolish. Only the Spirit can show us. But one thing is sure, Christians have reason to be courageous. God is our helper. And when we rely on Him, He'll enable us to stand firm no matter what danger we may face.

MRD

Ask God for good judgment and courage
To face unexpected events;
To follow the teachings of Scripture
Is the best, most effective defense. —Hess

Courage is fear that has said its prayers.

October 6

God Was at Columbine

Read: Job 23:8–17

I go forward, but He is not there, and backward,
but I cannot perceive Him. Job 23:8

This item appeared in a newspaper after the 1999 fatal shooting at Columbine High School in Colorado:

Dear God: Why didn't you save the children of the Littleton school? Sincerely, a student
Dear Student: I am not allowed in schools. Sincerely, God

The intended message seems clear: If we bring God back into the public schools by allowing prayer and Bible reading, then such tragedies would not occur. Whether you agree with that sentiment or not, one thing is sure—laws can't keep God out of school. They didn't that fateful day at Columbine High! God reached out to the gunmen through those who confessed their faith in Christ before being shot. He was there in the courage of a teacher who gave his life helping students escape.

God may be doing His greatest work when evil seems to triumph. When Job looked back, he saw that his suffering gave him a new understanding of God (Job 42:5–6). At Calvary, man crucified the only sinless One who ever lived, yet God turned history's darkest day into man's redemption.

Are you facing a great injustice? Keep trusting God. Those who go through the greatest darkness are those who most fully appreciate the glory of His light. —DJD

When tragedy, heartache, and sorrow abound,
When evil appears to have conquered the right,
We center our heart on our Father's great love,
For He will bring hope in the darkest of night. —DJD

God may be doing His greatest work
when evil seems to triumph.

October 7

He's Near to Hear

Read: Psalm 145:17–21

*The Lord is near to all who call upon Him, to all who
call upon Him in truth. Psalm 145:18*

When I was seven years old, my grandfather was caretaker of a wooded estate. One fall evening I took my toy gun, called for my dog Pal, and headed down a path into the forest. I walked bravely into the woods. Soon, though, it began to get dark and I panicked. "Grandpa!" I shouted.

"I'm right here," he said calmly, only a few yards away. He had seen me go into the woods and had followed me to make sure I was okay. Talk about being relieved!

As followers of Christ, we sometimes venture into unfamiliar territory. We try new things. We take on responsibilities in the work of the Lord that are bigger than we've ever attempted before. We risk rejection when we witness to friends about Christ. It can get pretty scary.

But wherever we go, God is there. His pledge to be near is backed up by His omnipresence. His promise to help us is backed up by His mighty power. He will hear the cries of those who fear Him (Psalm 145:19–20).

So take some risks in your walk with God. Venture out into the scary unknown in your service or giving or witnessing. God is nearer to you than Grandpa Hayes was to me in the darkening woods. He will always hear your cry.   DCE

The Lord is near to all who call;
He promised in His holy Word
That if we will draw near to Him,
Our faintest heart cry will be heard. —Hess

Dark fears flee in the light of God's presence.

It's Not Over Till It's Over

Read: Ecclesiastes 9:11–12

*The race is not to the swift, nor the battle
to the strong. Ecclesiastes 9:11*

The newspaper headline read, "Jockey Beats Horse over Finish Line." The jockey beat the pack by twenty lengths and his horse by one length when he was catapulted out of the saddle and over the finish line. His horse, who had tripped, followed soon after. But the victory went to the second-place finisher named Slip Up. A race official said that the jockey "was so far in front that only a freak accident would stop him,... and that's what happened."

We've all experienced life's unexpected happenings. The author of Ecclesiastes took note of them when he said, "The race is not to the swift, nor the battle to the strong" (9:11). He reflected on the fact that man is not the master of his destiny, as he so often thinks he is.

Life is filled with unpredictable experiences and events. They seem like stones dropped into the gears of human ingenuity. A strong, healthy man drops dead. A rising young athlete contracts a crippling disease. A person of means suddenly loses everything in a bad deal.

What can we learn from this? Not to trust our own strength, our own wisdom, or our own skill, but to depend on the Lord who alone knows the end from the beginning.

Life's race is not over till He says it's over.   MD

*There's so much now I cannot see,
My eyesight's far too dim;
But come what may, I'll simply trust
And leave it all to Him. —Overton*

Living without faith in God is like driving in the fog.

Prepare to Sleep

Read: Isaiah 26:1–9

*You will keep him in perfect peace, whose mind is stayed
on You, because he trusts in You. Isaiah 26:3*

We spend approximately 30 percent of our lives sleeping—or trying to sleep. Today there are more than three hundred sleep disorder clinics in the United States. There are also ninety million Americans who snore, and they (or the people who share a room with them) spend about two hundred million dollars a year on anti-snoring remedies.

Think of it! Nearly a third of our entire lives sleeping! Yet how much do we plan and prepare spiritually for those important hours of sleep?

For many years, a friend of mine has followed a simple guideline he refers to as HWLW, which stands for "His Word the Last Word." Every night, just before turning out the light, he reads a passage from the Bible or meditates on a verse he has memorized. Before he goes to sleep, he wants the last word he thinks about to be from God—not the evening news or the weather, not the late-night talk-show host or the celebrity guest, but a final word from the Lord.

Is it possible that the words of Isaiah 26:3 could apply to our subconscious as well as our conscious minds? Wouldn't "perfect peace" for the person "whose mind is stayed on" the Lord make for a good night's sleep?

Why don't we all try it? "His Word the Last Word"—spiritual preparation for a peaceful night's sleep!   DMC

PUTTING IT INTO PRACTICE

*Before going to sleep, read a portion from the Bible
or recall a verse you read earlier in the day.
Meditate on God and your relationship with Him.*

Before you turn out the light, turn to the light of God's Word.

In His Hands

Read: Isaiah 40:25–31

He heals the brokenhearted and binds up their wounds. He counts the number of the stars; He calls them all by name. Psalm 147:3–4

How big is the cosmos? Galaxies upon galaxies stretch into space farther than we can comprehend.

Two Harvard astronomers have discovered a "great wall" of galaxies that they estimate to be 500 million light-years long, 200 million light-years wide, and 15 million light-years thick. (One light-year is 5.88 trillion miles.) Those numbers are mind-boggling.

Here's something even more amazing. God created all of those galaxies and sustains everything that exists by His powerful hands. Yet that same mighty God, the one and only God, uses those hands to gently touch the lives of suffering men and women.

In Psalm 147:3–4 we read that the Lord not only knows all the stars by name, but He also "heals the brokenhearted and binds up their wounds." That truth is echoed in Isaiah 40:26–31, which states that the all-powerful Creator is the One who renews the strength of those who rely on Him. The God of the galaxies is the Great Physician who lovingly ministers to our needs. What a contrast—and what a comfort!

Regardless of how heavy your burdens, how tangled your problems, or how serious your diseases, the God of the galaxies has power enough to meet all your needs—and measureless power to spare. Put your problems in His hands.   VCG

Those who see God's hand in everything can leave everything in God's hands.

There Is Hope

Read: 1 Kings 19:1–7

*It is enough! Now, Lord, take my life, for I am
no better than my fathers. 1 Kings 19:4*

An old legend tells of an angel who was sent by God to inform Satan that all his methods to defeat Christians would be taken from him. The devil pleaded to keep just one. "Let me retain depression," he begged. The angel, thinking this a small request, agreed. "Good!" Satan exclaimed. He laughed and said, "In that one gift, I have secured all."

In a now out-of-print book about depression, author Roger Barrett describes it as a "wretched experience that leaves you exhausted, uninvolved, and in deep, hopeless despair... You feel doomed, trapped... It's awful!"

In every age, God's people have struggled with this crippling emotion. Elijah's cry "It is enough! Now, Lord, take my life!" is the cry of a despondent man (1 Kings 19:4). Others like Job and David knew similar agony of soul, but they emerged from it with stronger faith. That's encouraging!

Depression can be rooted in spiritual, mental, or physical causes, and we should not be afraid to seek godly counsel and medical help. Whatever the initial cause, Satan would love to defeat us by keeping us in our hope-starved condition. That's why we need to see that our ultimate help is in God—for He loves us and longs to shine His light through the clouds that surround us. He is the God of hope.

DJD

*Lord, give us grace to trust You when
Life's burdens seem too much to bear;
Dispel the darkness with new hope
And help us rise above despair. —Sper*

No one is hopeless who knows the God of hope.

October 12

Expert Restoration

Read: 2 Corinthians 5:14–21

If anyone is in Christ, . . . old things have passed away; behold,
all things have become new. 2 Corinthians 5:17

A woman who restores valuable paintings says many works of art that seem hopelessly damaged can be saved by an expert. Rebecca McLain has brought color and life back to dulled oil paintings by carefully removing dirt and discolored varnish. But she has also seen the damage done when people attempt to clean their own soiled art with oven cleaner or abrasive powders. Her advice? If you value the art, take it to an expert in restoration.

The same need exists in lives soiled by sin. Our efforts at ridding ourselves of the guilt and defilement of sinful actions and attitudes often end in frustration and despair. In our attempts to get rid of guilt, we sometimes blame others. Or we simply give up, thinking that we cannot be any different.

But Jesus our redeemer is the expert who can restore the most damaged, defiled, and discouraged person. Christ died so that anyone who by faith receives Him can be completely forgiven and restored. With His own blood He will cleanse us (1 John 1:7) and make us a new creation, God's own "workmanship" (2 Corinthians 5:17; Ephesians 2:10).

When it comes to cleansing the canvas of our souls, we cannot do it ourselves. Only Jesus Christ can. Call on Him today for expert restoration.   DCM

God sees in us a masterpiece
That one day will be done;
His Spirit works through all of life
To make us like His Son. —Sper

Only God can transform a sin-stained soul
into a masterpiece of grace.

October 13

Time Off

Read: 2 Thessalonians 3:6–13

Do not grow weary in doing good.
2 Thessalonians 3:13

The teenager's mom, a bit exasperated by the failure of her youngest child to show the desired maturity, sighed and said, "Two more years of junior high." To which he, in typical style, replied with a smile, "Mom, why don't you just take the next two years off!"

Often there are things we would simply like to avoid by taking "time off." When we have a chronically sick family member, we may be tempted to just "check out" for a while. When children rebel and make parenting a struggle, we'd prefer a long vacation from the hassle. Then there are those times when we face great spiritual battles that we would like to skip altogether.

Paul spoke briefly about such struggles in 2 Thessalonians 3. He mentioned the problem of dealing with people who "walk among you in a disorderly manner,... busybodies" (v. 11). Facing up to people problems can be frustrating. But Paul gave part of the solution when he said, "Do not grow weary in doing good" (v. 13). Another part of the equation is to listen to the psalmist, who said, "Cast your burden on the Lord, and He shall sustain you" (Psalm 55:22).

When it's not possible to "take the next two years off," we can gain hope from this advice: Keep doing good and keep casting your care on God. That's better than taking time off.   DB

Be not weary in well-doing
When you're tempted to give up;
Cast on God your every burden,
Trust in Him—keep looking up! —Fitzhugh

When God stretches your patience He is seeking
to enlarge your soul.

October 14

Changing Your World

Read: 1 Corinthians 13:1–7

I have been crucified with Christ; it is no longer I who live,
but Christ lives in me. Galatians 2:20

A young woman lived in a home where she was very unhappy. She often complained to her friends and told them how difficult it was for her to stay there. She blamed her parents and the other members of her family for her discontent and threatened to move out as soon as she could afford to be on her own.

One day, though, her face was graced with a happy smile. Gone was her usual glum expression. Her eyes were sparkling. There was a spring in her step.

When a friend noticed the difference, she exclaimed, "Things must have improved at home. I'm so glad!" "No," the young woman responded, "I'm the one who's different!"

That young woman's outlook was brighter and her relationships with others were transformed. It wasn't because her circumstances had improved, but because she had experienced a change in her heart.

When we are confronted with irritating situations and we begin to feel sorry for ourselves, we should ask these questions: Is the trouble really with others? Or could it be me? As we ask the Lord to fill us with His perfect love, it's amazing how life begins to look better. Letting God change us is the best way to change our world. —RDH

Lord, take my life and make it wholly Thine;
Fill my poor heart with Thy great love divine.
Take all my will, my passion, self, and pride;
I now surrender, Lord—in me abide. —Orr

When you stop changing, you stop growing.

October 15

Gratitude Is Contagious

Read: Psalm 103:1–22

Bless the Lord, O my soul, and forget not
all His benefits. Psalm 103:2

Although forgetfulness sometimes increases with age, it's really common to us all. Even children have lapses of memory and excuse themselves by saying, "I forgot!" But there's one kind of forgetfulness that is inexcusable at any age—forgetting to be grateful to God. The psalmist David was determined not to fail the Lord in this way, so he exhorted his soul: "Forget not all His benefits" (Psalm 103:2).

David didn't keep his thanksgiving to God a secret. In Psalm 34:2 he wrote, "The humble shall hear of it and be glad." And who were the humble? They were those who, like David, were going through tough times. Why would they be glad to hear his praises? Because their own faith was strengthened when he testified about God's help to him in times of fear (v. 4), trouble (v. 6), need (v. 10), sorrow (v. 18), or affliction (v. 19).

When was the last time you openly and unashamedly praised God for helping you in your difficulties? Someone has said, "If Christians praised God more, the world would doubt Him less." Not only is it appropriate, therefore, to express your gratitude for all His benefits, but your example may also encourage others to move from doubt to faith as you praise Him.   JY

Thank the Lord when trouble comes,
His love and grace expressing;
Grateful praise will strengthen faith,
Turn trials into blessing. —DCE

An attitude of gratitude can make your life a beatitude.

Lord, Hear Our Prayer!

Read: Psalm 6:1–10

The Lord has heard my supplication;
the Lord will receive my prayer. Psalm 6:9

During every morning worship service in a small church I attended, the congregation would share prayer requests. After each one, the pastor would say, "Lord, in your mercy," and the people would respond, "Hear our prayer." One Sunday, a four-year-old boy behind me became more intense after each request, until he finally shouted out, "Hear our prayer!" The little boy probably expressed what a lot of us were feeling that morning.

As Christians, we believe that God hears us when we pray not because we deserve it but because Christ has opened the way for us to talk directly to the Father. We often make our requests quietly and confidently, but there are times when we cannot help but cry out to God in heartbreak and anguish.

In Psalm 6 we can almost hear David's sobs as he pleaded with God for mercy, help, and healing. Yet, even though he was faced with difficult people and overwhelming circumstances, David affirmed his trust in God: "The Lord has heard the voice of my weeping. The Lord has heard my supplication; the Lord will receive my prayer" (vv. 8–9).

Today, in that mysterious blend of confidence and crying out, we can bring everything to our loving heavenly Father, saying, "Lord, in your mercy, hear our prayer!" DCM

God hears us when we call to Him,
Not one voice is ignored;
The sounds of praise, the pleas of pain
Are all heard by the Lord. —Sper

In prayer, God hears more than just words—
He listens to your heart.

He Quiets the Storms

Read: Psalm 46:1–11

*There is a river whose streams shall make
glad the city of God. Psalm 46:4*

In the fall of 2001, a thunderous storm blew across Lake Michigan for thirty-six hours straight. Sustained winds of sixty miles per hour, with gusts much stronger, whipped up the highest waves in fifteen years. One frothing roller after another, some up to eighteen feet high, crashed over the breakwaters and pounded the shore with great fury.

The writer of Psalm 46 must have experienced a sustained spiritual and emotional crisis like the incessant pounding of a giant storm, for he wrote of troubled waters and roaring seas. He also mentioned the quaking of the mountains (vv. 2–3).

That may describe how life in this world feels to you right now. If so, continue on to verse 4, which tells of a quiet river that delights and refreshes the people of God. Its cool, peaceful waters flow continually as a never-ending source of joy and blessing.

This psalm describes God as "our refuge and strength" (v. 1). We have no need to fear, even when the nations of the world are angry and pounding one another with their tools of war (vv. 2, 6), for "the Lord of hosts is with us" (v. 7).

Let the Lord quiet the storms in your heart. For He says, "Be still, and know that I am God; I will be exalted among the nations, I will be exalted in the earth!" (v. 10). DCE

*Give me a spirit of peace, dear Lord,
Midst the storms and the tempests that roll,
That I may find rest and quiet within,
A calm buried deep in my soul. —Dawe*

God does not shield us from life's storms;
He shelters us in life's storms.

Prescription for Anxiety

Read: Psalm 55:4–23

Cast your burden on the Lord, and He shall sustain you; He shall never permit the righteous to be moved. Psalm 55:22

According to a *Wall Street Journal* report, anxiety has overtaken depression as the leading mental health problem in the United States. Anxiety-fighting drugs are now the top-selling pharmaceutical products. Even with a booming economy and political stability, worry and apprehension remain part of our human condition—one that can never be adequately relieved by a pill.

When David composed Psalm 55, his mind was agitated by the same types of situations we struggle with today: He recoiled in horror from the violence, anger, and abuse that stalked the city streets (vv. 9–11). He suffered the anguish of being betrayed by a close friend (vv. 12–14). He longed to leave and escape to a place of peace (vv. 4–8).

Because David's anxious pain mirrors our own, his prescription for relief can be ours as well. He wrote, "I will call upon God, and the Lord shall save me… Cast your burden on the Lord, and He shall sustain you" (vv. 16, 22).

Anxiety is a burden we are not called to bear. Instead, we are to lay our concerns on Christ because He cares for us (1 Peter 5:7; see also Philippians 4:6–7).

If your heart is weighed down today, the Lord is ready to bear every burden you give Him.   DCM

All your anxiety, all your care,
Bring to the mercy seat, leave it there;
Never a burden He cannot bear,
Never a friend like Jesus. —Joy

God invites us to burden Him with what burdens us.

Down but Not Out

Read: Psalm 88:1–18

The peace of God . . . will guard your hearts and
minds through Christ Jesus. Philippians 4:7

The eighteenth-century author Samuel Johnson was noted for his wit, sensitivity, and encyclopedic knowledge. He found solitude depressing, so he often took in the poor and homeless so that he could be surrounded by people. He also confessed that he had a deep fear of dying.

An *Encyclopedia Britannica* article, however, speaks of Johnson's "zest for living." It characterizes him as a "Christian moralist" with a strong conviction of the reality of sin and of the redemption provided through faith in Jesus Christ. It also says that "his faith prevailed," for when he knew he was dying "he refused to take opiates because he had prayed that he might render his soul to God unclouded." The article concludes, "Few men have left finer examples of the art of living than Samuel Johnson."

I have known many believers with a disposition like that. Most of them went through repeated cycles of joy and gloom. And when they were down, merely quoting Bible verses helped little because they were already aware of them. But they kept living for God and praying, and their faith prevailed. The "peace of God" filled their hearts (Philippians 4:7). That's good news for all of us, especially for those who go through times of doubt and despair.　　　HVL

Whenever darkness grips your soul
And you are tempted to despair,
Remember Christ's unfailing love,
And trust His faithful, tender care. —Sper

When life is filled with shadows,
face the sunshine of God's love.

Seeing the Unseen

Read: Psalm 34:4–7

The angel of the Lord encamps all around those
who fear Him, and delivers them. Psalm 34:7

In a materialistic world like ours, we are tempted to conclude that the only real things are those we experience with our five senses. Yet "there are things we cannot see: things behind our backs or far away and all things in the dark," said C. S. Lewis.

There is another realm of reality, just as actual, just as factual, just as substantial as anything we see, hear, touch, taste, or smell in this world. It exists all around us—not out there "somewhere," but "here." There are legions of angels helping us, for which the world has no countermeasures (Hebrews 1:14). The psalmist David referred to them as a force of "thousands of thousands" of chariots (Psalm 68:17). We cannot see God nor His angels with our natural eyes. But they are there, whether we see them or not. I believe the world is filled with them.

Faith is the means by which we are able to "see" this invisible world. That is belief's true function. Faith is to the spiritual realm what the five senses are to the natural realm. The writer of Hebrews says that faith is "the evidence of things not seen" (Hebrews 11:1). By faith we recognize the existence of the spiritual world and learn to depend on the Lord for His help in our daily life. Our goal, then, as George MacDonald once said, is to "grow eyes" to see the unseen. DHR

At times our fears may loom so large,
We long for proof that God is near;
It's then our Father says to us,
"Have faith, My child, and do not fear." —DJD

Faith sees things that are out of sight.

How Will My Worry Look?

Read: Luke 12:22–34

Which of you by worrying can add one cubit
to his stature? Luke 12:25

Hans Christian Andersen, author of such well-known fairy tales as "The Emperor's New Clothes," had a phobia of being buried alive. As a result, he always carried a note in his pocket telling anyone who might find him unconscious not to assume he was dead. He often left another note on his bedside table stating, "I only seem dead." Such was his anxiety until he finally succumbed to cancer in 1875.

We may think such a fear is strange, but do we have fears that will someday look just as irrational? Is it possible that the day will come when we look back and marvel at our own anxieties? Will we one day wonder at that foolish person who chose to worry rather than to pray? Will time eventually cast us as a pitiful person who was plagued by fear because we did not face life with the resources lavished on us by the Almighty Lord of the universe?

Worrying doesn't change anything. But trusting the Lord changes everything about the way we view life.

Forgive us, Lord, for our inclination to worry. Help us to see how foolish it is for us to worry about what you have promised to provide. Don't let us bury ourselves alive with fears.   MD

A STRATEGY FOR WINNING OVER WORRY

Identify specific worries.
Work to change what you can.
Leave what you can't change with God.

When we put our cares in God's hands,
He puts His peace in our hearts.

God Is Great!

Read: Psalm 86:1–17

You are great, and do wondrous things;
You alone are God. Psalm 86:10

O nly God is great." That was the solemn and unexpected
declaration of Jean-Baptiste Massillon as he began his sermon at the funeral service of King Louis XIV.

The king, who liked to be referred to as Louis the Great, had
ruled France from 1643 to 1715 with absolute power and incredible
splendor. His funeral was held in a magnificent cathedral that was
lit by a single candle alongside the ornate coffin. When it was time
for Massillon to speak, he reached out and extinguished the flame.
Then he broke the silence with the words, "Only God is great."

We recognize and admire some of our fellow mortals who are
considered to be great thinkers, great scientists, great inventors,
great achievers in every field of endeavor. In many ways they tower
above all of us ordinary people, but they still have the same needs
we do. They experience aches and pains. They have troubled minds
and hungry hearts. They cannot stave off death nor guarantee life
beyond the grave.

Only God is truly great—great enough to meet all our needs,
great enough to forgive all our sins, and great enough to carry us
through the dark valley of death into eternity to be with Him forever. So we declare with the psalmist, "You are great,... You alone
are God" (Psalm 86:10).   VCG

Immortal, invisible, God only wise,
In light inaccessible hid from our eyes,
Most blessed, most glorious, the Ancient of Days,
Almighty, victorious—Thy great name we praise. —Smith

In a world of empty superlatives, God is the greatest.

God Is Down-to-Earth

Read: 1 Kings 19:1–18

*Arise and eat, because the journey is
too great for you. 1 Kings 19:7*

The more challenging life becomes, the more we long for a down-to-earth spirituality to help us with the challenge. We're skeptical of believers who are "so heavenly minded that they are no earthly good." Yet we seldom get the balance right.

Author Os Guinness writes that we usually end up "being either practical at the expense of being spiritual or spiritual at the expense of being practical." He points out that, paradoxically, it is God who gets it right. God was never more down-to-earth than when Jesus came into the world. It was Jesus, God's divine Son, who became truly human by taking on human flesh. Therefore, Guinness concludes, the one who is the most spiritual (God) ended up being the most practical!

How God dealt with Elijah is a prime example of His practicality. Guinness points out that "God's remedy for Elijah's depression was not a refresher course in theology but food and sleep." Only then did He confront Elijah gently about his spiritual error.

If you are discouraged because you are tired or overworked, God's initial remedy for you is probably extra sleep or a day off. The most practical remedy, if it's the right one, is usually the most spiritual one.   JY

*When we're discouraged spiritually
And fear and doubt assail our soul,
We may just need to rest awhile
Before God heals and makes us whole. —Sper*

If we don't come apart and rest awhile, we may
just plain come apart. —Havner

October 24

You Can Always Pray

Read: Acts 12:1–16

I called on the Lord in distress; the Lord answered me. Psalm 118:5

The young mother called out to the missionary, "Come quick! My baby is going to die." Gale Fields was in Irian Jaya helping her husband Phil translate the Bible into Orya, a tribal language. But they also provided medical help whenever possible. Gale looked at the malaria-stricken child and realized she didn't have the right medicine to help the infant.

"I'm sorry," she told the mother, "I don't have any medicine for babies this small." Gale paused, then said, "I could pray for her though."

"Yes, anything to help my baby," answered the mother.

Gale prayed for the baby and then went home feeling helpless. After a little while, she again heard the mother cry out, "Gale, come quick and see my baby!"

Expecting the worst, Gale went to the baby's side. This time, though, she noticed improvement. The dangerous fever was gone. Later, Gale would say, "No wonder the Orya Christians learned to pray. They know God answers."

The early Christians prayed for Peter to be released from prison and then were "astonished" when God answered them (Acts 12:16). We respond that way too, but we shouldn't be surprised when God answers our prayers. Remember, His power is great and His resources are endless.   DB

Forgive us, Lord, when we're surprised
By answers to our prayer;
Increase our faith and teach us how
To trust Your loving care. —Sper

The most powerful position on earth is kneeling
before the Lord of the universe.

His Goodness

Read: Psalm 33:1–11

The earth is full of the goodness of the Lord. Psalm 33:5

One Saturday my life came perilously close to being permanently altered. My brother and my nephew stopped by to pick up a desk. After loading it on the truck, they chatted for a few minutes and then drove off. I went into the house while my husband Jay pulled our car into the garage. Moments later I heard a loud crash, so I raced out to the garage. Jay was staring at the overhead garage door, which had suddenly slammed down. If the spring had broken a few minutes earlier, someone would have been hit by the two-hundred-pound door—and would have been seriously injured, or even killed.

It was not simply a matter of luck or coincidence that no one was hurt in that garage. God's protective hand was there—one more reminder of His goodness.

I sometimes long for a dramatic display of God's glory and power to show that He is with me. But He wants me to see Him in His little displays of goodness, which He demonstrates every day in hundreds of acts of mercy and compassion—just as He did in my garage that Saturday.

The psalmist reminds us that "the earth is full of the goodness of the Lord" (Psalm 33:5). May God open our eyes to His many acts of goodness so we'll never doubt His presence and His love.   JAL

As endless as God's blessings are,
So should my praises be
For all His daily goodnesses
That flow unceasingly! —Adams

If you know that God's hand is in everything,
you can leave everything in God's hand.

Turning Trials into Triumphs

Read: James 1:1–11

*My brethren, count it all joy when you fall
into various trials. James 1:2*

James's words "Count it all joy when you fall into various trials" (1:2) offer a vital key for turning trials into triumphs. Although we don't choose to have trials, we can choose how we respond. J. B. Phillips paraphrased it like this: "Don't resent them as intruders, but welcome them as friends!"

British counselor Selwyn Hughes reminds people that trials are our friends only if our goal is to become more like Jesus. If our goal is to avoid difficulties or mishaps, our trials will seem more like intruders.

Hughes admits that he often needs to take his own advice. He recalls a time when he and his wife had pulled off to the side of the road to look at a map. Then a truck swerved and slammed into their car. They escaped injury, but their car was totaled. Then it started to rain! Hughes immediately battled with frustration, apprehension, and anger toward the other driver, and found it extremely difficult to "count it all joy." But as they waited for the police, he began to focus on how God could use the trial to make him more like Jesus. Gradually, the crisis became his friend.

The next time you face a trial of some kind, make friends with it and allow God to use the situation to make you more like Jesus.

JY

*Our loving God transforms us
And makes us like His Son
By using trials and testings
Until His work is done. —Sper*

God chooses what we go through;
we choose how we go through it.

He Cares for His Own

Read: Psalm 145:8–21

The Lord preserves all who love Him. Psalm 145:20

A young girl traveling on a train for the first time heard that it would have to cross several rivers. She was troubled and fearful as she thought of the water. But each time the train came near to a river, a bridge was always there to provide a safe way across.

After passing safely over several rivers and streams, the girl settled back in her seat with a sigh of relief. Then she turned to her mother and said, "I'm not worried anymore. Somebody has put bridges for us all the way!"

When we come to the deep rivers of trial and the streams of sorrow, we too will find that God in His grace "has put bridges for us all the way." So we need not fall into hopelessness and anxiety. In delightful though often untraceable ways, He will provide for us and carry us through the difficulties to the other side. Even though we may not understand how He will meet our needs, we can be sure that He will provide a way.

Those who have given their situations over to God can exclaim with the psalmist, "The Lord is righteous in all His ways, gracious in all His works... The Lord preserves all who love Him" (Psalm 145:17, 20).

Instead of worrying about what's ahead, we can trust the Lord to be there to care for us. HGB

Where God guides, He provides.

Pleasure Versus Joy

Read: John 15:7–11

These things I have spoken to you, that My joy may remain in you, and that your joy may be full. John 15:11

The world offers "passing pleasures" (Hebrews 11:25), but the Lord Jesus offers to give us full and lasting joy (John 15:11). Pleasure is dependent on circumstances, but joy is inward and is not disturbed by one's environment.

Pleasure is always changing, but joy is constant! Worldly delights are often followed by depression. True joy is grounded in Jesus Christ, who is "the same yesterday, today, and forever" (Hebrews 13:8).

To keep experiencing pleasure, we must run from one stimulus to another, for it refuses to be permanently grasped. Joy is just the opposite. It is a gift we receive from God.

Pleasure is built on self-seeking, but joy is based on self-sacrifice. The more we pursue self-gratification, the more empty we feel. If a pint of pleasure gives momentary happiness today, a gallon of excitement and thrills is necessary for the same effect tomorrow. Joy, however, is based on the sacrificial giving of ourselves. As we learn what it means to focus on the needs of others, we find greater fulfillment in God himself, who meets our every need.

Only when you seek the things of Christ can you find abiding joy.   HGB

There is joy beyond all measure
In abiding in the Lord;
It is promised most abundant
And enduring in His Word. —*McQuat*

For joy that will last, always put Christ first.

Tomorrow's Terrors

Read: Hebrews 13:1–8

*Jesus Christ is the same yesterday,
today, and forever. Hebrews 13:8*

Peter Marshall, whose dynamic preaching attracted crowds of people, died suddenly on the morning of January 25, 1949, at the age of forty-six. In one of his sermons he had said: "When the clock strikes for me, I shall go, not one minute early, and not one minute late. Until then, there is nothing to fear. I know that the promises of God are true, for they have been fulfilled in my life time and time again. Jesus still teaches and guides and protects and heals and comforts, and still wins our complete trust and our love."

Do you and I share that same fear-dispelling conviction? Can each of us, like David, say to our Lord, "My times are in Your hand" (Psalm 31:15)? Are we confident that God holds us in His almighty hands? Can we boldly say, "The Lord is my helper; I will not fear. What can man do to me?" (Hebrews 13:6).

True, we may have concern about the days ahead. As Scripture reminds us, we "do not know what will happen tomorrow" (James 4:14). But we do know that whatever happens He will always be with us (Hebrews 13:5). That knowledge can lighten any burden of worry about the future.

Some anxiety about the process of dying is normal. Yet, by the grace of God and by the comfort of His Spirit, we can face tomorrow's terrors with courage.   VCG

*I don't know about tomorrow,
Nor what coming days will bring;
But I know my Lord is with me,
And His praise my heart will sing. —Fitzhugh*

Worry can do a lot of things to you;
prayer can do a lot of things for you.

From Bitter to Sweet

Read: Exodus 15:22–27

The Lord showed him a tree. When he cast it into the waters,
the waters were made sweet. Exodus 15:25

Joy and sorrow are often close companions. Just as the Israelites went from the thrill of victory at the Red Sea to the bitter waters of Marah just three days later (Exodus 15:22–23), our rejoicing can quickly turn into anguish.

At Marah, the Lord told Moses to throw a tree into the water, which made it "sweet" and drinkable (v. 25). Another "tree," when "cast into" the bitter circumstances of our lives, can make them sweet. It is the cross of Jesus (1 Peter 2:24). Our outlook will be transformed as we contemplate His sacrificial death and His submission to the will of God (Luke 22:42).

Our pain may come from the ill will of others, or worse, from their neglect. Nevertheless, our Lord has permitted it. We may not understand why, yet it is the will of our Father and Friend, whose wisdom and love are infinite.

When we say yes to God as His Spirit reveals His will to us through His Word, the bitter circumstances of our lives can become sweet. We must not grumble against what the Lord permits. Instead, we must do all that He asks us to do. Jesus said that we are to take up our cross daily and follow Him (Luke 9:23).

When we remember Jesus's cross and submit to the Father as He did, bitter experiences can become sweet. DHR

God uses our difficulties to make us better—not bitter.

October 31

Be Glad for Today

Read: Psalm 118:14-24

This is the day the Lord has made; we will rejoice
and be glad in it. Psalm 118:24

In Edith Schaeffer's book called *The Tapestry*, she describes a
summer when her husband Francis was away in Europe for three
months. During that time of missing him greatly, Edith and her sister Janet took their children to live in a former schoolhouse on Cape
Cod. On a shoestring budget they shared the rent, lived without a
car, and created daily adventures for the five young children.

Looking back years later, Edith said of that summer: "Never
again have I spent time of that sort with my own children or my
sister and nephews. The sudden precious moments in life need to be
recognized for the unique periods they are, not wasted by wishing
for something else."

Edith's perspective offers us a key to applying the words of Psalm
118:24, "This is the day the Lord has made; we will rejoice and be
glad in it." During difficult times, we are tempted to become pas-
sive while waiting for a storm of life to pass. But God invites us to
actively pursue the opportunities at hand instead of lamenting over
what we don't have.

Because the Lord has made this day, we can look past the closed
doors to see people and opportunities we had previously overlooked. In celebrating their value, we will discover joy and gladness
from God. DCM

The God who put us here on earth
Knows life is tinged with sadness,
And so He gives us many things
To fill our hearts with gladness. —Hess

You don't have to worry about eyestrain from
looking on the brighter side of life.

November 1

Shine On!

Read: Daniel 1:1–6

Let it be known to you, O king, that we do not serve your gods, nor will we worship the gold image which you have set up. Daniel 3:18

Ashpenaz, a high court official in ancient Babylon, was committed to banishing any testimony of Israel's God from his kingdom. His strategy focused on young leadership from the captive Hebrews. Ashpenaz gave the captives new names to honor the pagan gods of Babylon. This made sense to him, because their original Hebrew names honored their God (Daniel 1:6).

But the life choices of those captives were a far more powerful witness than any label put on them. When faced with a literal trial by fire, the young men would not bow down and worship the golden idol. Instead, they accepted the punishment of being cast into the fiery furnace—confident in God's sovereignty and care (Daniel 3).

Do you know unbelievers who try to pressure you to fit in with their lifestyle? If you don't party with them, follow a questionable business practice, or laugh at an offensive joke, do you get the cold shoulder? People may even call you names because you won't run with their crowd. But when you're rejected because of your loyalty to God, you can live in a way that honors the Father.

It doesn't matter what others call us. How we live our lives before God does. What's important is that we always let our light shine.   DF

Never mind what others call you—
God alone knows every heart;
Character is all that matters—
Lord, to us this grace impart. —Hess

A small light can dispel great darkness.

November 2

Everlasting Arms

Read: Deuteronomy 33:26–29

The eternal God is your refuge, and underneath are
the everlasting arms. Deuteronomy 33:27

After a pre-concert rehearsal in New York City's Carnegie Hall, Randall Atcheson sat on stage alone. He had successfully navigated the intricate piano compositions of Beethoven, Chopin, and Liszt for the evening program, and with only minutes remaining before the doors opened, he wanted to play one more piece for himself. What came from his heart and his hands was an old hymn by Elisha Hoffman:

> *What have I to dread,*
> *what have I to fear,*
> *Leaning on the everlasting arms?*
> *I have blessed peace*
> *with my Lord so near,*
> *Leaning on the everlasting arms.*

Those words echo the truth in the final blessing of Moses: "There is no one like the God of Jeshurun, who rides the heavens to help you, and in His excellency on the clouds. The eternal God is your refuge, and underneath are the everlasting arms" (Deuteronomy 33:26–27).

What a gift we have in our own arms and hands—they can swing a hammer, hold a child, or help a friend. But while our strength is limited, God's boundless power on our behalf is expressed in might and gentle care. "Behold, the Lord's hand is not shortened, that it cannot save" (Isaiah 59:1). "He will gather the lambs with His arm, and carry them in His bosom" (Isaiah 40:11).

Whatever challenge or opportunity we face, there is security and peace in His everlasting arms.   DCM

The heavenly Father's arms never tire of holding His children.

No Need Is Too Trivial

Read: Isaiah 49:13–18

*As a father pities his children, so the Lord pities
those who fear Him. Psalm 103:13*

Several mothers of small children were sharing encouraging answers to prayer. One woman admitted that she felt selfish when she troubled God with her personal needs. "Compared with the huge global needs God faces," she explained, "my circumstances must seem trivial to Him."

Moments later, her little son pinched his fingers in a door and ran screaming to his mother. She didn't say, "How selfish of you to bother me with your throbbing fingers when I'm busy!" No, she showed him great compassion and tenderness.

As Psalm 103:13 reminds us, this is the response of love, both human and divine. In Isaiah 49, God said that even though a mother may forget to have compassion on her child, the Lord never forgets His children (v. 15). God assured His people, "I have inscribed you on the palms of My hands" (v. 16).

Such intimacy with God belongs to those who fear Him and who rely on Him rather than on themselves. As that child with throbbing fingers ran freely to his mother, so may we run to God with our daily problems.

Our compassionate God doesn't neglect others to respond to your concerns. He has limitless time and love for each of His children. No need is too trivial for Him.   JY

*No heart too small, no world too wide
To feel the Master's touch;
Dear Lord of all, we give Thee thanks
For Thou hast sent so much.* —Michael

God bears the world's weight on His shoulder, and
He holds His children in the palm of His hand.

Strength and Support

Read: Job 4:1–11

Your words have upheld him who was stumbling, and you have strength-
ened the feeble knees. Job 4:4

The local newspaper reported that a mother is devastated because her twenty-one-year-old son, who had always seemed like an upright young man, had been arrested for dealing drugs.

Also in our community, the parents and siblings of a fifteen-year-old are grieving because he was killed in a gun accident.

An aged friend is heartbroken because her only daughter, the person she depended on more than all others, died from cancer.

People who are hurting have a common need: the comfort that comes from trusting God. They need to be assured that tragedy and grief are not a mark of God's disfavor but that He weeps with them, He loves them, and He will never leave those who are His.

Eliphaz said to Job: "Your words have upheld him who was stumbling, and you have strengthened the feeble knees" (Job 4:4). Job earned this tribute despite his own deep suffering. And when we offer comfort to sorrowing and suffering people, we not only emulate Job—we emulate Jesus.

In the midst of a host of hurting people, each one of us can reach out to become a comforter like Job. Let's ask God to make our hearts tender enough to support and strengthen those who are hurting.   HVL

God doesn't comfort us to make us comfortable,
but to make us comforters.

November 5

A Living Hope

Read: 1 Peter 1:3–9

Blessed be [God]... who according to His abundant mercy has begotten us again to a living hope. 1 Peter 1:3

Life is hard for everybody, but it's much harder for some than for others. Putting our trust in Christ as our Savior does little to change that. Nothing in the Bible promises us a free pass merely because we are Christ's followers. In fact, some of our wounds may not heal and some of our deficiencies may not be corrected during our lifetime. They may even get worse. Yet our deformities and weaknesses are only temporary.

Anticipating what God has in store for us can put a smile in our heart. Hope gives us poise and lets us live with inner strength, because we know that one day we will be dramatically different than we are now.

If you are in some way damaged by past abuse or feeling defeated by sin, or if you feel so inferior to others that you walk with your eyes to the ground, take heart in what God has in store for you. Live today with the courage God gives you. Make what you can of your afflictions. But rejoice, because all that degrades and limits you is only temporary. It will be gone—some of it sooner rather than later.

If you have a living hope in Christ, you can deal with your past because of your future. God's glorious best for you lies ahead.

HWR

Lord, give us grace to trust You when
Life's burdens seem too much to bear;
Dispel the darkness with new hope
And help us rise above despair. —Sper

Christians can cope with their past because they have hope for the future.

The Good That Pain Can Do

Read: 1 Peter 4:1–3

*It is good for me that I have been afflicted, that
I may learn Your statutes. Psalm 119:71*

Affliction, when we accept it with humility, can be instructive, a discipline that leads us to a deeper, fuller life. "Before I was afflicted I went astray," David said, "but now I keep Your Word" (Psalm 119:67). Peter would agree: Affliction leads us to live not for ourselves, "but for the will of God" (1 Peter 4:2).

Far from being an obstacle to our spiritual growth, pain can be the instrument of it—if we're trained by it. It can push us closer to God and deeper into His Word. It is a means by which He graciously shapes us to be like His Son, gradually giving us the compassion, contentment, tranquility, and courage we long and pray for. Without pain, we wouldn't be all that God wants us to be. His strength shines brightest through human weakness.

Has God set you apart today to receive instruction through suffering and pain? Endure this training patiently. He can turn the trial into a blessing. He can use it to draw you close to His heart and into His Word, teach you the lessons He intends for you to learn, and use it to bestow His grace on you.

God is making more of you—something much better—than you ever thought possible. DHR

*By faith a Christian can have poise
And rise above all that annoys—
Sustained and strengthened by God's power
To live in victory hour by hour.* —Hess

Whatever God teaches us through pain is gain.

How to Face Another Day

Read: James 4:13–17

This is the day the Lord has made; we will rejoice and be glad in it.
Psalm 118:24

World-famous cellist Pablo Casals once gave this challenging testimony: "For the past 80 years I have started each day in the same manner... I go to the piano and I play two preludes and fugues of Bach. I cannot think of doing otherwise. It is a benediction on the house. But that is not its only meaning for me. It is a rediscovery of the world of which I have the joy of being a part."

If that is how a dedicated musician daily started his waking hours, we Christians—by the enabling grace of the Holy Spirit—can surely dedicate each new day to our Lord. No matter where we are or what our situation may be, each day we can resolve to dedicate the hours before us to God's praise. As David wrote, "This is the day the Lord has made; we will rejoice and be glad in it" (Psalm 118:24).

If you are facing loneliness or pain as once again you pick up your burden, you can draw on the Lord's resources and be a living testimony of His all-sufficiency. If you're filled with thanksgiving and praise, you can tell others of God's goodness.

James reminded us that we "do not know what will happen tomorrow" (4:14). All the more reason, then, to dedicate each day to rejoicing in the Lord.   VCG

This is the day the Lord hath made,
He calls the hours His own;
Let heaven rejoice, let earth be glad,
And praise surround the throne. —Watts

If you know Jesus, you always have a reason to rejoice.

Life Is Real

Read: Psalm 56

Whenever I am afraid, I will trust in You. Psalm 56:3

In the comic strip *Peanuts,* Lucy had just broken the news to Linus that children cannot live at home forever. Eventually they grow up and move away. Then she said that when he left she would get his room. But Linus quickly reminded her that at some time she too would have to leave home. When this realization hit Lucy, she was shocked, but she quickly came up with a solution. She turned the TV up loud, crawled into her beanbag chair with a bowl of ice cream, and refused to think about it.

Avoiding unpleasant circumstances is not as easy as Lucy thinks. Life's realities cannot be avoided. We may try to run and hide, but struggles and trials have a way of dogging our footsteps and eventually catching up with us.

Instead, we should face up to our problems. The psalmist David did this when beset by persistent foes and false friends. He didn't try to minimize his danger; he acknowledged the storm that was raging around him and looked to the Lord. He wrote, "In God I have put my trust" (Psalm 56:4).

Let's follow David's example—not Lucy's. Facing up to life's difficulties may be a frightening experience. But when we trust God and draw close to Him, we'll experience real deliverance.

PVG

When troubles call on you, call on God.

November 9

A Tender and Mighty God

Read: Psalm 147:1–5

[God] heals the brokenhearted and binds up their wounds. He counts the number of the stars; He calls them all by name. Psalm 147:3–4

God knows and numbers the stars, yet He is concerned about you and me, even though we're broken by sin. He binds our shattered hearts with sensitivity and kindness, and He brings healing into the depths of our souls. The greatness of God's power is the greatness of His heart. His strength is the measure of His love. He is a tender and mighty God.

The psalmist tells us that God "counts the number of the stars," and even "calls them all by name" (147:4). Would He care for the stars that are mere matter and not care for us, who bear His image? Of course not. He knows about our lonely struggles, and He cares. It is His business to care.

God, in the form of His Son Jesus, was subject to all our passions (Hebrews 2:18). He understands and does not scold or condemn when we fall short and fail. He leans down and listens to our cries for help. He gently corrects us. He heals through time and with great skill.

The stars will fall from the sky someday. They are not God's major concern—you are! He "is able to keep you from stumbling, and to present you faultless before the presence of His glory with exceeding joy" (Jude 1:24). And He will do it!   DHR

The God who made the firmament,
Who made the deepest sea,
The God who put the stars in place
Is the God who cares for me. —Berg

Because God cares about us,
we can leave our cares with Him.

Two Great Fears

Read: Psalm 107:23–32

He guides them to their desired haven. Psalm 107:30

Psalm 107 tells of "those who go down to the sea in ships" (v. 23). Along their journey at sea, they see God as the One behind the tempestuous storm and the One who calms it. In the world of sailing vessels there were two great fears. One fear was of a terrible gale, and the other was of having no wind at all.

In "The Rime of the Ancient Mariner," English poet Samuel Taylor Coleridge (1772–1834) describes tempests and doldrums at sea. Two lines have become household words:

Water, water everywhere,
Nor any drop to drink.

In doldrum latitudes, the wind dies down and a sailing ship remains stationary. Captain and crew are "stuck" with no relief in sight. Eventually, with no wind, their water supply runs out.

Sometimes life demands that we weather a storm. At other times it puts us to the test of tedium. We may feel stuck. What we want most is just out of reach. But whether we find ourselves in a crisis of circumstance or in a place where the spiritual wind has been taken out of our sails, we need to trust God for guidance. The Lord, who is sovereign over changing circumstances, will eventually guide us to our desired haven (v. 30). DF

I will not fear the howling storms of doubt,
Nor shudder when I feel I'm all alone;
But I will trust my Savior as I shout:
"The Lord's my helper—He is on the throne!" —Hess

God orders our stops as well as our steps.

November 11

Father Knows Best

Read: 2 Samuel 16:5–12

It may be that the Lord will look on my affliction, and that the Lord will repay me with good for his cursing. 2 Samuel 16:12

Unlike David in 2 Samuel 16, we like to take revenge, silence our critics, insist on fairness, and set everything right. But David told those who wanted to defend him: "Let [Shimei] alone, and let him curse; for so the Lord has ordered him" (v. 11).

It seems to me that as the years go by, we grow—as David did—in the awareness of God's protective love. We become less concerned with what others say about us and more willing to give ourselves over to our Father. We learn humble submission to God's will.

We may, of course, ask our opponents to justify their charges, or we may meet them with steadfast denial if they charge us falsely. But when we have done all we can do, the only thing left is to wait patiently until God vindicates us.

In the meantime, it's good to look beyond the words of those who vilify us to the will of the One who loves us with infinite love. We need to say that whatever God permits is for His ultimate good in us or in others—even though our hearts break and we shed bitter tears.

You're in God's hands, no matter what others say about you. He sees your distress, and in time will repay you with good. Trust Him and abide in His love.   DHR

Each day we learn from yesterday
Of God's great love and care;
And every burden we must face
He'll surely help us bear. —DJD

It takes the storm to prove the real shelter.

Prosperity and Adversity

Read: Proverbs 30:1-9

*Give me neither poverty nor riches—feed me with
the food allotted to me. Proverbs 30:8*

Prosperity and adversity are equal-opportunity destroyers. The extremes of life can be hazardous because a person with too much may encounter as much difficulty as one with too little.

Agur, the writer of Proverbs 30, must have sensed this danger when he prayed: "Remove falsehood and lies far from me; give me neither poverty nor riches—feed me with the food allotted to me; lest I be full and deny You, and say, 'Who is the Lord?' or lest I be poor and steal, and profane the name of my God" (Proverbs 30:8–9).

A similar request occurs in a beautiful choral anthem composed by Benjamin Harlan:

Write Your blessed name,
O Lord, upon my heart,
There to remain so indelibly engraved
That no prosperity, nor adversity
Shall remove me from Your love.

In Proverbs 30 the focus is on circumstances, while the song centers on the state of our heart. Perhaps we should pray that God would guard us in both areas of our lives.

The late Dr. Carlyle Marney, a prominent pastor, often said that most of us need to have our "wanter" fixed. Instead of always asking for more, we should seek the balance expressed in Proverbs 30.

When we invite the Lord to place His mark of ownership on our lives, we acknowledge His wise and loving provision for all our needs.   DCM

Contentment is realizing that God
has already given me all I need.

The Struggle

Read: 2 Timothy 3

In the last days perilous times will come. 2 Timothy 3:1

Have you ever heard someone suggest that if you just trust Jesus, He'll solve all your problems and you'll float through life with riches and peace?

If that were the way God planned it for the people who serve Him, then what was Paul's problem? After his conversion, he was as godly as they come, yet he had problems galore. He was one of the greatest missionaries of all time—and what did he get for his trouble? Beaten up. Arrested. Nearly drowned. Run out of town.

Look at Joseph, Abraham, Job, Jeremiah, Peter—godly men one and all. Yet they all faced dangers and trouble none of us would ever desire.

So, why the struggle? Why is it that tragedy strikes Christians with the same blunt force that it strikes the most antagonistic atheists? Why are we not exempt from natural disasters, serious illness, interpersonal squabbles, and mistreatment by others?

Somehow, in God's way of making things work out, our troubles can advance His kingdom and purposes (Romans 8:28; Philippians 1:12). Our task is to glorify God, no matter what the circumstances. If we do, our struggle can direct others to the Savior as we make our way toward our ultimate goal of rest and reward in heaven.   DB

To make us good ambassadors
God sends us trials along the way,
But we become true conquerors
When in life's struggles we obey. —Hess

God allows trials in our lives not to impair us
but to improve us.

November 14

Sustained in the Silence

Read: Psalm 94:16–23

In the multitude of my anxieties within me,
Your comforts delight my soul. Psalm 94:19

Hudson Taylor (1832–1905) was the founder of the China Inland Mission and a great servant of God. But after the ferocious Boxer Rebellion of 1900, in which hundreds of his fellow missionaries were killed, Taylor was emotionally devastated and his health began to fail. Nearing the end of life's journey, he wrote, "I am so weak that I cannot work. I cannot read my Bible; I cannot even pray. I can only lie still in God's arms like a child and trust."

Have you been passing through a time when you are tired of body and sick of heart? Do you find it difficult to focus your mind on biblical promises? Has it become hard for you to pray? Don't write yourself off as a spiritual castaway. You are joining a host of God's people who have experienced the dark night of the soul.

When we endure such times, all we can do—indeed, all we *need* do—is lie still like a child in the arms of our heavenly Father. Words aren't necessary. A comforting father doesn't expect his child to make speeches. Neither does God. He knows we need His soothing care. In times of trouble, His mercy holds us up (Psalm 94:18). We may trust Him to carry us through that dark night of the soul and on into the dawning light. VCG

Under His wings I am safely abiding,
Though the night deepens and tempests are wild;
Still I can trust Him; I know He will keep me,
He has redeemed me, and I am His child. —Cushing

When we have nothing left but God,
we'll find that God is enough.

November 15

Be Glad!

Read: Psalm 69:29–36

I will praise the name of God with a song... The humble
shall see this and be glad. Psalm 69:30, 32

For several days after my husband and my brother sang a duet in church of "Be Ye Glad," I was unable to get the lyrics by Michael Blanchard out of my mind. But they're good words to get stuck on, reminding us to be glad because the Lord's grace has paid our debts in full.

Ancient Israel's beloved songwriter and king often wrote about gladness. In three consecutive songs, David spoke of being glad: Psalms 68:3; 69:32; 70:4. His lyrics assure us that it's not the rich or the powerful who have reason to be glad but those who are humble and right with God.

David expanded on this theme in another song: "Blessed is he whose transgression is forgiven, whose sin is covered... Be glad in the Lord and rejoice, you righteous; and shout for joy, all you upright in heart!" (32:1, 11).

If you are feeling poor and powerless today, you can still be glad. You can have something of far more value: a debt-free relationship with God.

When we stop defending our own sinful ways and humbly acknowledge that God's ways are right, true gladness will spring forth in songs of glorious praise. JAL

We can rejoice, our debt's been paid;
All of our sin on Christ was laid;
He wants us now to live our days
In thankfulness and endless praise. —Sper

Joy is the result of a right relationship with God.

Hope for the Blues

Read: Psalm 62

Pour out your heart before Him;
God is a refuge for us. Psalm 62:8

You've felt it yourself, or at least listened to other people talk about it—the blues, times of dark discouragement. Lynette Joy, in an article for christianwomentoday.com, tells of several steps we can take during those dark times to turn toward Jesus, the Light of the World:

Light up your heart through prayer. Pour out your heart to God when you're feeling overwhelmed (Psalm 62:8). Take your anxieties to Him in prayer (Philippians 4:6–7). And if you journal or write down your prayers, you can look back later to see how the Lord has answered you.

Light up your mind with truth. Read the Word of God every day, at least for a few minutes. Let His truth challenge, permeate, and transform your incorrect thinking that life is hopeless (Psalm 46:1; Romans 12:2).

Light up your life by doing God's will. His will for you is to worship and serve Him. Stay involved in your church where you can worship and fellowship with others and serve Him (Hebrews 10:25). This will help you grow in your trust of God.

When we feel darkness begin to close in on us, we need to turn to Jesus, the Light. He will be a refuge (Psalm 62:7–8) and will give us the strength to keep going. AC

You won't stumble in the dark if you
walk in the light of God's Word.

November 17

Is He Listening?

Read: Matthew 26:39–42; 27:45–46

My God, My God, why have
You forsaken Me? Matthew 27:46

S ometimes it feels as if God isn't listening to me." Those words, from a woman who tried to stay strong in her walk with God while coping with an alcoholic husband, echo the heart cry of many believers. For eighteen years, she asked God to change her husband. Yet it never happened.

What are we to think when we repeatedly ask God for something good—something that could easily glorify Him—but the answer doesn't come? Is He listening or not?

Let's look at the life of the Savior. In the Garden of Gethsemane, He agonized for hours in prayer, pouring out His heart and pleading, "Let this cup pass from Me" (Matthew 26:39). But the Father's answer was clearly no. To provide salvation, God had to send Jesus to die on the cross. Even though Jesus felt as if His Father had forsaken Him, He prayed intensely and passionately because He trusted that God was listening.

When we pray, we may not see how God is working or understand how He will bring good through it all. So we have to trust Him. We relinquish our rights and let God do what is best.

We must leave the unknowable to the all-knowing One. He is listening and working things out His way.   DB

When we bend our knees to pray, God bends His ear to listen.

Peaceful Anxiety

Read: Philippians 4:4–13

*The peace of God . . . will guard your hearts and
minds through Christ Jesus. Philippians 4:7*

I was scheduled to teach at a Bible conference outside the U.S. and was waiting for my visa to be approved. It had been rejected once, and time was slipping away. Without the visa, I would lose an opportunity for ministry, and my colleagues in that country would have to find another speaker at the last minute.

During those stressful days, a coworker asked how I felt about it all. I told him I was experiencing "peaceful anxiety." When he looked at me rather quizzically, I explained: "I have had anxiety because I need the visa and there is nothing I can do about it. But I have great peace because I know that, after all, there is nothing I can do about it!"

It's comforting to know that such things are in our Father's hands. My inability to do anything about the problem was more than matched by my confidence in God, for whom all things are possible. As I prayed about the situation, my anxiety was replaced by His peace (Philippians 4:6–7).

The problems of life can be taxing on us—physically, emotionally, and spiritually. Yet, as we learn to trust in the Father's care, we can have the peace that not only surpasses all understanding but also overcomes our anxiety. We can be at rest, for we are in God's hands. BC

Oh, the peace I find in Jesus,
Peace no power on earth can shake,
Peace that makes the Lord so precious,
Peace that none from me can take. —Beck

When we keep our minds on God,
God will keep our minds at peace.

November 19

Coping While Caring

Read: Psalm 46

God is our refuge and strength, a very present
help in trouble. Psalm 46:1

A survey titled "Caregiving in the U.S." estimates that more than forty-four million Americans are unpaid caregivers, and a majority of them currently work or have worked while providing care. The survey also found that God, family, and friends were most often cited as sources of strength by people who are caring for others.

Three-fourths of the respondents said they relied on prayer to deal with the demands of caregiving. "Prayer is the best way to refresh yourself," said one person. "I find a quiet place and pray and cry and get relief. Then I can go back into the room calm."

"God is our refuge and strength," wrote the psalmist, "a very present help in trouble" (Psalm 46:1). Eugene Peterson's vivid paraphrase says: "God is a safe place to hide, ready to help when we need Him."

Through prayer, we can step into the calming presence of the Lord and find strength to go on. As we bring our heartaches and needs to God, He meets us where we are and gives us His peace. He is an ever-present help who cares for us in every situation.

Caregiving is a high calling and a difficult task. But there is strength from the Lord to help us as we care for those who need us.   DCM

I must tell Jesus all of my trials,
I cannot bear these burdens alone;
In my distress He kindly will help me,
He ever loves and cares for His own. —*Hoffman*

Prayer puts us in touch with God—our greatest caregiver.

Turning Pain into Praise

Read: 2 Corinthians 1:7–11

As you are partakers of the sufferings, so also you will
partake of the consolation. 2 Corinthians 1:7

After years of a remarkable and fruitful ministry in India, Amy Carmichael became a bedridden sufferer. As the courageous founder and dynamic heart of the Dohnavur Fellowship, she had been instrumental in rescuing hundreds of girls and boys from a terrible life of sexual servitude.

While she carried on her rescue operation of bringing young people into spiritual freedom through faith in Jesus Christ, she wrote books and poems that are still blessing readers around the world.

Then arthritis made Amy a pain-wracked invalid. Did she bemoan her affliction or question God? No. Amy was still the guiding inspiration of Dohnavur, and she still kept on writing. Her meditations, letters, and poems are filled with praise to God and encouragement to her fellow pilgrims.

When affliction strikes us, how do we react? Are we embittered, or do we trustfully appropriate God's sustaining grace? (2 Corinthians 12:9). And do we prayerfully encourage those around us by our Spirit-enabled cheerfulness, our courage, and our confidence in God?

When we rely on the Lord, He will help us turn pain into praise. VCG

Can God trust you with sorrow,
With anguish, and with pain,
Or would your faith soon falter
And faint beneath the strain? —Nicholson

Praise is the song of a soul set free.

Mixing-Bowl Musings

Read: Luke 18:18–27

The things which are impossible with men
are possible with God. Luke 18:27

Countless times I've heard myself say, "I'm going to bake a cake." Then one day I realized that I've never baked a cake in my life—only my oven can do that. I simply mix the right ingredients and allow the oven to do its part. Through that division of labor, I have the joy of seeing others taste and enjoy delicious cake.

God used my mixing-bowl musings to clarify a dilemma I once had after starting a neighborhood Bible study. It was one thing to bring my neighbors together to study the Bible, but seeing them believe and follow Christ was another. I felt powerless. Suddenly I saw the obvious. Like baking cakes, making Christians was impossible for me, but not for God. I had blended the right ingredients—an open home, friendship, love. Now I had to trust the Holy Spirit, through His Word, to do His work. When I cooperated with that division of labor, I had the joy of seeing others taste of God's goodness.

In Luke 18:18–27, Jesus so vividly described some hindrances to saving faith that His listeners began to wonder if anyone could be saved. Do you feel that way about someone? Be encouraged by the Lord's strong reminder that there are some things that only God can do. Saving people is one of them.   JY

The Lord's the only one who can
Transform a person's heart;
But when we share God's saving truth,
We play a crucial part. —Sper

We sow the seed, but God brings the harvest.

No Terror

Read: Psalm 31:9–24

Make Your face shine upon Your servant;
save me for Your mercies' sake. Psalm 31:16

After the terrorist bombing in Bali in 2002, one man reacted by giving up traveling. Three years later, he finally took his family for a holiday in Bali, together with fifty tourists from Newcastle, Australia. The trip ended in tragedy when his family was caught in a suicide bombing at a café on Jimbaran Beach.

From New York to Indonesia, warnings and threats of terrorist attacks continue. Terrorism derives its sting by exporting fear. No one feels safe.

In Psalm 31, David was in the grip of surrounding threats that terrorized both his reputation and his life. He wrote, "Fear is on every side," and said, "They scheme to take away my life" (v. 13).

When everything seemed bleakest, David cried in despair, "I trust in You, O Lord" (v. 14). He began to find peace when he acknowledged, "My times are in Your hand" (v. 15).

In our world, perfect safety is not possible. But David's God is our God. Though our earthly security may be threatened, we can never lose God's eternal, unfailing love.

To those who trust in the Lord, David wrote these hope-filled words: "[The Lord] shall strengthen your heart" (v. 24). When we place our times in His hand, we can exchange the fear of terror for peace and praise. AL

Peace, perfect peace,
Death shadowing us and ours?
Jesus has vanquished
Death and all its powers. —Bickersteth

Putting your faith in the living God takes the fear out of living.

Always Thankful

Read: Habakkuk 3:17–19

*I will rejoice in the Lord, I will joy in the
God of my salvation. Habakkuk 3:18*

Perhaps Habakkuk 3:17–19 was an unusual Bible passage to read as our family and guests sat down to a traditional feast of turkey with all the trimmings. But I had a reason for choosing it. Simply to bow my head and give thanks didn't seem to be enough. Compared with the poverty of many of the world's people, I am wealthy.

The prophet Habakkuk was awaiting the destruction of his country by the ruthless Chaldeans, whose army was called by God to punish His people for their disobedient and evil ways (Habakkuk 1:5–6). He said, "Though the fig tree may not blossom, nor fruit be on the vines; though the labor of the olive may fail, and the fields yield no food; though the flock may be cut off from the fold, and there be no herd in the stalls—yet I will rejoice in the Lord" (3:17–18).

Those words made me stop and ask, "Am I thankful to God regardless of what He gives or withholds?" Habakkuk pondered how he would respond to the loss of every material blessing. He concluded, "I will joy in the God of my salvation" (v. 18).

Circumstances may change, but God remains the same. That's always cause for thanksgiving.   DCM

*We can give thanks in every trial
And say, "Your will be done,"
For God's at work in everything
To make us like His Son. —DJD*

Thankfulness depends on what is in your heart,
not what is in your hand.

November 24

A Gratitude Visit

Read: Romans 16:1–16

*I commend to you Phoebe, . . . for indeed she has been a
helper of many and of myself also. Romans 16:1–2*

Counting your blessings promotes good physical health, according to a study by some U.S. doctors. Volunteers who kept weekly gratitude journals reported fewer aches and pains than those who recorded daily hassles or neutral events.

A "gratitude visit" was developed by Dr. Martin E. P. Seligman to promote strong emotional health. He tells people to think of someone who has made an important difference in their lives. He asks them to write the story of how that person has helped them, and then to visit that person and read the story aloud. Tests show that a year later the people who had done so were happier and reported fewer episodes of depression. Even more important, think of what it must have done for those who were thanked!

The apostle Paul had a long list of people who had helped him and for whom he was grateful (Romans 16:1–16). He wrote that Phoebe had "been a helper," Priscilla and Aquila had "risked their own necks" for his life, and Mary had "labored much" for him. And he took time to write his thanks in a letter to the church at Rome.

Who has helped to shape your life? Could you make a gratitude visit—for their sake, and for yours? AC

*Consider what the Lord has done
Through those who've shown you love;
Then thank them for their faithful deeds,
For blessings from above. —Sper*

Gratitude should not be an occasional incident
but a continuous attitude.

Peace in the Storm

Read: Isaiah 26:1–4

You will keep him in perfect peace, whose mind is stayed
on You, because he trusts in You. Isaiah 26:3

Life can seem unbearable at times. Physical pain, difficult decisions, financial hardships, the death of a loved one, or shattered dreams threaten to engulf us. We become fearful and perplexed. Plagued by doubts, we may even find it difficult to pray.

Those of us who know the Lord through personal faith in Christ have in Him a calm retreat in the storms of life, even while the howling winds of trial are sweeping over us. We can experience peace of mind and calmness of spirit.

Richard Fuller, a nineteenth-century minister, told of an old seaman who said, "In fierce storms, we must put the ship in a certain position and keep her there." Said Fuller, "This, Christian, is what you must do... You must put your soul in one position and keep it there. You must stay upon the Lord; and, come what may—winds, waves, cross seas, thunder, lightning, frowning rocks, roaring breakers—no matter what, you must hold fast your confidence in God's faithfulness and His everlasting love in Christ Jesus."

Do you feel overwhelmed by your troubles? Learn a lesson from that old sailor. Fix your mind on the Lord. Ask for His help. Then trust Him to give you peace in your storm (Philippians 4:6–7).

RDH

Stayed upon Jehovah,
Hearts are fully blest—
Finding, as He promised,
Perfect peace and rest. —Havergal

The secret of peace is to give every anxious care to God.

A Surprise Answer

Read: 1 John 3:16–23

Whatever we ask we receive from Him, because
we keep His commandments and do those things
that are pleasing in His sight. 1 John 3:22

When Josh McDowell's mother died, he was not sure of her salvation. He became depressed. Was she a Christian or not? "Lord," he prayed, "somehow give me the answer so I can get back to normal. I've just got to know." It seemed like an impossible request.

Two days later, Josh drove out to the ocean and walked to the end of a pier to be alone. There sat an elderly woman in a lawn chair, fishing. "Where's your home originally?" she asked. "Michigan—Union City," Josh replied. "Nobody's heard of it. I tell people it's a suburb of—" "Battle Creek," interrupted the woman. "I had a cousin from there. Did you know the McDowell family?"

Stunned, Josh responded, "Yes, I'm Josh McDowell." "I can't believe it," said the woman. "I'm a cousin to your mother." "Do you remember anything at all about my mother's spiritual life?" asked Josh. "Why sure—your mom and I were just girls—teenagers—when a tent revival came to town. We both went forward to accept Christ." "Praise God!" shouted Josh, startling the surrounding fishermen.

God delights to give us what we ask when it is in His will. Never underestimate His desire to respond to our prayers. A surprise may be just around the corner.   DJD

That long-sought wish, oh, how I prayed,
I thought it not divinely willed,
And then the joyous, tear-stained smile
Of faith triumphant, hope fulfilled! —Brandt

If you get definite with God, He'll get definite with you.

November 27

Three Certainties

Read: 1 Thessalonians 4:13–18

O Death, where is your sting? O Hades,
where is your victory? 1 Corinthians 15:55

As I waited outside the Intensive Care Unit for changes in the condition of a loved one, I was reminded that death affects all of us: old and young, male and female, rich and poor.

In 1 Thessalonians 4, the apostle Paul comforted those who mourned the death of their loved ones. He told them that excessive grief resulted from being uninformed. Weeping for our loss is good, but we need not weep like those who have no hope. Instead, we must rely on three certainties of death.

The first certainty is that the soul does not die. The souls of departed believers are with the Lord (v. 14). They have retired from this problematic world, and they "sleep in Jesus."

Second, Jesus will come for every believer. Whether a Christian is alive on earth or asleep in death, Jesus will return for all His children (vv. 16–17).

Third, there will be a joyous reunion. "Then we who are alive and remain shall be caught up together with them in the clouds to meet the Lord in the air. And thus we shall always be with the Lord" (v. 17).

Knowing these certainties brings comfort to believers when their friends and loved ones depart. Although we are separated from them for a while, we will meet again in the presence of our Lord.

AL

When facing death's shadow, remember the Light;
The shadows bring fear, and the dark shrouds our eyes;
But if we will turn to face Jesus the Light,
The shadows will fade as He brightens our skies. —Lee

Sunset in one land is sunrise in another.

Love That Lifts

Read: Psalm 40:1–3

They called upon the Lord, and He answered them. Psalm 99:6

When King David looked back on his life, he remembered some painful experiences. In Psalm 40, he recalled one especially severe difficulty, a time when he felt as if he had sunk deep into "the miry clay" (v. 2).

In his despair David kept pleading with God for deliverance, and graciously the Lord answered his desperate cries. Lifting him out of the "horrible pit," He set his feet on solid ground (v. 2). No wonder David broke out into this hymn of praise and gratitude! As you look back on your own life, do you remember any experience when you felt as if you had fallen into a pit? Perhaps it was the pit of failure, the pit of bereavement, the pit of painful illness, the pit of dark doubt, the pit of some persistent sin. Did you keep crying out to God, and did He mercifully deliver you?

If so, are you still praising the Lord for that answer to your cries and thanking Him for His grace? And are you now walking with Him in obedient fellowship?

You can confidently trust the Lord to help you in whatever experience comes your way in the days ahead. Rejoice that in His time He can—and will—bring you through and bring you out.

VCG

Why must I bear this pain? I cannot tell;
I only know my Lord does all things well.
And so I trust in God, my all in all,
For He will bring me through, whate'er befall. —Smith

God can bring showers of blessing out of storms of adversity.

A Sure Hope

Read: 1 Corinthians 15:12–20

Christ is risen from the dead, and has become the firstfruits
of those who have fallen asleep. 1 Corinthians 15:20

Konrad Adenauer, former chancellor of West Germany, said, "If Jesus Christ is alive, then there is hope for the world. If not, I don't see the slightest glimmer of hope on the horizon." Then he added, "I believe Christ's resurrection to be one of the best-attested facts of history."

Christ's resurrection and ours go together. So reasoned the apostle Paul in 1 Corinthians 15. And if Christ didn't rise from the grave, what's left? Empty preaching (v. 14), false witnesses (v. 15), a futile faith (v. 17), unforgiven sins (v. 17), no life after death (v. 18), and hopelessness (v. 19).

But Christ did rise from the grave. Paul asserted the proof for the resurrection in verses 1 through 11, listing many credible witnesses who saw the risen Lord: Peter (v. 5), 500 people (v. 6), all the apostles (v. 7), and Paul himself (v. 8).

When the Greek philosopher Socrates lay dying, his friends asked, "Shall we live again?" He could only say, "I hope so." In contrast, the night before author and explorer Sir Walter Raleigh was beheaded, he wrote in his Bible, "From this earth, this grave, this dust, my God shall raise me up."

If we trust in Christ as our Savior, we won't say "I hope so" about our own resurrection. Jesus's resurrection gives us a sure hope. DJD

Rejoice in glorious hope!
Our Lord the Judge shall come
And take His servants up
To their eternal home. —Wesley

Christ's resurrection is the guarantee of our own.

Keeping Away the Elephants

Read: Philippians 4:6–13

Be anxious for nothing, but in everything by prayer, . . .
let your requests be made known to God. Philippians 4:6

A man was sitting on a park bench shredding old newspapers and spreading them around. "What are you doing?" asked a bystander. "I'm spreading this paper around to keep the elephants away." The visitor looked around the well-kept city park. "I don't see any elephants," he said. The man smiled. "Works pretty good, doesn't it," he replied.

Worry is like that. We expend a lot of energy on problems that don't exist. Yes, I know we all face real problems, but we often create additional ones by thinking of all the bad things that might happen but never do.

One of the great challenges for worriers is to turn every care into a prayer and then to stop there, leaving it with God. Some people find this difficult to do, perhaps because they are pessimistic or sensitive by nature. But there is hope!

Paul's counsel in Philippians 4:6 is not a mechanical formula but a tested reality. He had found peace and contentment (vv. 7, 11). Yet, notice the phrase in verse 12: "I have learned." Learning takes time. It is a process marked by trial and error, and by perseverance. Aren't you glad that our teacher, the Lord Jesus, is patient with us—even when we tear up papers and spread them around?   DJD

Help me, Lord, to place my worries
At Your feet in prayer,
Then to trust Your love and goodness
As I leave them there. —Sper

Worry is carrying a burden that God
never intended us to bear.

December 1

Still Trusting

Read: Psalm 139:1–16

In Your book they all were written,
the days fashioned for me. Psalm 139:16

How could this happen? How could God allow our beautiful daughter Melissa to be taken from us in a car accident at age seventeen? And it's not just us. It's also our friends Steve and Robyn, whose daughter Lindsay, Melissa's friend, died nine months earlier. And what about Richard and Leah, whose son Jon—another of Melissa's friends—lies in a gravesite within fifty yards of both Lindsay and Melissa?

How could God allow these three Christian teens to die within sixteen months of each other? And how can we still trust Him?

Unable to comprehend such tragedies, we cling to Psalm 139:16—"In Your book they all were written, the days fashioned for me." By God's design, our children had a specific number of days to live, and then He lovingly called them home to their eternal reward. And we find comfort in God's mysterious words: "Precious in the sight of the Lord is the death of His saints" (116:15).

The death of those close to us could rob us of our trust in God—taking with it our reason for living. But God's unfathomable plan for the universe and His redemptive work continue, and we must honor our loved ones by holding on to His hand. We don't understand, but we still must trust God as we await the great reunion He has planned for us. DB

Though tragedy, heartache, and sorrow abound
And many a hardship in life will be found,
I'll put all my trust in the Savior of light,
For He can bring hope in the darkest of night. —DJD

Don't let tragedy steal your trust in God.

God Cares for You

Read: Matthew 14:1–14

Jesus . . . saw a great multitude; and He was moved
with compassion for them. Matthew 14:14

John the Baptist had been martyred by King Herod. John was Jesus's cousin and friend, and his death must have touched Jesus deeply. I believe that's why He sought refuge from the crowds. Matthew wrote, "He departed from there [His hometown and place of ministry] by boat to a deserted place by Himself" (14:13).

Jesus wanted to be alone to grieve, but the crowd pressed Him with their needs and wouldn't let Him get away (v. 13). Seeing the multitudes and their pain, Jesus was moved with compassion for them. Despite His own heartache, He began to heal their sick (v. 14). He didn't let His own grief keep Him from ministering to them.

Perhaps you're a caregiver—a pastor, a teacher, a nurse, or a counselor. Maybe you're a mother with small children or the spouse of an invalid. You have your own struggles, disappointments, heartaches—and no one seems to care about you.

But there is someone who cares. God does. He knows your sorrow as no one else does, and He understands the depths of your misery. You can give your cares to Him (1 Peter 5:7) and find in His presence His love, consolation, and the strength you need to move from your own grief to the grief of others. You can care for others because God cares for you.   DHR

O yes, He cares; I know He cares,
His heart is touched with my grief;
When the days are weary, the long nights dreary,
I know my Savior cares. —Graeff

Because God cares for us, we can care for others.

December 3

Lift Up Your Eyes

Read: Psalm 121:1–8

I will lift up my eyes to the hills—from whence comes my help?
My help comes from the Lord. Psalm 121:1–2

A woman whose work demanded constant reading began to have difficulty with her eyes, so she consulted a physician. After an examination he said, "Your eyes are just tired; you need to rest them."

"But," she replied, "that is impossible in my type of work."

After a few moments the doctor asked, "Do you have windows at your workplace?"

"Oh, yes," she answered with enthusiasm. "From the front windows I can see the noble peaks of the Blue Ridge Mountains, and from the rear windows I can look out at the glorious Allegheny foothills."

The physician replied, "That is exactly what you need. When your eyes feel tired, go look at your mountains for ten minutes—twenty would be better—and the far look will rest your eyes!"

What is true in the physical realm is true in the spiritual realm. The eyes of the soul are often tired and weary from focusing on our problems and difficulties. The upward look—the far look—will restore our spiritual perspective.

At times we feel overwhelmed by life's troubles. If we look to the Lord in His Word and in prayer, however, He will put our problems in perspective and renew our strength.

Let's lift up our eyes! (Psalm 121:1).   HGB

For the right spiritual focus, fix your eyes on the Lord.

December 4

Hug of the Heart

Read: Mark 10:13–16

He took [little children] up in His arms . . .
and blessed them. Mark 10:16

A friend told me about a touching conversation between her two grandchildren, five-year-old Matthew and three-year-old Sarah. The boy said, "I talk to Jesus in my head!" The girl responded, "I don't—I just cuddle with Him!"

While Jesus lived on earth, He took little children in His arms and blessed them (Mark 10:16). And He is still in the child-embracing ministry today.

Many of God's children, much older ones, have experienced His unseen everlasting arms around them and beneath them. Brother Lawrence, the seventeenth-century monk known for sensing the presence of God even amid the pots and pans of the monastery kitchen, spoke of being "known of God and extremely caressed by Him." And Hudson Taylor, the pioneer missionary to China, scrawled this note as he neared the end of his life: "I am so weak that I cannot work; I cannot read my Bible; I cannot even pray. I can only lie still in God's arms like a child, and trust."

Whether we're young or old, strong or weak, God wants us to cuddle close to Him in childlike trust. He will respond through His indwelling Spirit by drawing us to himself to comfort and to bless.

Have you and God had a "hug of the heart" today?   JY

The Lord took children in His arms
To bless them and to show
That if we come in childlike faith
His presence we will know. —Sper

Jesus longs for our fellowship even more than we long for His.

Seeing God's Glory

Read: Ezekiel 43:1–5

*Behold, the glory of the God of Israel came
from the way of the east. Ezekiel 43:2*

I've had the privilege of viewing some glorious sights in my life. I've seen an awe-inspiring nighttime launch of the space shuttle, the majesty of Mount Fuji in Japan, the sparkling beauty of ocean sea life off the coast of the Philippine Islands, the architectural wonders of New York City, and the gleaming midsummer spectacle of a night baseball game in a major league stadium.

But nothing I've ever seen comes close to what some Old Testament people saw. Moses, the people he led, Ezekiel, and others witnessed the most breathtaking sight of all time. They had a glimpse of the glory of God—a visible manifestation of the Lord's invisible being and character.

Moses experienced it on Mount Sinai, and his face shone (Exodus 34:29). The Israelites saw it in the cloud, before God provided them with quail (16:10). Ezekiel saw God's glory return to the temple, and he fell to the ground (Ezekiel 43:1–5).

Someday we who have been redeemed by Jesus will experience that inspiring sight. God's glory will shine in the heavenly Jerusalem (Revelation 21:10–11). And we will see our risen and glorified Savior, the Lord Jesus (1 John 3:2).

This hope encourages us as Christians to keep going. For nothing in this world compares to seeing God's glory!　　　　DB

*The glory of God
In the face of His Son
To us who behold Him
Is heaven begun. —Hess*

The world's greatest glory is but a spark compared to the
radiance of God's glory.

December 6

A Little Perspective

Read: 2 Corinthians 4:16–18

*Our light affliction . . . is working for us a far more exceeding
and eternal weight of glory. 2 Corinthians 4:17*

A college student wrote a startling letter to her parents:

Dear Mom and Dad:

*I have so much to tell you. Because of the fire in my room set by riot-
ing students, I suffered lung damage and had to go to the hospital.
While there, I fell in love with an orderly. Then I got arrested for my
part in the riots. Anyway, I'm dropping out of school, getting married, and moving to Alaska.*

Your loving daughter

*P.S.: None of this really happened, but I did flunk a chemistry class,
and I wanted you to keep it in perspective.*

We might question this student's method of breaking bad news
to her parents, but her approach highlights a truth: Proper perspective is essential.

When Paul encouraged the church in Corinth, he wrote a litany
of his own very real trials and tribulations. To gain perspective, he
shifted his focus to the eternal. "Our light affliction," he said, "is
working for us a far more exceeding and eternal weight of glory"
(2 Corinthians 4:17).

In some ways, our perspective is more important than our experiences. Paul continued, "The things which are seen are temporary,
but the things which are not seen are eternal" (v. 18). Our sufferings will diminish in importance when compared to the glory that
awaits us.   HWR

The supreme need in every hour of difficulty
is a vision of God. —G. C. Morgan

December 7

Are You a Worrywart?

Read: Matthew 6:25–34

*Do not worry about tomorrow... Sufficient for
the day is its own trouble. Matthew 6:34*

Worry is sin. It is caused by lack of faith, a failure to believe God's Word. Yet it is a sin that many Christians find hard to overcome.

Stop and think of the things you have worried about. How many actually happened? And how many of the things that did happen had never entered your mind? We tend to be filled with anxiety over what might happen but never does.

I once read about a paratrooper in the U.S. Army who had made more than fifty successful parachute jumps without a single serious injury. But the first day back home after being discharged, he stumbled over a rug, fell against a table, and broke four of his ribs! He had worried a great deal about his parachute jumps, but then something happened he had never worried about: He tripped over a rug.

So why worry? Jesus said that it's futile to fret, for worrying can't change anything (Matthew 6:27). We need to remember that our heavenly Father knows all about our situation and watches over us (vv. 28–34). We can be sure that He will take care of our needs no matter what tomorrow brings. It's better, therefore, to be wise and trust the Lord.   MRD

Worry doesn't improve the future, it only ruins the present.

December 8

Our Refuge

Read: Leviticus 23:37–43

God is our refuge and strength, a very
present help in trouble. Psalm 46:1

Most homes are built to keep its inhabitants safe from ill effects of the weather, but not the dwellings built for *Succoth*. During this Jewish holiday, also known as the Feast of Tabernacles, worshipers live in dwellings made of leaves and branches. One requirement is that the stars must be visible through the "roof."

Obviously, this dwelling provides little protection from inclement weather. And that's the point. Living in this vulnerable shelter reminds the Jews of their dependency on God.

During the days of the prophet Isaiah, the people bragged about a very different kind of dwelling place; they had made lies their refuge and falsehood their hiding place (Isaiah 28:15). Because of the Israelites' dependence on ungodly things, the Lord said to them through the prophet, "Hail will sweep away the refuge of lies, and the waters will overflow the hiding place" (v. 17).

Succoth calls us to examine our lives to make sure that our security rests not on lies but on God's truth. The Feast of Tabernacles reminds us that all of life is sustained by God's goodness.

When we make truth our refuge, no storm can threaten us, for we can depend on God to sustain us.   JAL

No storm can shake my inmost calm
While to that refuge clinging;
Since Christ is Lord of heaven and earth,
How can I keep from singing? —Lowry

God is a safe dwelling place in life's storms.

Grumblers

Read: Proverbs 18:1–7

A fool has no delight in understanding, but in expressing his own heart. Proverbs 18:2

Mrs. Grumpty complained bitterly because her friends seemed to avoid her, and she just couldn't understand why. If only she could have heard a recording of her own voice, she would have known the reason for her unpopularity. She always talked about her complaints, weaknesses, aches, and pains, and insisted on relating in wearying detail her stay in the hospital.

If you want to keep friends, don't be a grumbler. Most people have enough problems of their own and don't need to hear all of yours.

In one of the churches I pastored, a dear old soul expected me to visit her at least once a week. I don't know of a visit in my entire ministry that I dreaded as much as that one. Every week she insisted on entertaining me with a recital of her five surgeries. She never expressed happiness and joy for her current good health or her wonderful recovery, but she always went back to her days of suffering. She seemed to "enjoy" poor health. Incidentally, she lived many more years. She reminds me of the saying: "A creaking wagon will last the longest."

Today, fix your eyes on the doughnut, not on the hole. Share your joys with others, and leave your troubles with the Lord.

MRD

Go bury your sorrow, the world has its share;
Go bury it deeply, go hide it with care,
Go think of it calmly, when curtained by night,
Go tell it to Jesus, and all will be right! —Bachelor

Spend your time counting your blessings,
not airing your complaints.

December 10

Bite-Size Requests

Read: Mark 11:20–24

*Whatever things you ask when you pray, believe that you
receive them, and you will have them. Mark 11:24*

Lots of things are easier to do when they're bite-size. If you have
a major task to get done, for example, it helps to divide it into
smaller units and tackle them one at a time. This is true whether
you are redecorating the house, packing for a vacation, or directing
a church project.

Rosalind Rinker suggests that the same is true of prayer. She
found that when she made very general, all-inclusive requests of
God, it seemed that nothing happened. But when she began making specific, bite-size requests, she saw results.

She recommends that we make our requests very specific, and
ask for what we really believe is according to God's will. Rinker
adds that as we see God's answers to relatively small requests, we
will find that we are asking for bigger needs with a greater degree
of faith.

Have you been praying general, world-encompassing prayers
without seeing results? It's wiser to ask for something smaller and
more specific and really believe that it will be answered. For example, if you've been asking God to destroy all the pornography in the
world, it would be better to pray that the convenience store on the
corner would stop selling it. Then ask God what you can do to help
bring that about.

Let's begin making bite-size requests!   DCE

PRAYER SUGGESTION

*If you don't already have one, make a prayer list that includes
several bite-size requests.
Keep the list, and then record how God answers.*

Be specific in your prayers if you want specific answers.

December 11

Is God Unfair?

Read: Acts 12:1–25

All His ways are justice, a God of truth and without injustice;
righteous and upright is He. Deuteronomy 32:4

A couple I knew some years ago questioned God's fairness after both of their school-aged children were killed in auto accidents within a period of three years. Like most parents, they had anticipated much happiness with their son and daughter. Their friends saw their own children graduate from high school, but these parents were deprived of that joy.

I wonder if the family of the apostle James may have questioned God's fairness too. He was executed, but Peter was miraculously rescued from the same fate (Acts 12:2, 5–11).

It's true that life is often unfair. Some seem to be blessed with far more opportunities than others, but let's not blame God. These injustices are here because mankind's sin has invaded God's creation. The Lord allows them, but He has not caused them. He grieves over them more than we do, loves us equally, has made eternal salvation available to all, and will judge everyone by the principle: "To whom much is given, from him much will be required" (Luke 12:48).

At the end of time, the Lord will right all the wrongs of the ages, and even the people most deprived and mistreated in this life will be satisfied with God's justice. Ultimately, no one will have reason to accuse Him of being unfair. —HVL

Life can be lived with joy and song
Amid its heartache and its pain,
For one day God will right each wrong—
With peace and justice He will reign. —DJD

We can endure life's wrongs, knowing that
God will make all things right.

Calm Under Pressure

Read: Isaiah 30:15–18

*In returning and rest you shall be saved; in quietness and
confidence shall be your strength. Isaiah 30:15*

At the farewell for a minister who had served his church for
twenty years, several preachers eloquently extolled his many
virtues. One layman, however, paid a tribute that the pastor considered to be the most gratifying. He said, "I have observed him
nearly every day for the past twenty years, and I've never seen him
in a hurry!"

The pastor said that for years he had asked God to teach him
how to renew his strength through "quietness and confidence," as
he had read in Isaiah 30:15. In this verse Isaiah was calling rebellious Israel to return to God and rely on Him to find new strength.
The pastor, however, saw in that verse a principle applicable to his
own life.

Some people are calm by nature; others are high-strung. But
Christians, regardless of their temperament, can come to God in
prayer and learn to renew their strength in quietness and confidence. Martin Luther said that he could get so busy that he first
needed to spend at least three hours a day in prayer to get anything
done. Often we reverse that order. We rush from task to task feeling
flustered because we haven't taken time to be with the Lord.

Let's learn the principle set forth in Isaiah 30:15. In quietness and
confidence before God we find the real source of strength to stay
calm.   RDH

We oft grow weary in life's race,
We're driven by its hurried pace;
But when we wait upon the Lord,
His strength becomes our sure reward. —DJD

Never take on more work than you have time to pray about.

December 13

At Just the Right Time

Read: Galatians 4:1–7

When the fullness of the time had come,
God sent forth His Son. Galatians 4:4

Why is being on time so challenging for some of us? Even when we start early, something inevitably gets in our way to make us late.

But here's the good news: God is always on time! Speaking of the arrival of Jesus, Paul said, "When the fullness of the time had come, God sent forth His Son" (Galatians 4:4). The long-awaited, promised Savior came at just the right time.

Jesus's arrival during the Roman Empire's *Pax Romana* (the peace of Rome) was perfect timing. The known world was united by one language of commerce. A network of global trade routes provided open access to the whole world. All of this guaranteed that the gospel could move rapidly in one tongue. No visas. No impenetrable borders. Only unhindered access to help spread the news of the Savior whose crucifixion fulfilled the prophecy of the Lamb who would be slain for our sins (Isaiah 53). All in God's perfect timing!

All of this should remind us that the Lord knows what time is best for us as well. If you're waiting for answered prayer or the fulfillment of one of His promises, don't give up. If you think He has forgotten you, think again. When the fullness of time is right for you, He'll show up—and you'll be amazed by His brilliant timing! JS

God's timing is always perfect.

December 14

Square Watermelons?

Read: Romans 12:1–5

*Do not be conformed to this world, but be transformed
by the renewing of your mind. Romans 12:2*

Farmers in Zentsuji, Japan, are preparing full-grown watermelons for shipment—only these are no ordinary melons, they're *square*! They were placed in tempered-glass cubes while they were still growing. Why would anyone want a square watermelon? They're much easier to store in a refrigerator!

It's amusing to think of how a naturally round watermelon can become square because of the shape of the container in which it's grown. This reminds me of the forces in the world that exert their influence on us and attempt to shape us. That's why in Romans 12:2 we are told not to be "conformed to this world," but to be "transformed by the renewing of [our] mind." The idea is rather simple: We are to allow the transforming Word of God to work within us and produce outward results, instead of permitting external pressures to shape us.

If we meditate on God's Word daily, it will influence our thoughts and help us grow to be more like Jesus Christ (2 Corinthians 3:18). Then we will act in a manner that pleases Him. Pressures of the world will continue to try to shape our character, but they will not succeed if God's Word is changing us from within.   AL

*The Savior can satisfy fully
The heart that the world cannot fill;
His presence will sanctify wholly
The soul that is yielded and still. —Smith*

If we are being transformed by the Word,
we won't be conformed to the world.

Thankful for Seasons

Read: Ecclesiastes 3:1–8

To everything there is a season, a time for
every purpose under heaven. Ecclesiastes 3:1

I grew up on the West Coast of the U.S. The possibility of snow for Christmas was so remote that my mom would point to fog in the early morning as evidence that the holidays were just around the corner.

My wife and I now live in the Midwest. There's a lot of snow when the yuletide season comes around. And I couldn't be happier with four distinct seasons. But I don't find that same response from many who have grown up in the Midwest. I find it amusing that they don't share my appreciation for the wonderful cycles of change God has built into nature for our good.

In Ecclesiastes 3:1–8, Solomon acknowledged the cycles of life. He observed a time to sow and to reap, to weep and to laugh, to mourn and to dance, to gain and to lose, to keep silent and to speak, to love and to hate.

Just as God determines the weather, He also controls the cycles in our lives: "To everything there is a season, a time for every purpose under heaven" (Ecclesiastes 3:1). Do we resist those seasons and complain about the "snowy" conditions on the horizon? Or do we trust God and thank Him for whatever He has planned for us?

Whatever our situation is today, we can be thankful for God's seasons. DF

Just as the winter turns to spring,
Our lives have changing seasons too;
So when a gloomy forecast comes,
Remember—God has plans for you. —Sper

Rather than praying for a change in circumstances,
pray for a change of heart.

Weighed Down at Christmas

Read: Luke 4:14–21

He has sent Me to heal the brokenhearted, . . . to set at liberty those who are oppressed. Luke 4:18

During a December visit to New York City's Metropolitan Museum of Art, I paused to admire the magnificent Christmas tree. It was covered with angels and surrounded at its base by an elaborate eighteenth-century nativity scene. Nearly two hundred figures, including shepherds, the Magi, and a crowd of townspeople, looked in anticipation toward the manger or gazed up in awe at the angels.

But one figure appeared different from the rest—a barefoot man, who carried a heavy load on his back and looked at the ground. It struck me that this man, like so many people today, was so weighed down that he couldn't see the Messiah.

Christmas can be a difficult time for those who carry the burden of hard work, stressful family situations, and personal loss. But we should remember that Christ came into our world to lift up all those who are bowed down. Jesus used the words of Isaiah to announce His God-given mission on earth: "To preach the gospel to the poor; . . . to heal the brokenhearted, to proclaim liberty to the captives and recovery of sight to the blind, to set at liberty those who are oppressed" (Luke 4:18).

Jesus came to lift our burdens so we can raise our eyes to welcome Him at Christmas. DCM

Help us, Lord, to give our burdens
To Your tender, loving care;
Grant us faith to trust You fully,
Knowing that each one You bear. —DJD

To find true joy at Christmas, look to Jesus.

December 17

Change of Plans

Read: Proverbs 16:1–9

A man's heart plans his way, but the
Lord directs his steps. Proverbs 16:9

It was Christmas Eve in Oberndorf, Austria, in 1818. Joseph Mohr, the vicar of the church, had written a new song for the Christmas Eve service and the organist Franz Gruber had set it to music. But the organ in the village church broke down. So Gruber grabbed a guitar and accompanied Mohr in the first-ever rendition of "Silent Night."

The story doesn't end there, however. When a man came to fix the organ, Gruber tested it by playing the new song. The repairman liked the song so much that he took a copy of it back to his own village. There, four daughters of a village glove maker learned the song and began singing it in concerts all over the region. Because of that faulty organ, this new Christmas song blessed people all over Austria—and eventually the world.

When things break or when plans change, how should we respond? Often we fret and worry because we don't have the control we would like to have. That's when we need to step back, trust God, and wait to see how He is going to use the situation for His glory. The changes in our lives may not give the world something as remarkable as "Silent Night," but because God is in charge we can be sure that "all is calm, all is bright."   DB

Sometimes our plan does not unfold
The way we thought it would,
But God is always in control
To use it for our good. —Sper

In the drama of life, God is the director behind the scenes.

December 18

Crushing Responsibilities

Read: Nehemiah 4:1–14

*Do not be afraid of them. Remember the Lord,
great and awesome. Nehemiah 4:14*

While the outcome of the Second World War was still uncertain, Franklin Roosevelt died and Harry Truman was sworn in as the next president of the United States. The following day, President Truman told reporters, "When they told me yesterday what had happened, I felt like the moon, the stars, and all the planets had fallen on me." Certainly Truman faced crushing responsibilities.

Nehemiah was a great leader who also faced overwhelming burdens. Accompanied by Jewish exiles who had returned from Babylon, Nehemiah was given the task of rebuilding the walls of Jerusalem. Amid terrible opposition, he refused to be intimidated by the jeers and threats of the enemy. Instead, the man of God organized a dual strategy of construction and military defense—bathing their efforts in prayer: "We made our prayer to our God, and because of them we set a watch against them day and night" (Nehemiah 4:9). Nehemiah addressed the ongoing threats the workers faced by getting their focus back on God: "Do not be afraid of them. Remember the Lord, great and awesome" (v. 14).

Are you facing crushing responsibilities today? Praying for God's help and putting together a practical plan can give you strength to complete the task. DF

God invites us to burden Him with what burdens us.

December 19

On the Winning Side

Read: Colossians 2:6–15

Having disarmed principalities and powers, He made a public spectacle
of them, triumphing over them. Colossians 2:15

Few today believe the pagan idea that the world is under the control of warring gods like Artemis, Pan, and Apollo. Yet even sophisticated skeptics readily acknowledge the reality of "forces" over which we have no control. For example, they attribute our inability to prevent violence in various places around the world to what they vaguely call "international forces." And they speak of "economic forces" beyond our control. For example, millions of people are starving despite the fact that there is more than enough food in the world to provide for every person on the earth.

The Bible clearly acknowledges the presence of invisible but very real spiritual beings, or powers. In Ephesians 6:11–12, Paul declared that our primary warfare is against an army of rebellious angels headed by Satan. The bad news is that they are more intelligent and powerful than we are. The good news is that Jesus defeated them by His death on the cross: "Having disarmed principalities and powers, He made a public spectacle of them, triumphing over them" (Colossians 2:15).

There are many things beyond our control, but we need not fear. We who have placed our trust in Jesus are on the winning side. HVL

Satan may win some battles, but he cannot win the war.

Keep Laughing

Read: Psalm 126

A merry heart does good, like medicine,
but a broken spirit dries the bones. Proverbs 17:22

A judge has ordered a German man to stop bursting into laughter in the woods. Joachim Bahrenfeld, an accountant, was taken to court by one of several joggers who say their runs have been disturbed by Bahrenfeld's deafening squeals of joy. He faces up to six months in jail if he is caught again. Bahrenfeld, 54, says he goes to the woods to laugh nearly every day to relieve stress. "It is part of living for me," he says, "like eating, drinking, and breathing." He feels that a cheerful heart, expressed through hearty laughter, is important to his health and survival.

A cheerful heart is vital in life. Proverbs 17:22 says, "A merry heart does good, like medicine." A happy heart affects our spirit and our physical health.

But there is a deeper, abiding joy for those who trust the Lord that is based on much more than frivolity and circumstances. It is a joy based on God's salvation. He has provided forgiveness of sin and a restored relationship with himself through His Son Jesus. That gives us a deep joy which circumstances cannot shake (Psalm 126:2–3; Habakkuk 3:17–18; Philippians 4:7).

May you experience the joy of knowing Jesus Christ today!

MW

To take a glimpse within the veil,
To know that God is mine,
Are springs of joy that never fail:
Unspeakable! Divine! —Newton

Joy comes from the Lord who lives in us, not from what's happening around us.

December 21

Unlimited Power

Read: Isaiah 40:25–31

[God] brings out their host by number;
He calls them all by name. Isaiah 40:26

"Why don't the stars fall down?" A child may ask that question, but so does an astronomer. And they both get essentially the same answer: A mysterious power or energy upholds everything and prevents our cosmos from collapsing into chaos.

Hebrews 1:3 tells us that it is Jesus who upholds all things by the word of His power. He is the source of all the energy there is, whether the explosive potential packed inside an atom or the steaming kettle on the kitchen stove.

That energy is not simply a mindless force. No, God is the personal power who created everything out of nothing, including the stars (Genesis 1, Isaiah 40:26); who divided the Red Sea and delivered the Israelites from Egyptian bondage (Exodus 14:21–22); who brought to pass the virgin birth of Jesus (Luke 1:34–35); and who raised Him from the dead and conquered death (2 Timothy 1:10). Our God, the one and only true God, has the power to answer prayer, meet our needs, and change our lives.

So when life's problems are baffling, when you face some Red Sea impossibility, call upon the wonder-working God who upholds all things. And remember that with our Almighty God, nothing is impossible. VCG

Thou art coming to a King—
Large petitions with thee bring;
For His grace and power are such
None can ever ask too much. —Newton

God is greater than our greatest problem.

December 22

A Boost of Courage

Read: Hebrews 12:1–11

*Looking unto Jesus, the author and finisher
of our faith. Hebrews 12:2*

When my son Joe was a child, I took him to the local YMCA for swimming lessons. I could almost see an Olympic gold medal swinging around his neck.

To my chagrin, Joe didn't "wow" the class. Instead, he took one look at the water, one look at the instructor, and started bawling.

To make matters worse, the instructor motioned for me to take Joe back to the locker room. In the midst of his sobs and pleas to go home, I gave him a little pep talk: "You can do it, Joe! I'll come to all your lessons, and we'll have a signal. When you get scared you can look up at me, and when I hold my thumb up you'll know it's going to be okay because I'm here cheering you on." Joe finally agreed, and today he can swim circles around me.

How often we too face situations that seem overwhelming and impossible. It's in those times that we need to find our confidence in Jesus. Our first instinct may be to back away in fear. But that's exactly when we need to look to Jesus, "the author and finisher of our faith" (Hebrews 12:2), who will raise His nail-scarred hand and say, "Stay with it. Run the race. I've run it before you, and in My power you can win. You can do it!"   JS

*Hold fast to Christ and He will give
The will to see you through;
And if you keep on keeping on,
Your strength He will renew.* —DJD

Christ's victory in the past gives courage
for the present and hope for the future.

December 23

Ordinary Days

Read: Luke 2:8–20

*Behold, an angel of the Lord stood before them, and the glory
of the Lord shone around them. Luke 2:9*

Writer Anita Brechbill observed in *God's Revivalist* magazine: "Most often the Word of the Lord comes to a soul in the ordinary duties of life." She cites the examples of Zacharias performing his duties as a priest and the shepherds watching their flocks. They were at work as usual with no idea that they were about to receive a message from God.

Luke describes the ordinary days when these men received their message from God: "While [Zacharias] was serving as priest before God in the order of his division, ... an angel of the Lord appeared to him" (1:8, 11). While the shepherds were "living out in the fields, keeping watch over their flock by night... an angel of the Lord stood before them, and the glory of the Lord shone around them" (2:8–9).

In *My Utmost for His Highest* Oswald Chambers said: "Jesus rarely comes where we expect Him; He appears where we least expect Him, and always in the most illogical situations. The only way a worker can keep true to God is by being ready for the Lord's surprise visits."

On this ordinary day, the Lord may have a word of encouragement, guidance, or instruction for us, if we're listening and ready to obey.   DCM

I wonder what I did for God today:
How many times did I once pause and pray?
But I must find and serve Him in these ways,
For life is made of ordinary days. —Macbeth

God speaks to those who are quiet before Him.

December 24

A Gift of Shelter

Read: Luke 2:1–7

There was no room for them in the inn. Luke 2:7

Life was tough for Datha and her family. At age thirty-nine, she had a heart attack and bypass surgery and learned that she had coronary artery disease. A year later, her fifteen-year-old daughter Heather became paralyzed as the result of a car accident. Datha quit her job to take care of Heather, and the bills started piling up. Soon they would be facing eviction. Datha was so angry with God that she stopped praying.

Then came Christmas Eve 2004. A young girl knocked on Datha's door. The girl wished her a "Merry Christmas," gave her an envelope, and left quickly. Inside was a gift that would cover Datha's housing needs for the next year. The attached note read, "Please accept this gift in honor of the Man whose birthday we celebrate on this holy night. Long ago, His family also had a shelter problem."

Luke 2 tells the story of Joseph and Mary as they searched for a shelter for Mary to deliver her baby. They found a place with the animals. Later in His life, Jesus said of himself, "The Son of Man has nowhere to lay His head" (Matthew 8:20).

Jesus understood Datha's troubles. He brought her hope and met her needs through others who contributed funds.

We can cast all our cares on Him (1 Peter 5:7). In Christ, we find shelter (Psalm 61:3–4). AC

God will take care of you still to the end;
O what a Father, Redeemer, and Friend!
Jesus will answer whenever you call;
He will take care of you: trust Him for all! —Crosby

You do the casting, God will do the caring.

December 25

Wonder

Read: Luke 2:15–20

*All those who heard it marveled at those things which were
told them by the shepherds. Luke 2:18*

Elmer Kline, a bakery manager in 1921, was given the job of
naming the company's new loaf of bread. As he struggled
to come up with something "catchy," he found his answer in an
unlikely place. While visiting the grounds of the Indianapolis Motor
Speedway, he stopped to watch the International Balloon Festival.

Later he described the sight of the beautiful hot-air balloons
launching into the Indiana sky as one of "awe and wonderment."
The thought stuck, and he called the new product Wonder Bread.
To this day, the packaging for Wonder Bread is brightened by col-
orful balloons.

Wonder, however, is a word that evokes something more significant than a loaf of bread or hot-air balloons. One dictionary defines
wonder as "a cause of astonishment or admiration." It's a word that
captures the experience of all the people surrounding the events of
the coming of Jesus into the world—the angels, Mary, Joseph, the
shepherds, and all the people they told. Luke said they "marveled"
(2:18). For all of them, trying to understand the birth of Christ was
an exercise in wonder.

As we celebrate Christmas, may we be filled with wonder at His
love and His coming!   BC

Have you felt the joy of the shepherds,
Who were first to behold the sight
Of that holy Child of Mary
On that wonderful Christmas night? —Brill

A wonder-filled life is yours when you know
the Christ of Christmas.

The Great Earthquake

Read: John 10:22–30

*I give them eternal life, and they shall never perish; neither
shall anyone snatch them out of My hand. John 10:28*

On December 26, 2004, an earthquake shook the whole earth. Many people didn't feel it, but the South Asian region and parts of Africa suffered a devastating tsunami as a result. According to reporter Randolph Schmid, however, "No point on Earth remained undisturbed." That earthquake, he tells us, "shook the ground everywhere on Earth's surface."

The 19th-century Danish philosopher Søren Kierkegaard says that his world was rocked when his religious father told him he had cursed God for the mistreatment he was getting from others. His father's actions shook Søren so much that he called the event "The Great Earthquake." He wondered for the rest of his life if his family was cursed by God for his father's actions.

We too have had or possibly will have "earthquakes" in our lives. But it's comforting to know that under the worst of circumstances, our faith in God can—and will—hold us fast. After all, "He's got the whole world in His hands," and that means "He's got you and me, brother and sister, in His hands."

No one, nor any disaster, can snatch us out of our heavenly Father's hands (John 10:28–29). His grip will hold us into all eternity. VCG

Neither life nor death can ever
From the Lord His children sever,
For His love and deep compassion
Comforts them in tribulation. —*Berg*

Our unknown future is secure in the hands
of our all-knowing God.

December 27

No Need to Panic

Read: 1 Peter 4:12–19

Do not think it strange concerning the fiery trial which is to try you, as
though some strange thing happened to you. 1 Peter 4:12

On a Bible-teaching cruise in the Caribbean, I was listening to the customary first-day safety briefing. The precautions were vital in case the ship should have to be evacuated.

The instructions from the ship's personnel concluded with a simple but significant explanation. A specific combination of air-horn blasts, indicating a drill, would be distinctly different from those indicating a real emergency. The distinction was critical. A drill did not constitute a need to evacuate. If passengers were to panic during the drill, it could result in chaos.

When we don't understand the circumstances that surround us, it's easy to be shaken by life's alarms. Peter's generation experienced the same thing. His warning was simple: "Do not think it strange concerning the fiery trial which is to try you" (1 Peter 4:12).

The trials and heartaches of life may sound like a call to evacuate—to run away or to respond to life in ways that are disheartening and destructive. But we would do well to listen more closely to our Lord. The trial may be nothing more than a reminder that our trust is to be in God, not in people. We can trust Him in those times when the alarms start to sound.   BC

We can trust our loving Savior
To protect from life's alarms;
He's prepared a place of refuge
Safe within His mighty arms. —Hess

Life's challenges are not designed to break us
but to bend us toward God.

God's Training School

Read: Romans 8:12–17

[We are] heirs of God and joint heirs with Christ,
if indeed we suffer with Him. Romans 8:17

Lew Wallace's book *Ben-Hur* tells the story of a Jewish aristocrat betrayed by his best friend and condemned to serve as a galley slave in the Roman navy. On a forced march to the ship, Judah Ben-Hur meets Jesus of Nazareth, whose compassion fills him with hope. Eventually, Ben-Hur saves the Roman commander during battle. In gratitude, the commander adopts Ben-Hur as his son, instantly elevating him from slave to heir.

That's what happens to us when God adopts us into His family. But great privilege brings great responsibility. Paul said that we become "heirs of God and joint heirs with Christ, if indeed we suffer with Him" (Romans 8:17). The gospel does not say, "Come to Jesus and live happily ever after." God's syllabus for His children's education includes training through hardships.

Ben-Hur's years of enduring hardship as a Roman slave strengthened him and increased his endurance. He eventually defeated his "friend-turned-enemy" in a chariot race.

As endurance and training were key to Ben-Hur's victory, so are they vital to victory in the Christian's war with sin and evil. The hard times we endure are God's way to prepare us for greater service for His glory.   CPH

We conquer by continuing.

What God Owes Us

Read: Colossians 1:9–14

Walk worthy of the Lord, fully pleasing Him. Colossians 1:10

A story is told about a vendor who sold bagels for fifty cents each at a street corner food stand. A jogger ran past and threw a couple of quarters into the bucket but didn't take a bagel. He did the same thing every day for months. One day, as the jogger was passing by, the vendor stopped him. The jogger asked, "You probably want to know why I always put money in but never take a bagel, don't you?" "No," said the vendor. "I just wanted to tell you that the bagels have gone up to sixty cents."

Too often, as believers, we treat God with that same kind of attitude. Not only are we ungrateful for what He's given us—but we want more. Somehow we feel that God owes us good health, a comfortable life, material blessings. Of course, God doesn't owe us anything, yet He gives us everything.

G. K. Chesterton wrote, "Here dies another day, during which I have had eyes, ears, hands, and the great world round me. And with tomorrow begins another. Why am I allowed two?" The psalmist said, "This is the day the Lord has made; we will rejoice and be glad in it" (Psalm 118:24).

Each day, whether good or bad, is one more gift from our God. Our grateful response should be to live to please Him.   CHK

Living for Jesus a life that is true,
Striving to please Him in all that I do;
Yielding allegiance, glad-hearted and free,
This is the pathway of blessing for me. —Chisholm

Life is a gift from God to be lived for God.

December 30

Our Changing World

Read: Psalm 102:25–27

I am the Lord, I do not change. Malachi 3:6

Change is one thing we can be sure of in this life. Our relationships change as we move to new places, experience illness, and ultimately face death. Even the cells in our bodies are always in the process of change. When cells wear out, most are replaced by new ones. This is especially noticeable with our skin—we shed and regrow outer skin cells about every twenty-seven days.

Yes, change is the one certainty in our world. Henry Lyte's melancholy line in his hymn "Abide with Me" is true: "Change and decay in all around I see." But the hymn immediately adds, "O Thou who changest not, abide with me!"

By faith in Jesus Christ we can have a relationship with the unchanging God, who says of himself in Malachi 3:6, "I am the Lord, I do not change." We can depend on God to be the same forever, as the psalmist says (Psalm 102:27). Hebrews 13:8 adds this reassuring testimony: "Jesus Christ is the same yesterday, today, and forever." He is our firm foundation, who can give us confidence and security in this changing world.

We creatures, caught up in the swirling tide of time, can rest our souls on the everlasting arms, which will never let us go.   VCG

Swift to its close ebbs out life's little day,
Earth's joys grow dim, its glories pass away;
Change and decay in all around I see—
O Thou who changest not, abide with me! —Lyte

To face life's changes, look to the unchanging God.

Look Both Ways

Read: Joshua 1:1–9

Moses My servant is dead. Now therefore, arise. Joshua 1:2

During our church's annual New Year's Eve Communion service, we say this prayer together: "Father, we surrender this past year and give it up to you. We give you our failures, our regrets, and our disappointments, for we have no more use for them. Make us now a new people, forgetting what lies behind and pressing on toward that which lies ahead of us.

"We give you all our hopes and dreams for the future. Purify them by your Spirit so that our wills shall truly reflect your will for us.

"As we stand on the threshold of another year, encourage us by our successes of the past, challenge us by the power of your Word, and guide us by the presence of your Holy Spirit."

In every transition, it's good to look both ways. When Joshua assumed leadership of Israel, God told him to consider the past and the future: "Moses My servant is dead. Now therefore, arise, go over this Jordan, you and all this people, to the land which I am giving to them" (Joshua 1:2). Then He promised, "As I was with Moses, so I will be with you... Do not be afraid, nor be dismayed, for the Lord your God is with you wherever you go" (vv. 5, 9).

With confidence in God, we can look back and look ahead, then walk boldly into a new year. DCM

Forgive us, Lord, for failures past,
Then help us start anew
With strength and courage to obey
And closely follow You. —Sper

The victories of the past give courage for the future.

Contributors

Henry G. Bosch . . . . HGB
Dave Branon . . . . DB
Anne Cetas . . . . AC
Bill Crowder . . . . BC
Dennis J. DeHaan . . . . DJD
Mart DeHaan . . . . MD
M. R. DeHaan . . . . MRD
Richard DeHaan . . . . RDH
David C. Egner . . . . DCE
Dennis Fisher . . . . DF
Vernon C. Grounds . . . . VCG
C. P. Hia . . . . CPH
Cindy Hess Kasper . . . . CHK
Albert Lee . . . . AL
Julie Ackerman Link . . . . JAL
David C. McCasland . . . . DCM
Our Daily Bread Ministries . . . . ODB
Haddon W. Robinson . . . . HWR
David H. Roper . . . . DHR
Joe Stowell . . . . JS
Herbert Vander Lugt . . . . HVL
Paul Van Gorder . . . . PVG
Marvin Williams . . . . MW
Philip Yancey . . . . PY
Joanie Yoder . . . . JY

Scripture Index

Old Testament

New Testament

Enjoy this book? Help us get the word out!

Share a link to the book
or mention it on social media

Write a review on your blog, on a retailer site,
or on our website (dhp.org)

Pick up another copy to share with someone

Recommend this book for your
church, book club, or small group

Follow Discovery House on
social media and join the discussion

Contact us to share your thoughts:

 @discoveryhouse   @DiscoveryHouse

Discovery House
P.O. Box 3566
Grand Rapids, MI 49501 USA

Phone: 1-800-653-8333
Email: books@dhp.org
Web: dhp.org

HELPING YOU CONNECT WITH GOD EVERY DAY

You can receive your daily devotional by mail, email, web, app, or e-book. *Sign up today!*

odb.org/subscribe

God said, "Let the water under the sky be gathered to one place, and let dry ground appear.". . . And God saw that it was good.